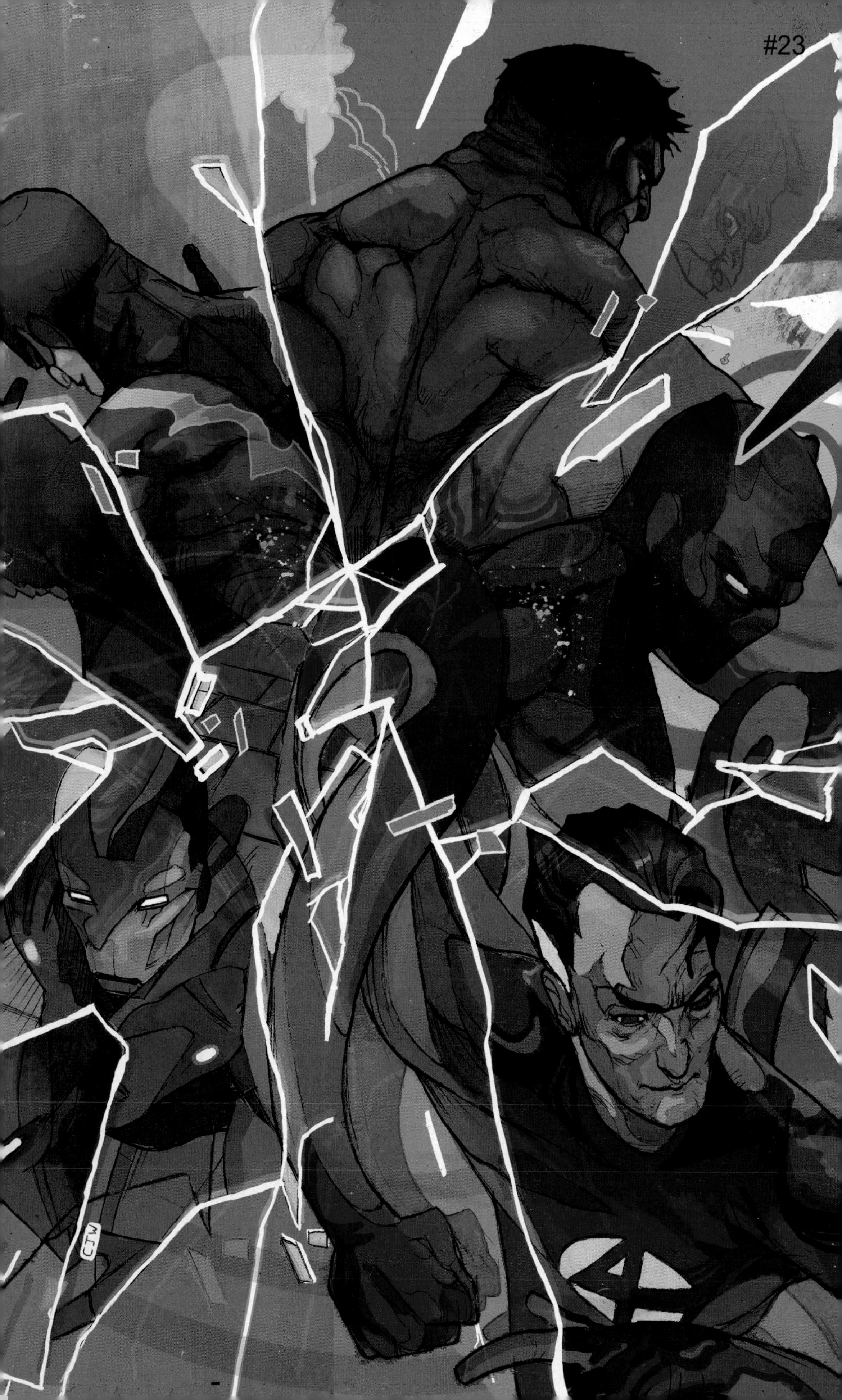
#23
CJW

#18 VARIANT BY **CHRISTIAN WARD**

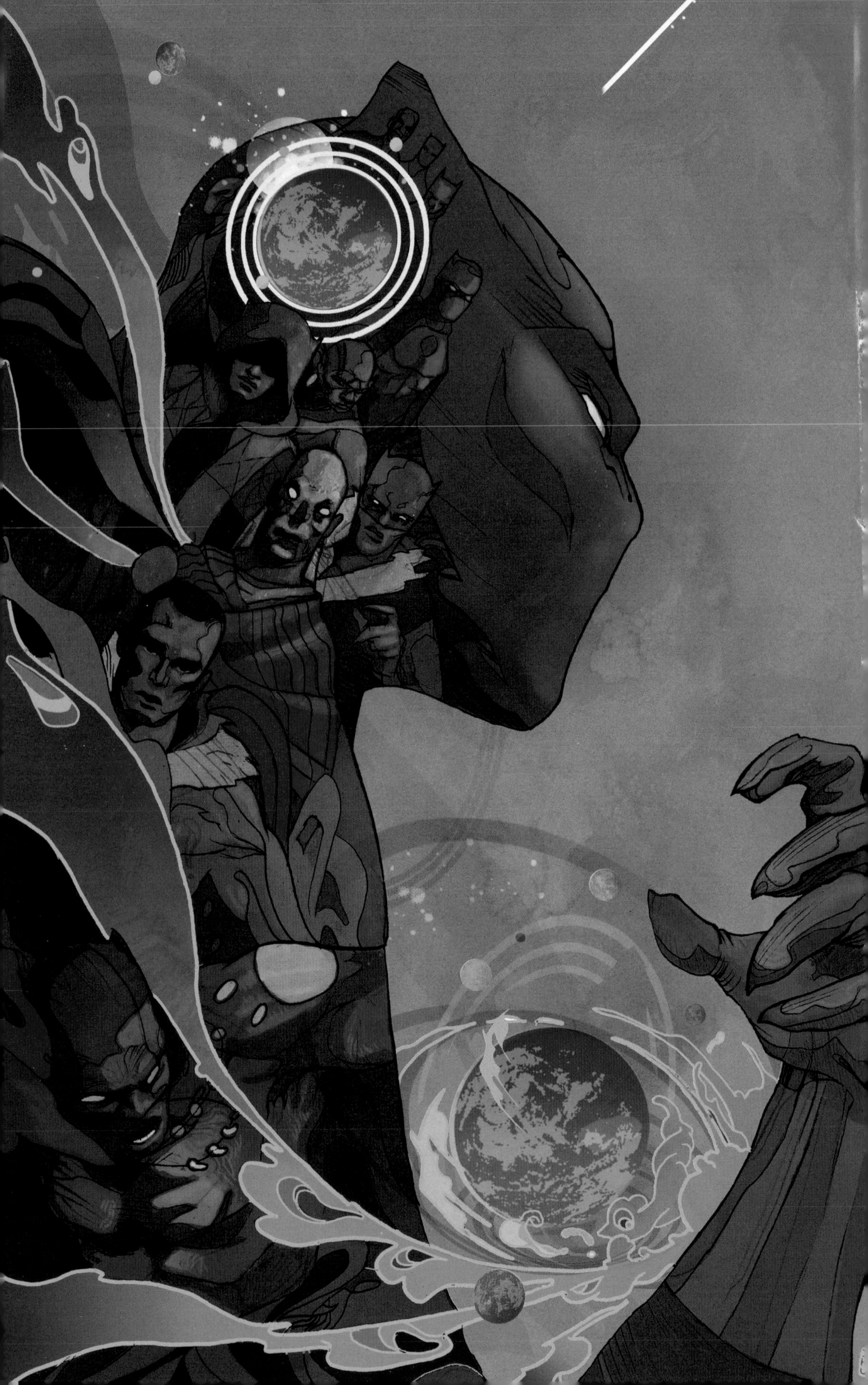

#21 GUARDIANS OF THE GALAXY VARIANT BY
PASQUAL FERRY & JASON KEITH

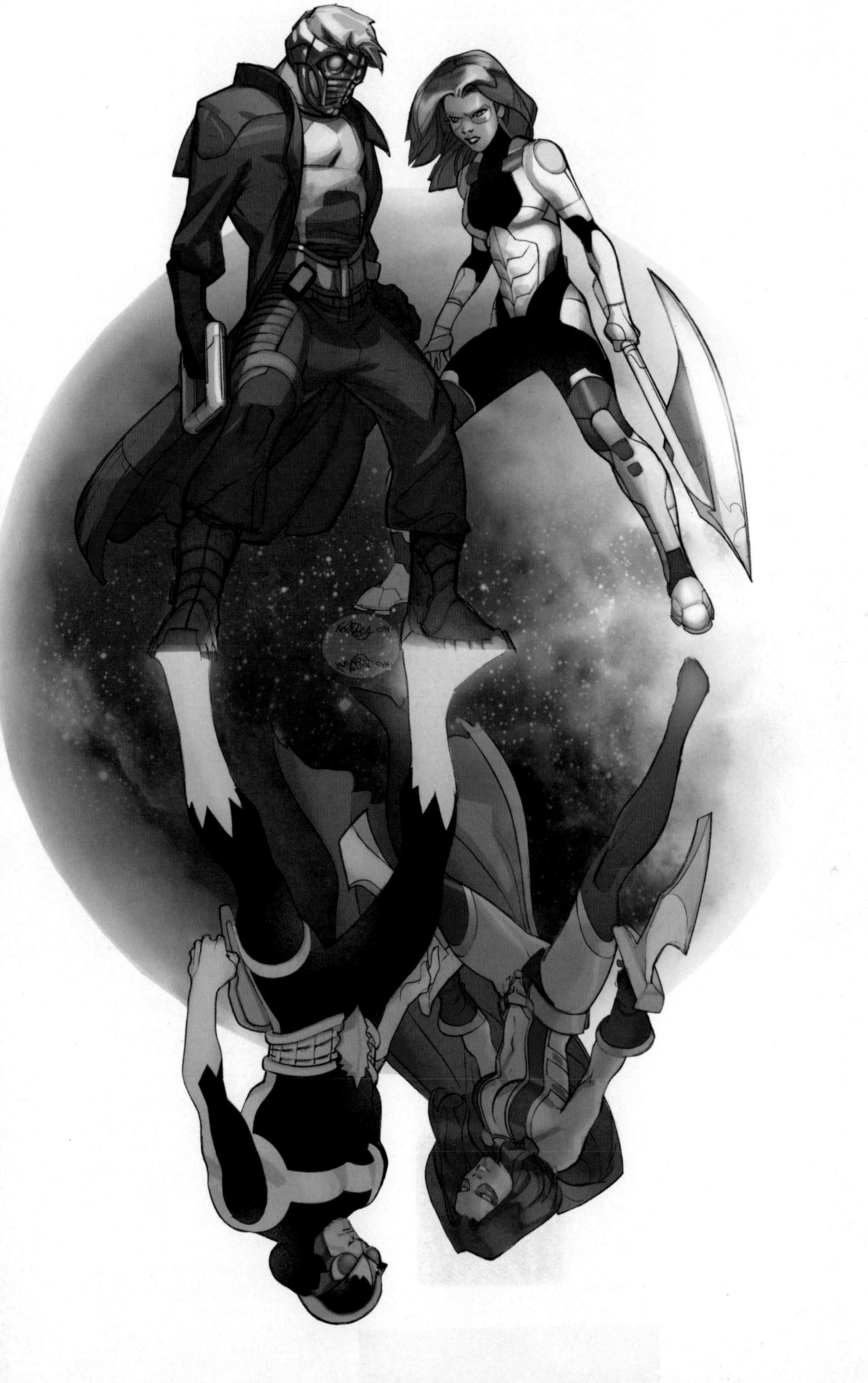

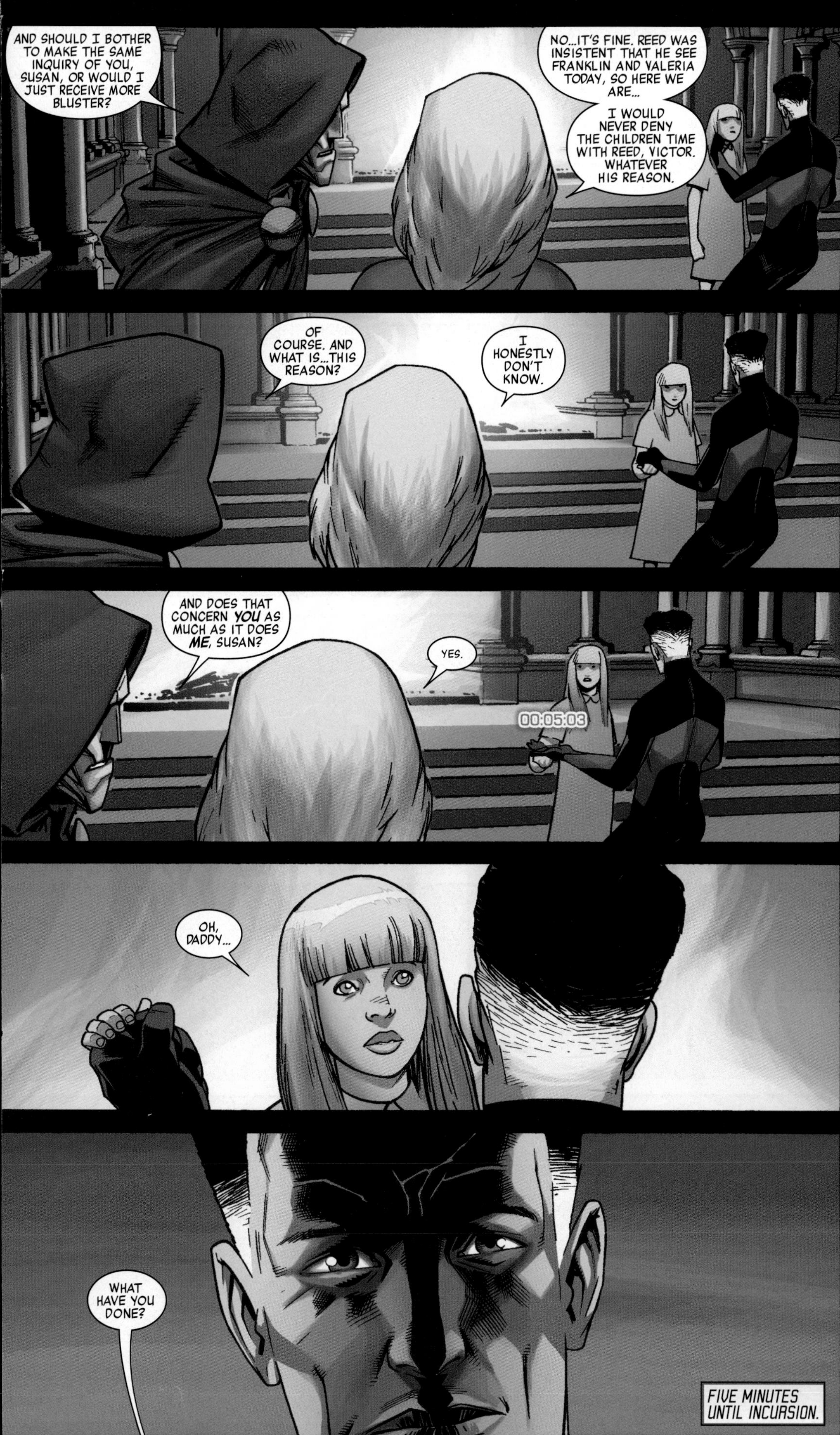
AND SHOULD I BOTHER TO MAKE THE SAME INQUIRY OF YOU, SUSAN, OR WOULD I JUST RECEIVE MORE BLUSTER?
NO...IT'S FINE. REED WAS INSISTENT THAT HE SEE FRANKLIN AND VALERIA TODAY, SO HERE WE ARE...
I WOULD NEVER DENY THE CHILDREN TIME WITH REED, VICTOR. WHATEVER HIS REASON.
OF COURSE. AND WHAT IS...THIS REASON?
I HONESTLY DON'T KNOW.
AND DOES THAT CONCERN YOU AS MUCH AS IT DOES ME, SUSAN?
YES.
00:05:03
OH, DADDY...
WHAT HAVE YOU DONE?
FIVE MINUTES UNTIL INCURSION.

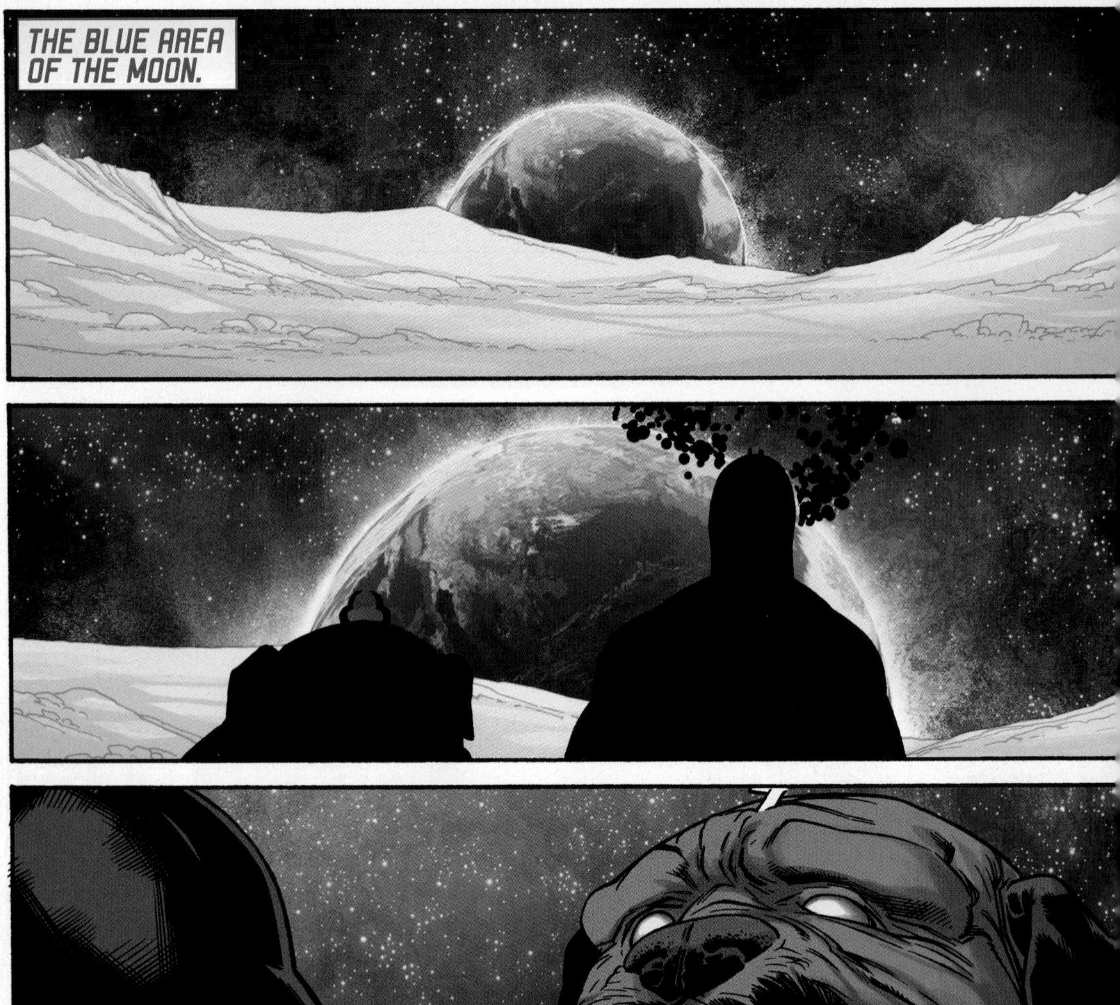
THE BLUE AREA OF THE MOON.
ONE MINUTE UNTIL INCURSION.

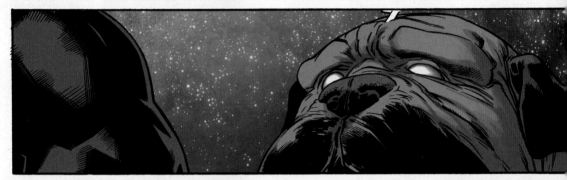

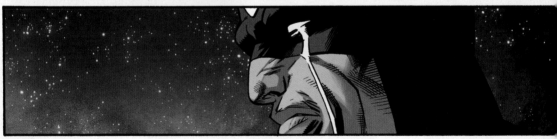

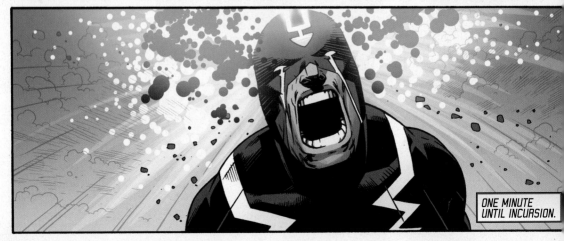

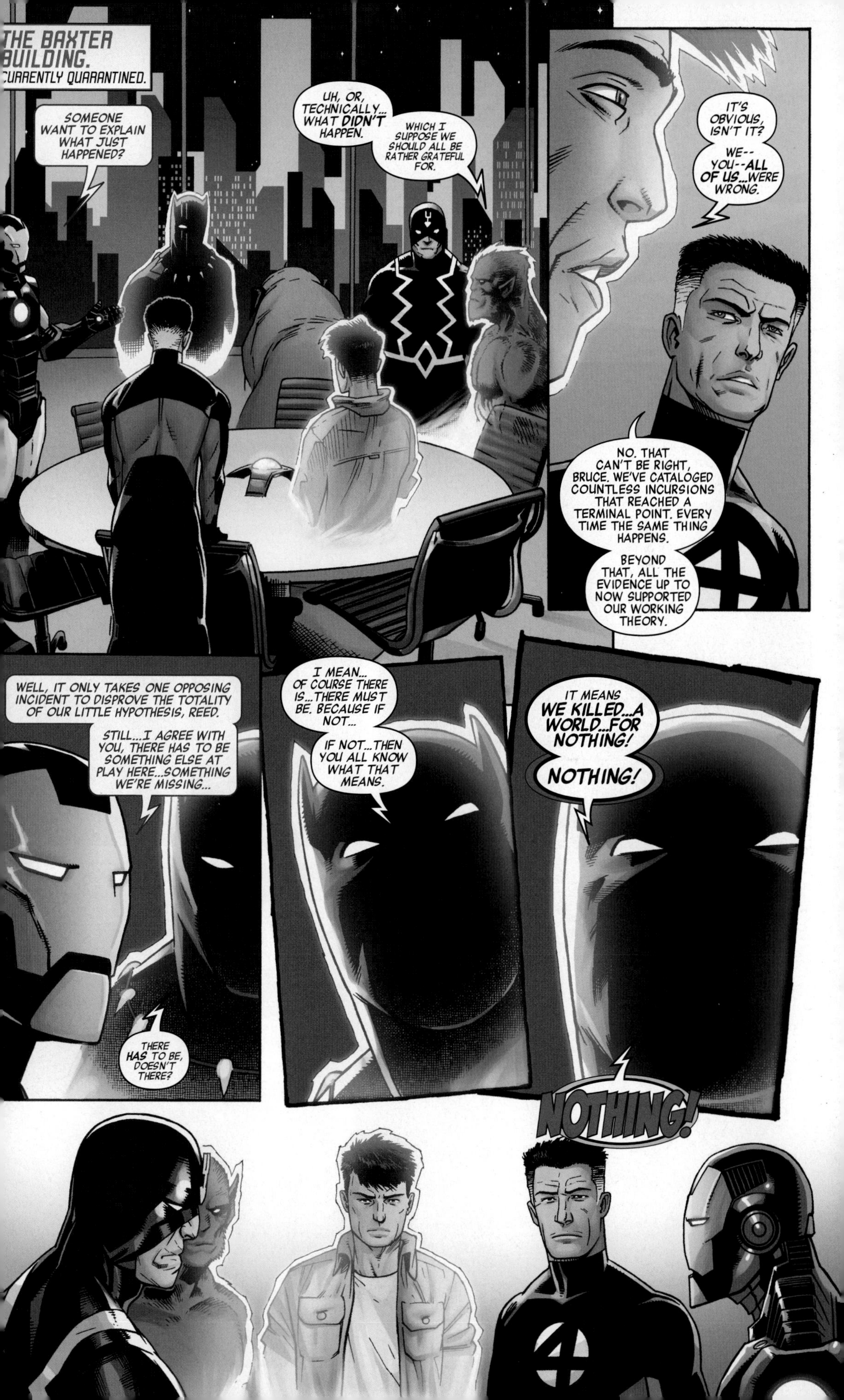
THE BAXTER BUILDING. CURRENTLY QUARANTINED.
SOMEONE WANT TO EXPLAIN WHAT JUST HAPPENED?
UH, OR, TECHNICALLY... WHAT DIDN'T HAPPEN.
WHICH I SUPPOSE WE SHOULD ALL BE RATHER GRATEFUL FOR.
IT'S OBVIOUS, ISN'T IT?
WE-- YOU--ALL OF US...WERE WRONG.
NO. THAT CAN'T BE RIGHT, BRUCE. WE'VE CATALOGED COUNTLESS INCURSIONS THAT REACHED A TERMINAL POINT. EVERY TIME THE SAME THING HAPPENS.
BEYOND THAT, ALL THE EVIDENCE UP TO NOW SUPPORTED OUR WORKING THEORY.
WELL, IT ONLY TAKES ONE OPPOSING INCIDENT TO DISPROVE THE TOTALITY OF OUR LITTLE HYPOTHESIS, REED.
STILL...I AGREE WITH YOU, THERE HAS TO BE SOMETHING ELSE AT PLAY HERE...SOMETHING WE'RE MISSING...
THERE HAS TO BE, DOESN'T THERE?
I MEAN... OF COURSE THERE IS...THERE MUST BE. BECAUSE IF NOT...
IF NOT...THEN YOU ALL KNOW WHAT THAT MEANS.
IT MEANS WE KILLED...A WORLD...FOR NOTHING!
NOTHING!
NOTHING!

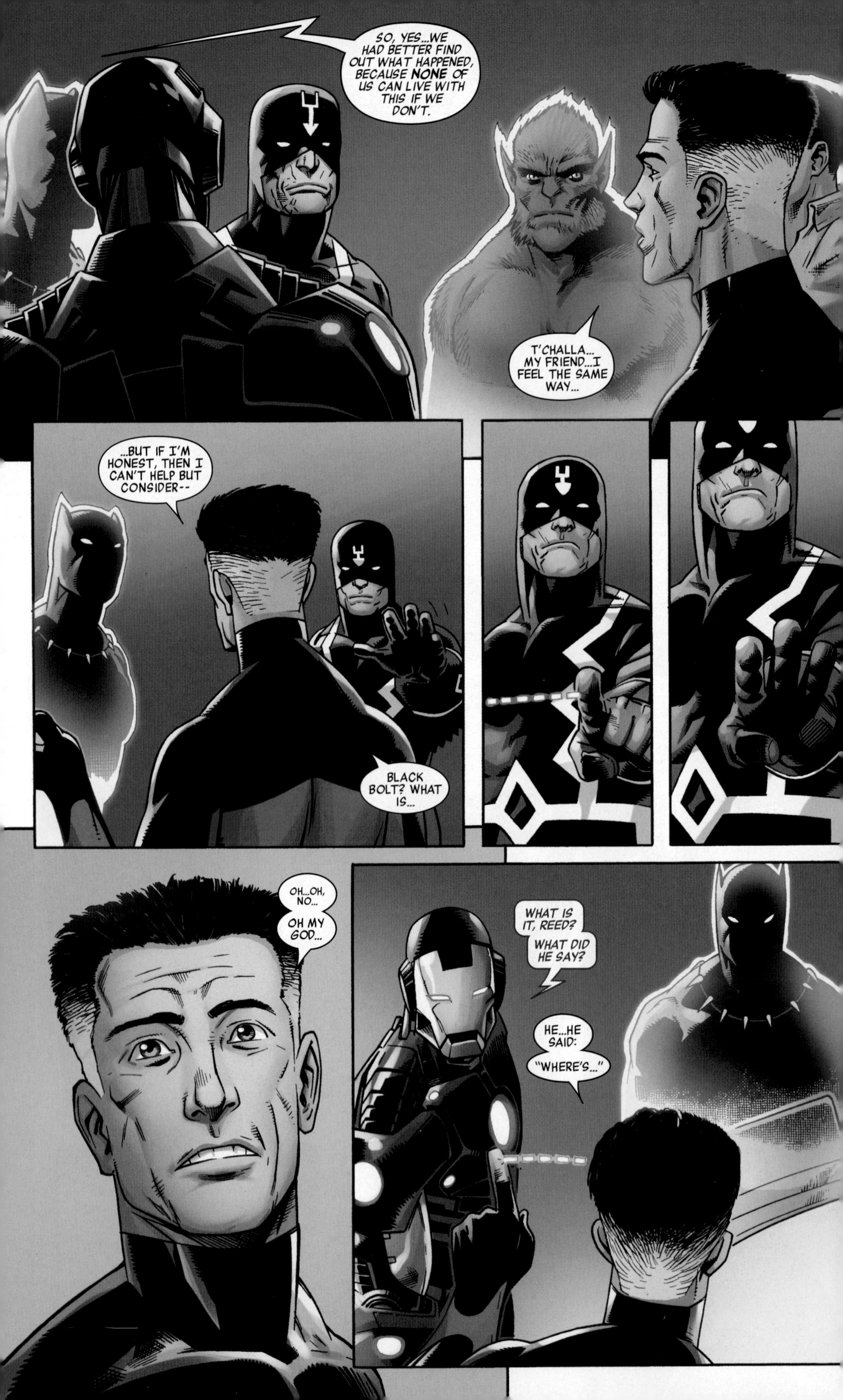

SO, YES...WE HAD BETTER FIND OUT WHAT HAPPENED, BECAUSE **NONE** OF US CAN LIVE WITH THIS IF WE DON'T.
T'CHALLA... MY FRIEND...I FEEL THE SAME WAY...
...BUT IF I'M HONEST, THEN I CAN'T HELP BUT CONSIDER--
BLACK BOLT? WHAT IS...
OH...OH, NO...
OH MY GOD...
WHAT IS IT, REED?
WHAT DID HE SAY?
HE...HE SAID:
"WHERE'S..."

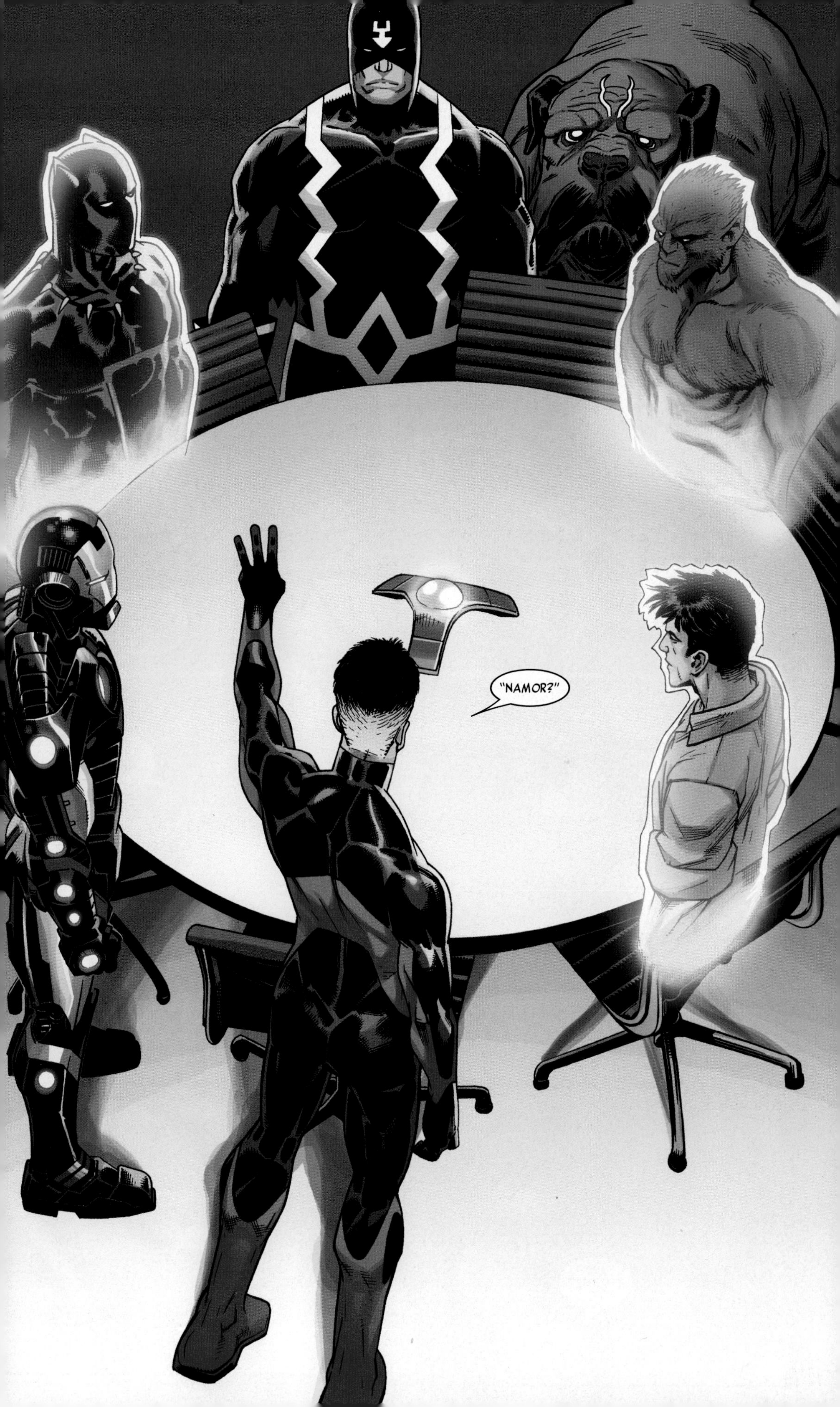
"NAMOR?"

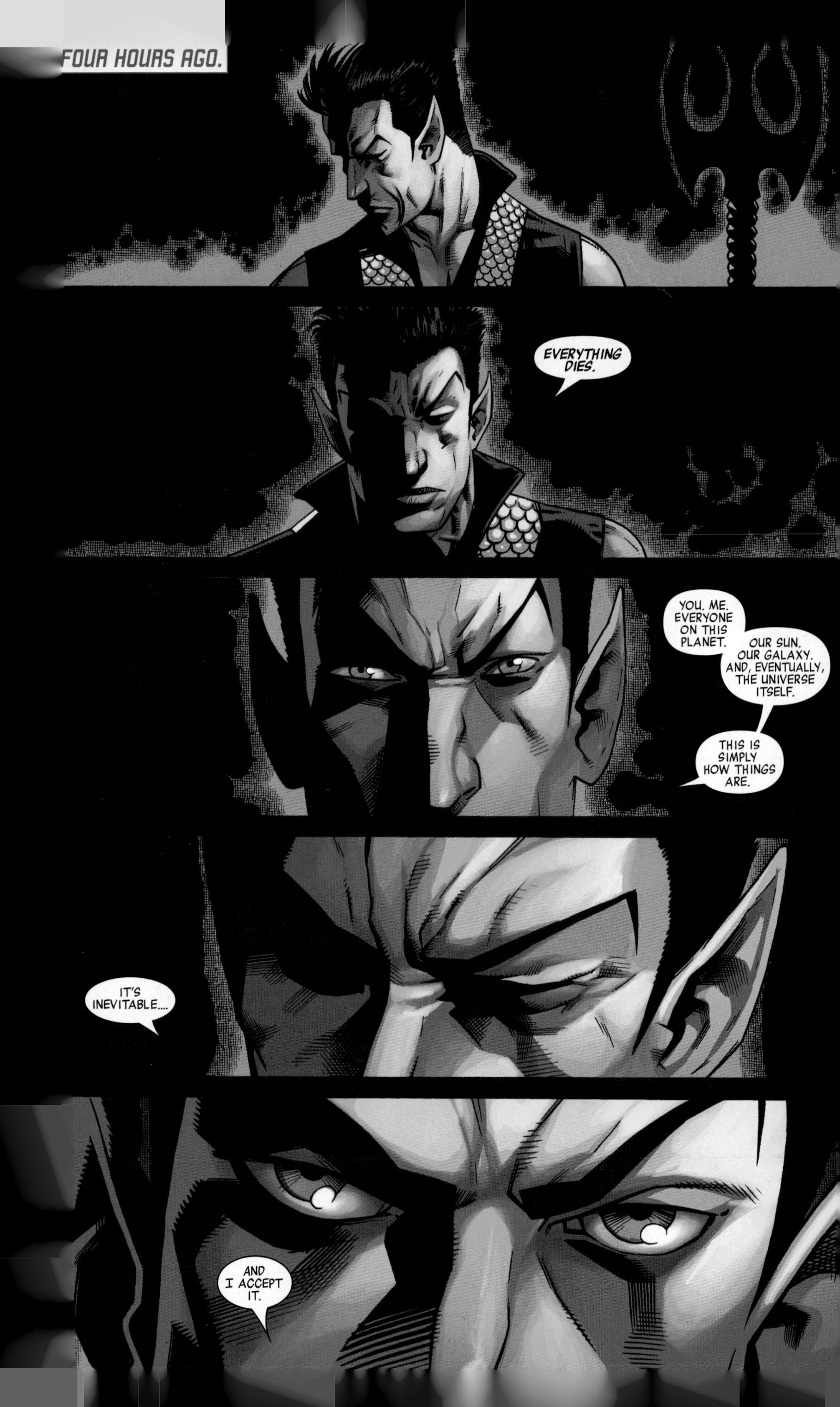
FOUR HOURS AGO.
EVERYTHING DIES.
YOU. ME. EVERYONE ON THIS PLANET.
OUR SUN. OUR GALAXY. AND, EVENTUALLY, THE UNIVERSE ITSELF.
THIS IS SIMPLY HOW THINGS ARE.
IT'S INEVITABLE....
AND I ACCEPT IT.

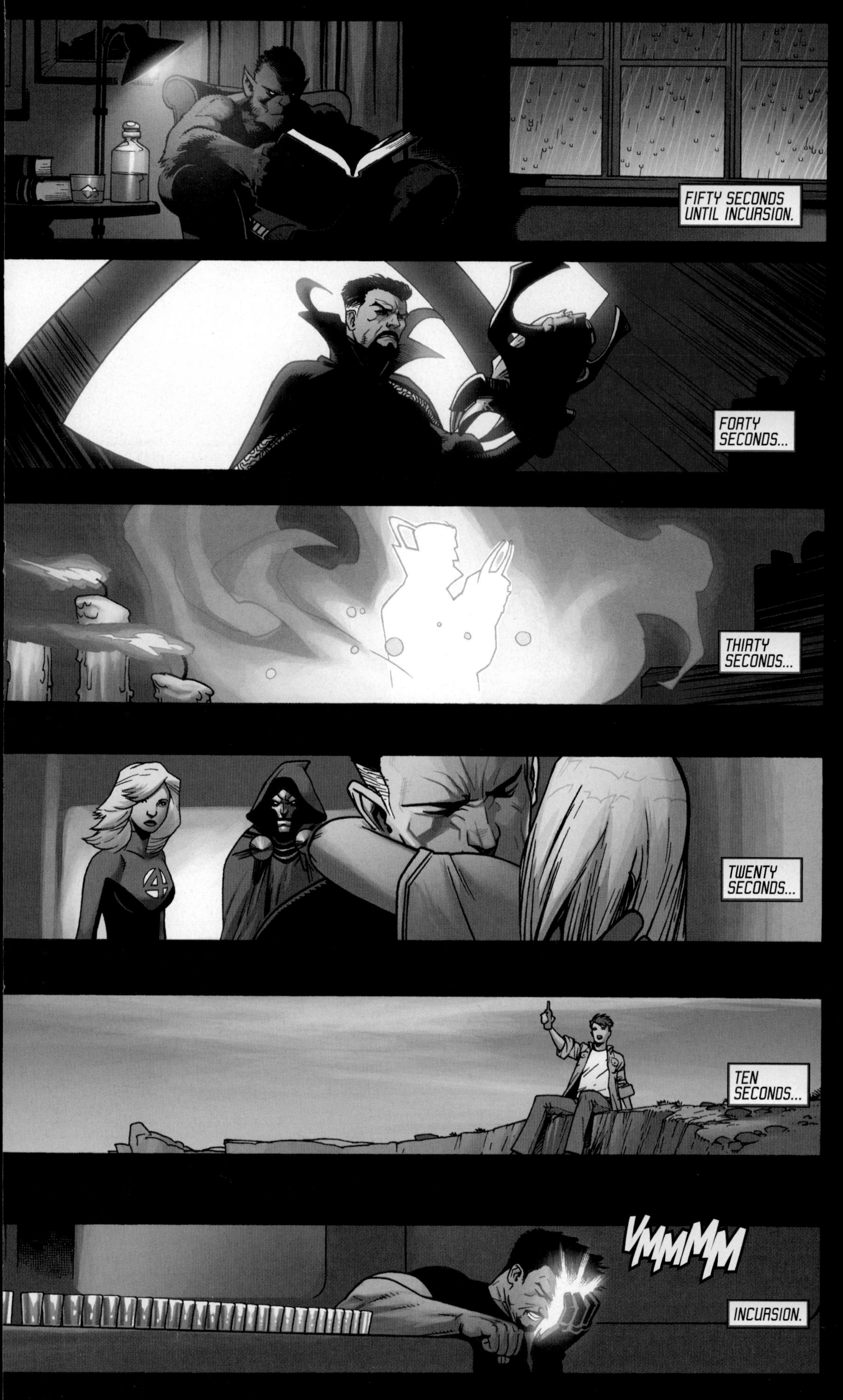

FIFTY SECONDS UNTIL INCURSION.
FORTY SECONDS...
THIRTY SECONDS...
TWENTY SECONDS...
TEN SECONDS...
VMMMM
INCURSION.

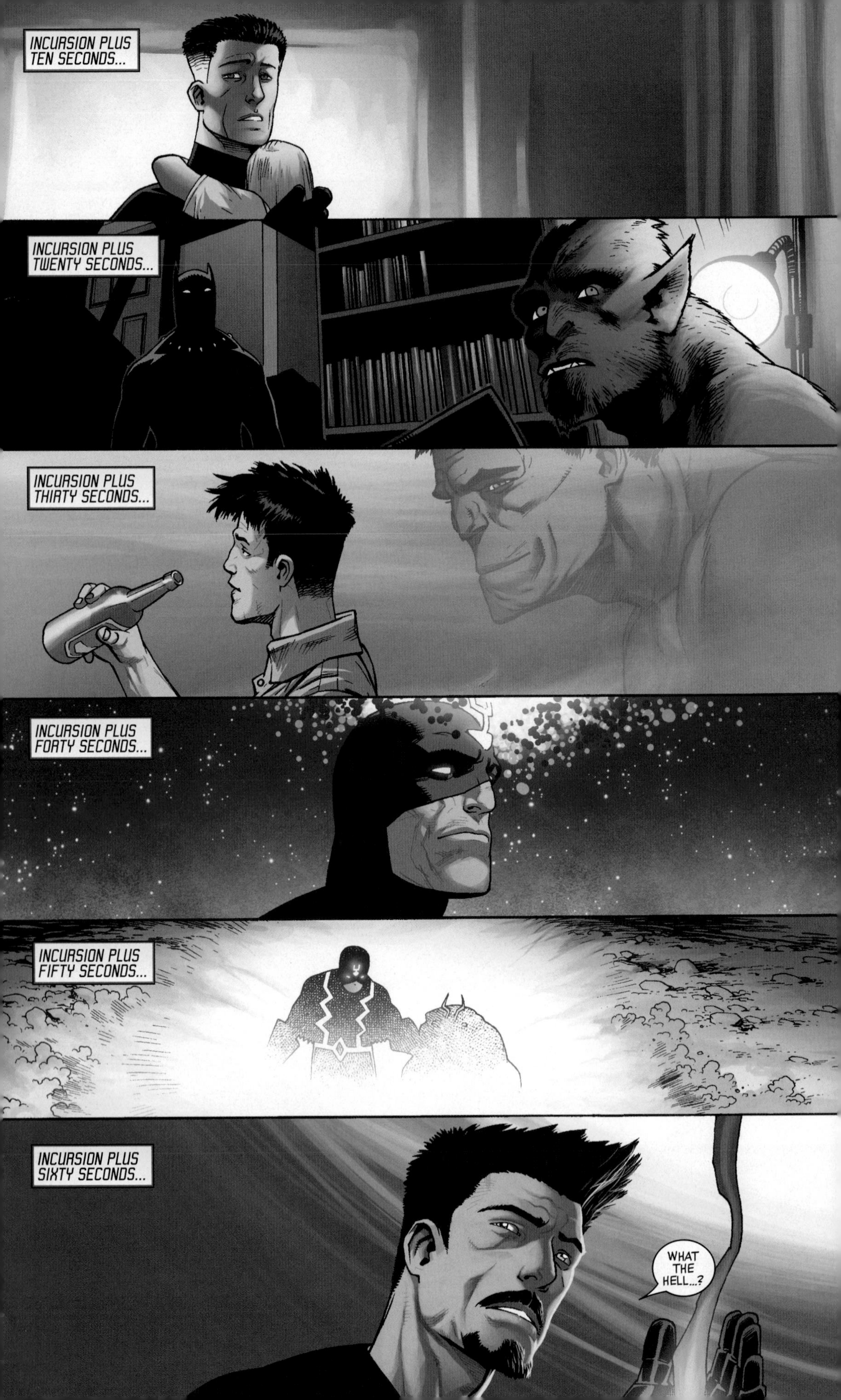
INCURSION PLUS TEN SECONDS...
INCURSION PLUS TWENTY SECONDS...
INCURSION PLUS THIRTY SECONDS...
INCURSION PLUS FORTY SECONDS...
INCURSION PLUS FIFTY SECONDS...
INCURSION PLUS SIXTY SECONDS...
WHAT THE HELL...?

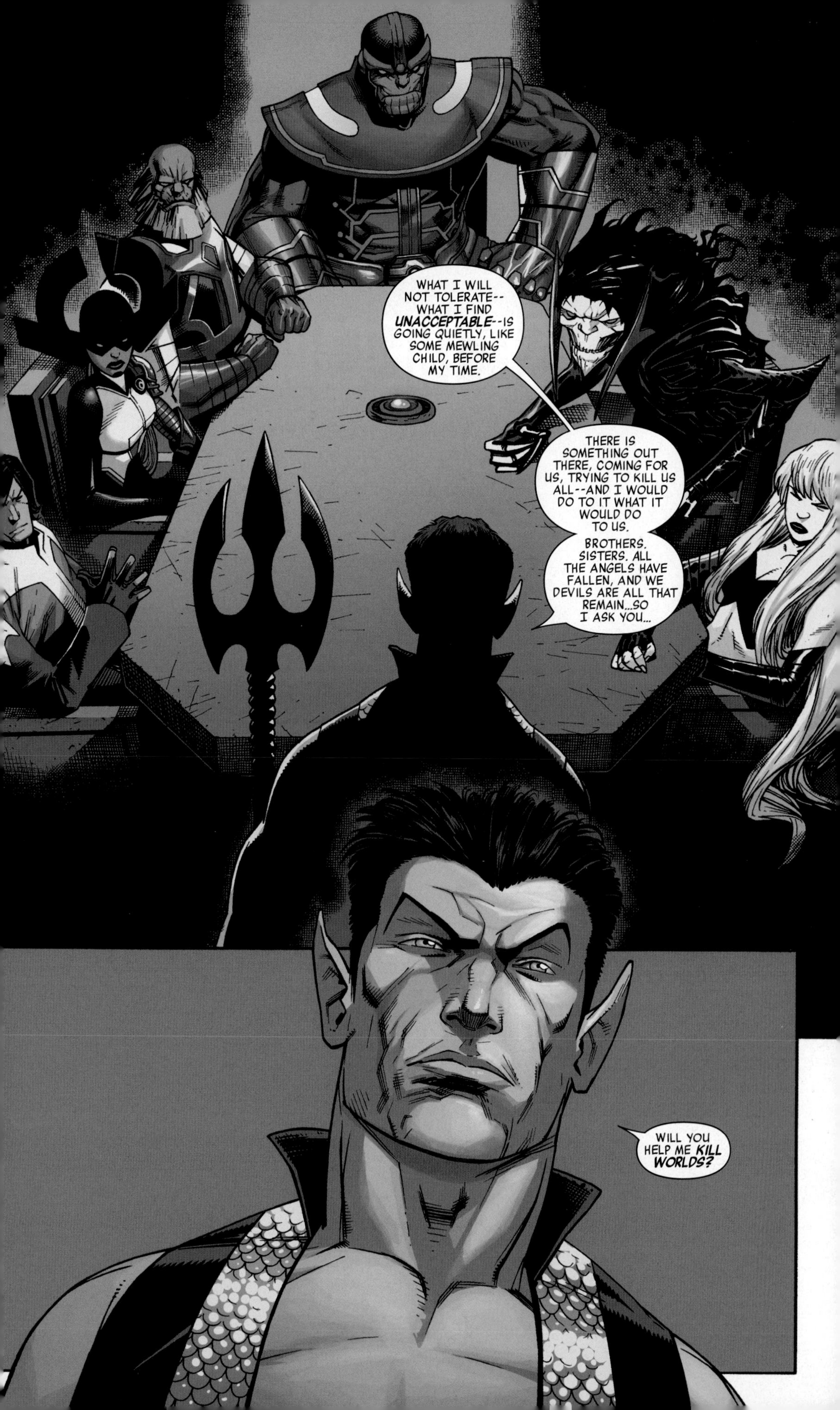
WHAT I WILL NOT TOLERATE-- WHAT I FIND UNACCEPTABLE--IS GOING QUIETLY, LIKE SOME MEWLING CHILD, BEFORE MY TIME.
THERE IS SOMETHING OUT THERE, COMING FOR US, TRYING TO KILL US ALL--AND I WOULD DO TO IT WHAT IT WOULD DO TO US.
BROTHERS. SISTERS. ALL THE ANGELS HAVE FALLEN, AND WE DEVILS ARE ALL THAT REMAIN...SO I ASK YOU...
WILL YOU HELP ME KILL WORLDS?

RISE, THE CABAL.

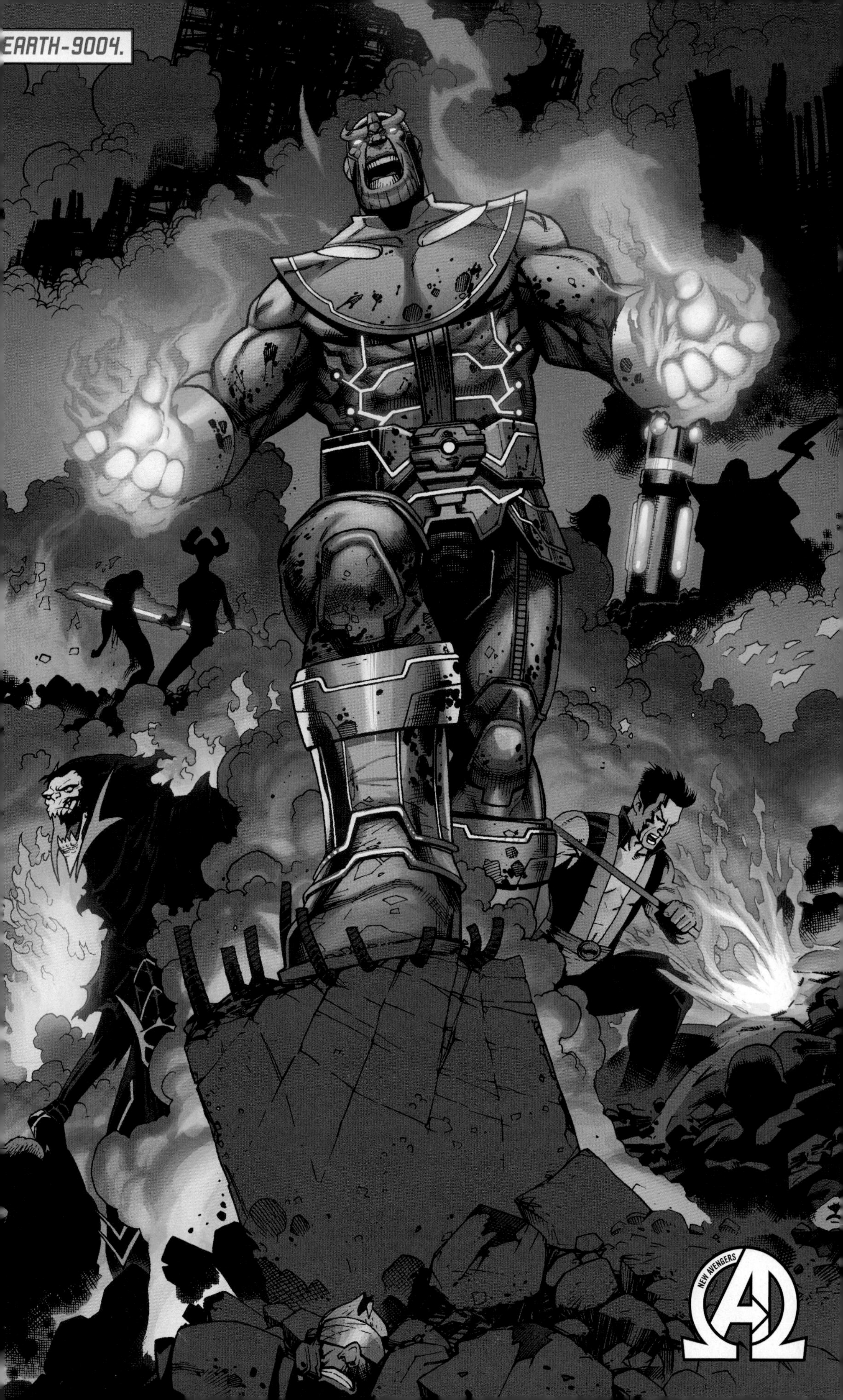
EARTH-9004.

COVER GALLERY

#18

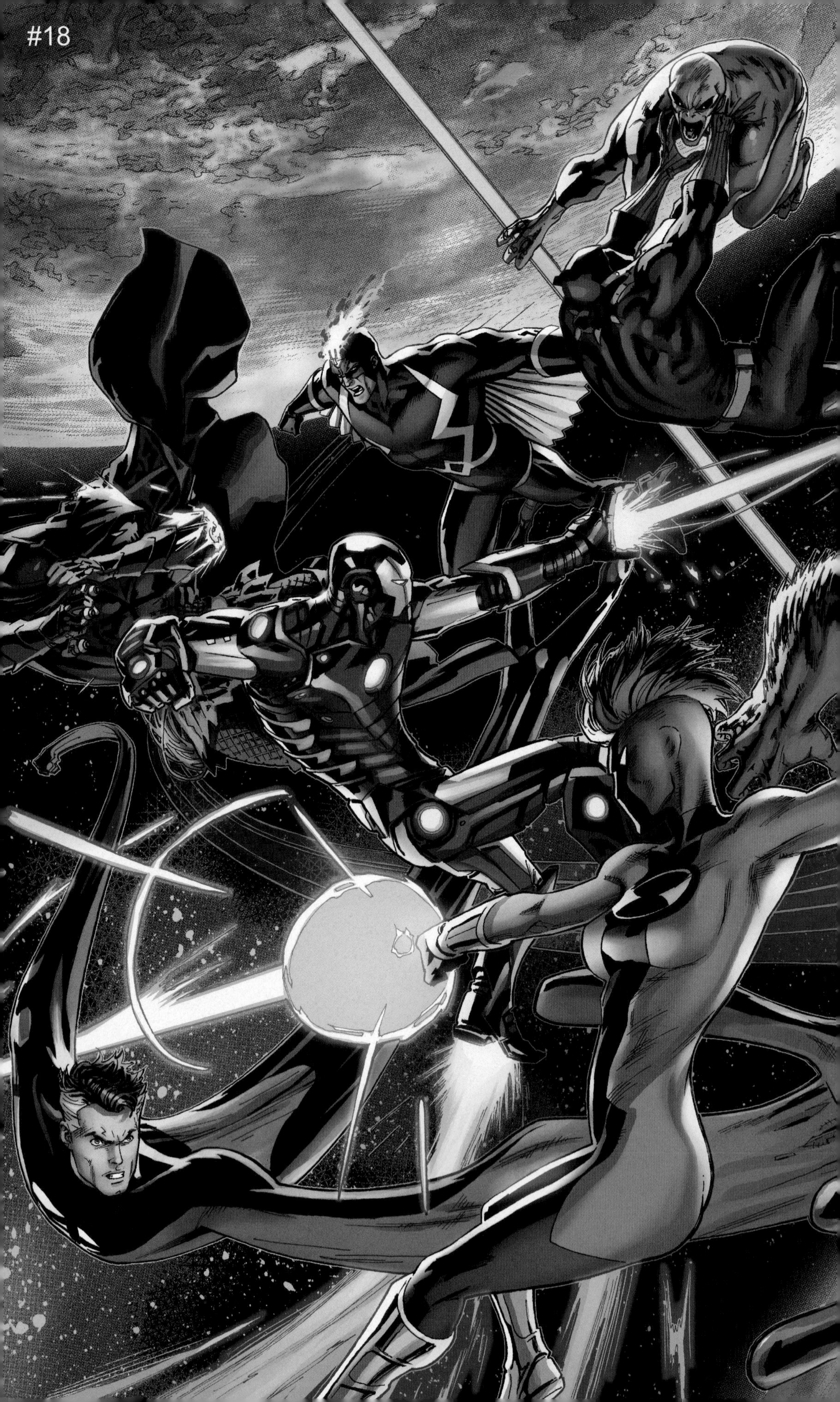

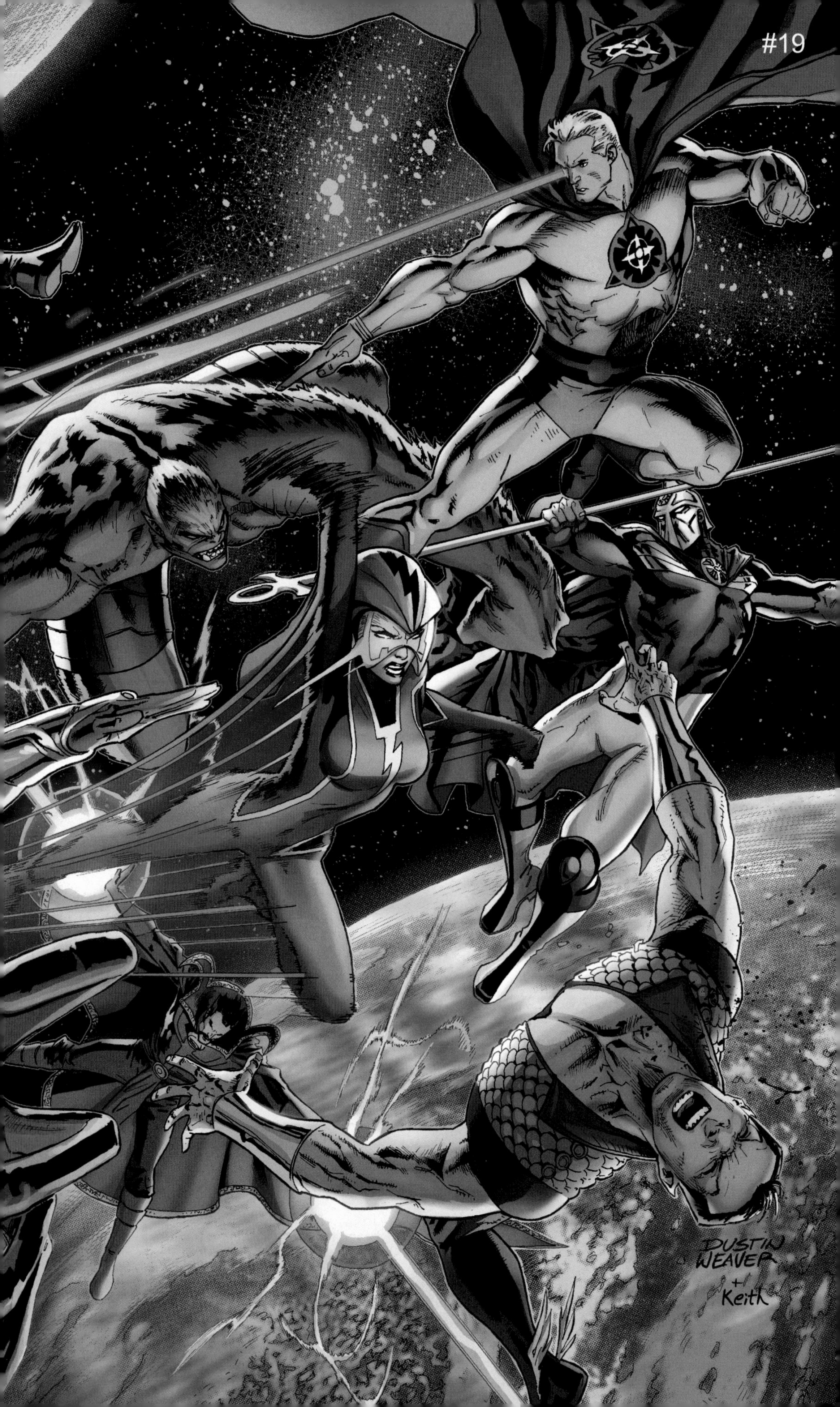
#19
DUSTIN WEAVER
+
Keith

#20

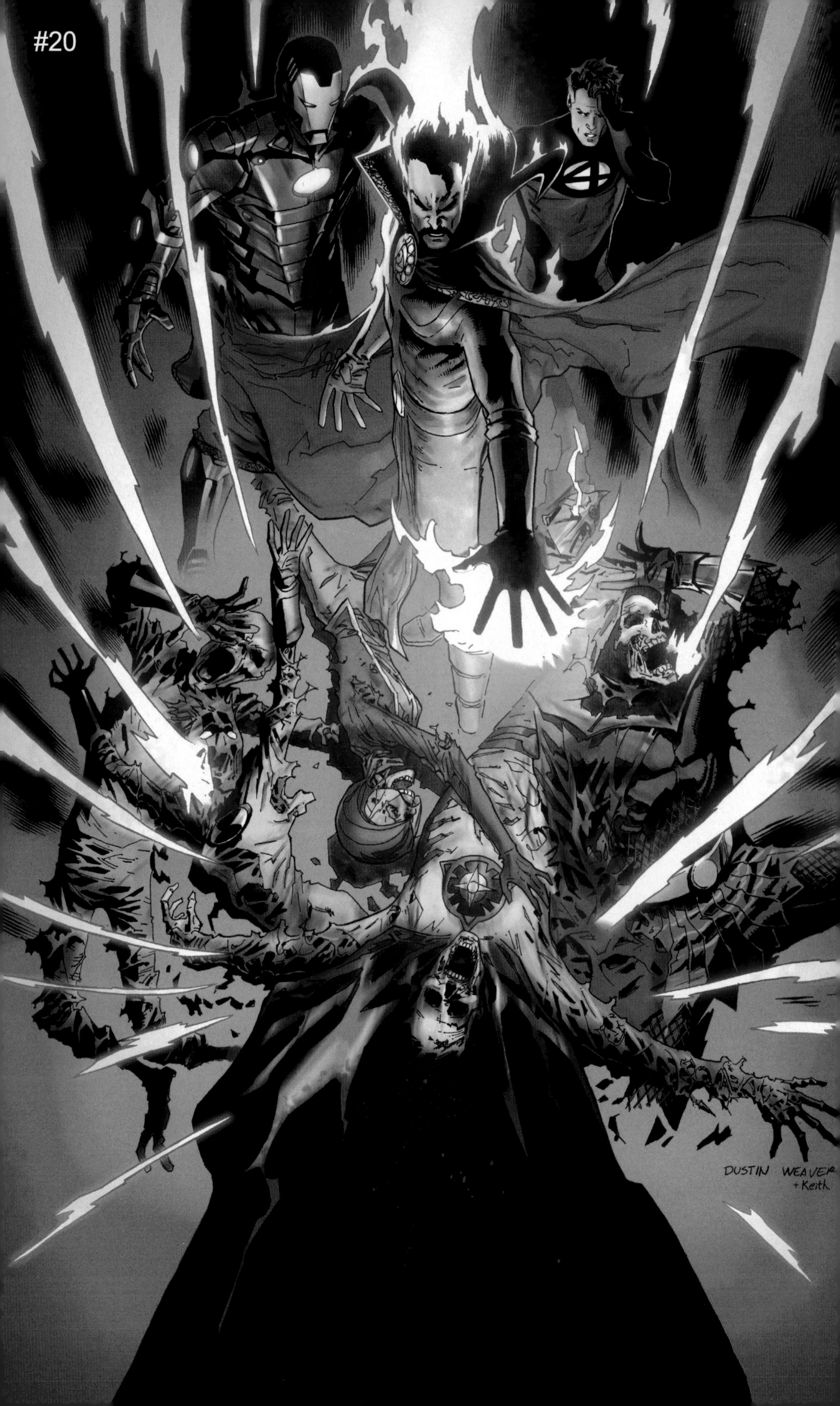
DUSTIN WEAVER
+ Keith

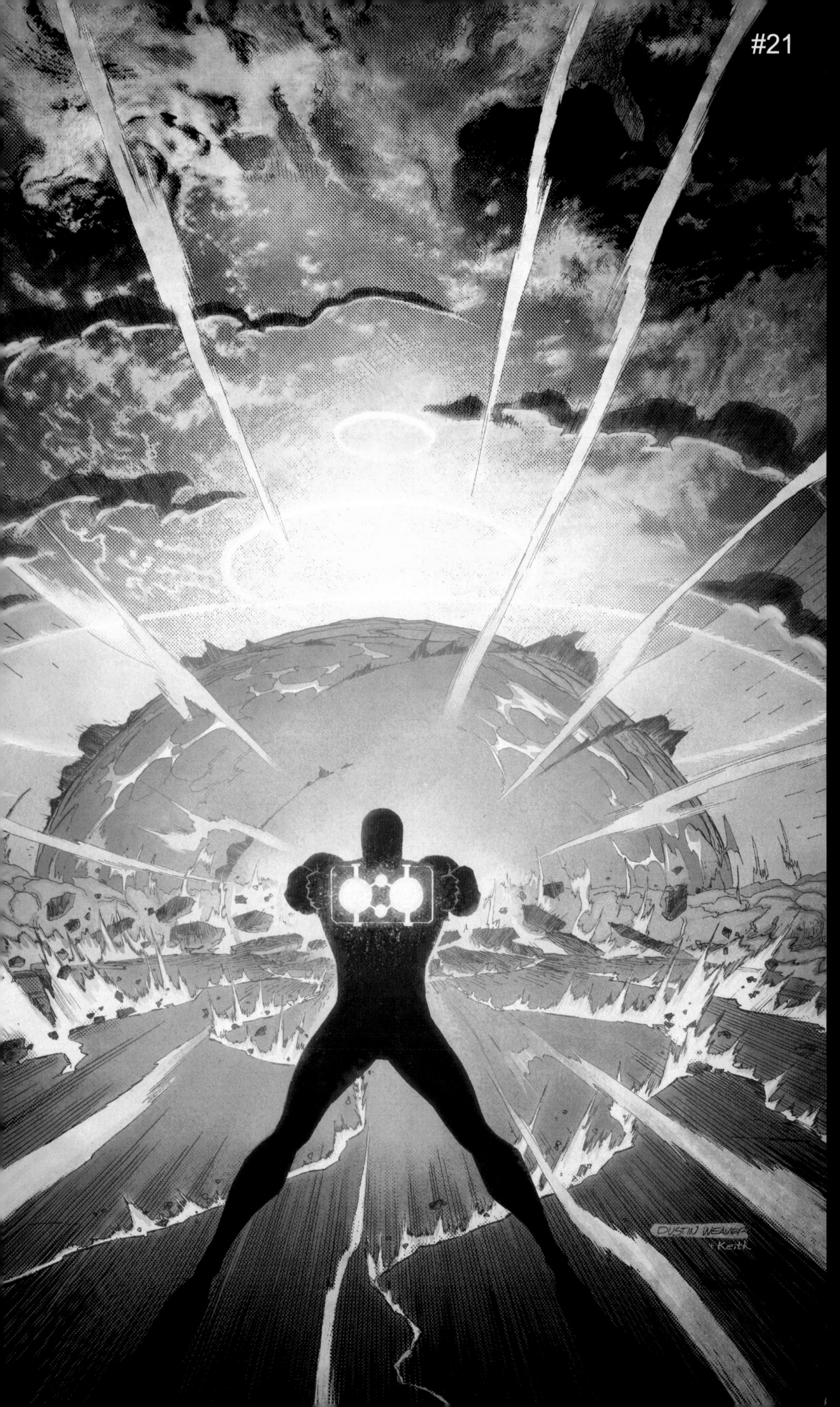
#21
DUSTIN WEAVER
+ Keith

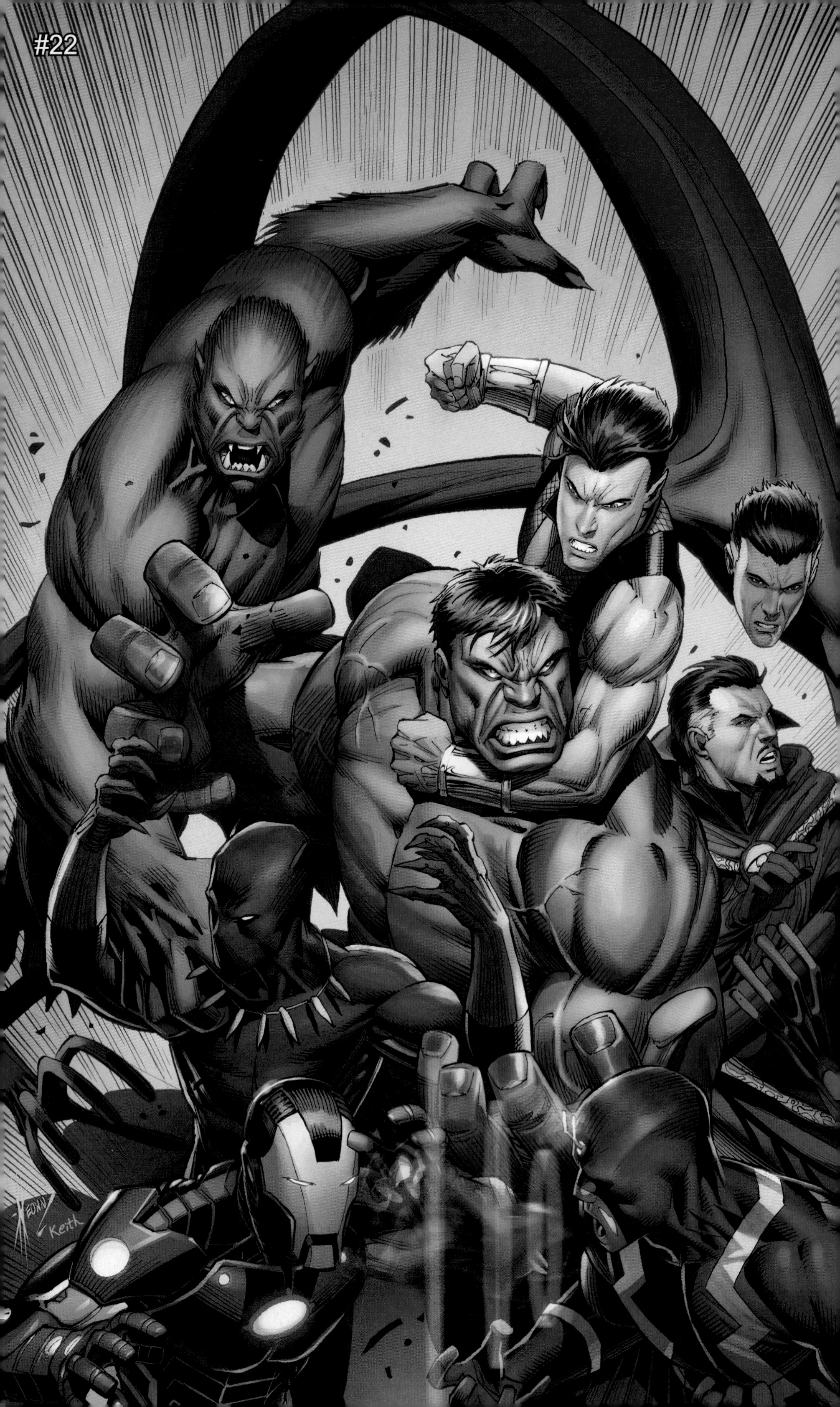
#22
Keith

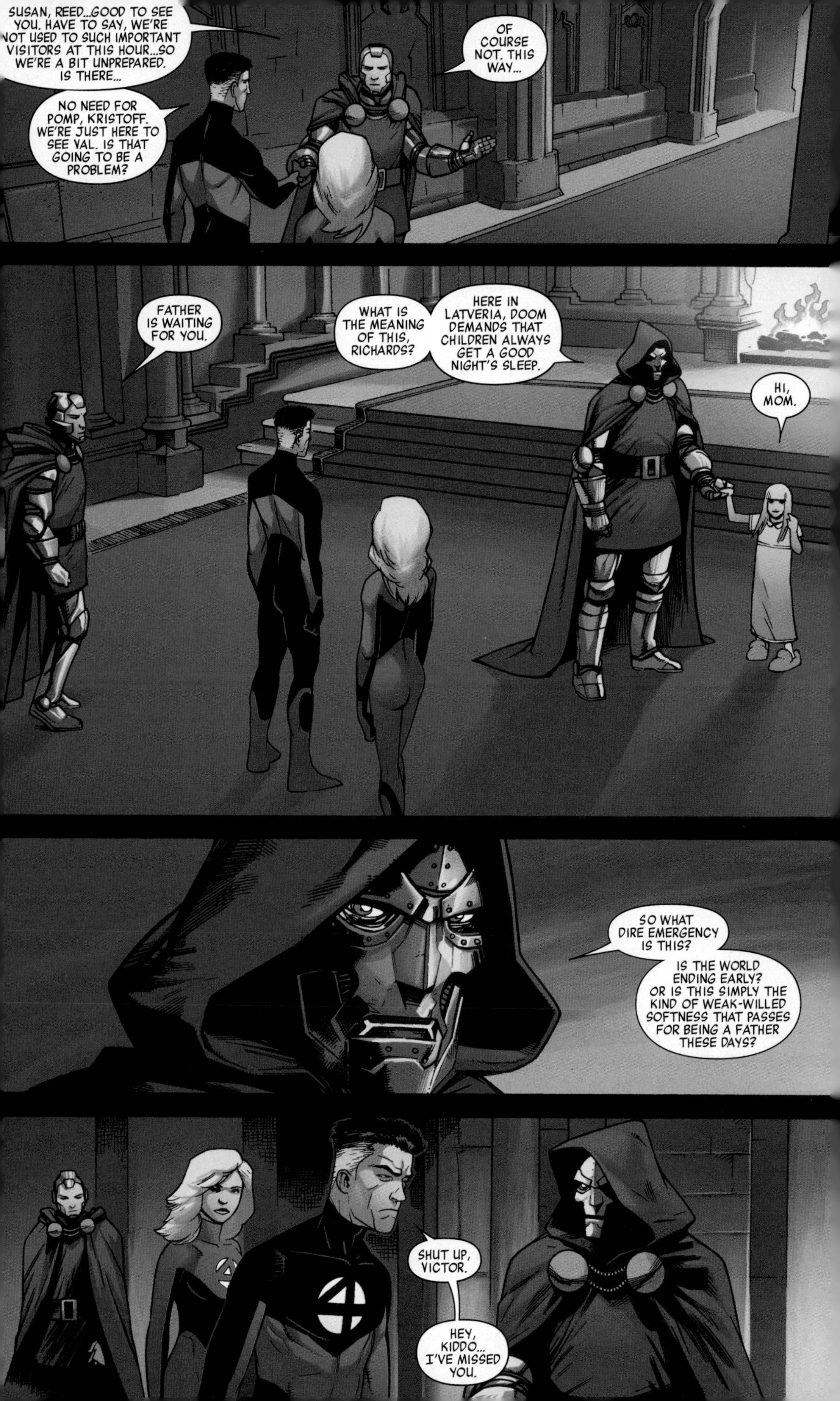
SUSAN, REED...GOOD TO SEE YOU. HAVE TO SAY, WE'RE NOT USED TO SUCH IMPORTANT VISITORS AT THIS HOUR...SO WE'RE A BIT UNPREPARED. IS THERE...
NO NEED FOR POMP, KRISTOFF. WE'RE JUST HERE TO SEE VAL. IS THAT GOING TO BE A PROBLEM?
OF COURSE NOT. THIS WAY...
FATHER IS WAITING FOR YOU.
WHAT IS THE MEANING OF THIS, RICHARDS?
HERE IN LATVERIA, DOOM DEMANDS THAT CHILDREN ALWAYS GET A GOOD NIGHT'S SLEEP.
HI, MOM.
SO WHAT DIRE EMERGENCY IS THIS?
IS THE WORLD ENDING EARLY? OR IS THIS SIMPLY THE KIND OF WEAK-WILLED SOFTNESS THAT PASSES FOR BEING A FATHER THESE DAYS?
SHUT UP, VICTOR.
HEY, KIDDO... I'VE MISSED YOU.

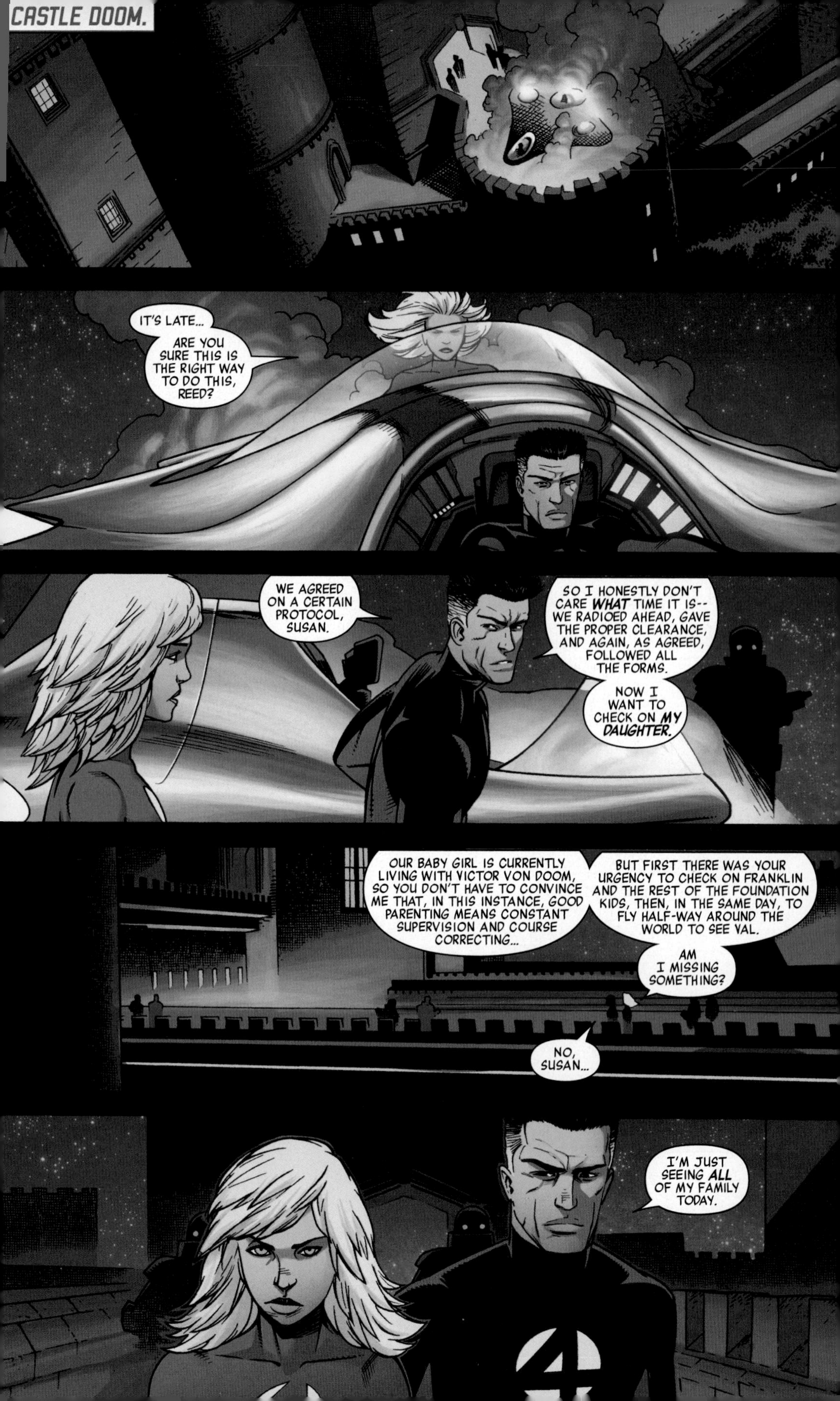
CASTLE DOOM.
IT'S LATE...
ARE YOU SURE THIS IS THE RIGHT WAY TO DO THIS, REED?
WE AGREED ON A CERTAIN PROTOCOL, SUSAN.
SO I HONESTLY DON'T CARE WHAT TIME IT IS-- WE RADIOED AHEAD, GAVE THE PROPER CLEARANCE, AND AGAIN, AS AGREED, FOLLOWED ALL THE FORMS.
NOW I WANT TO CHECK ON MY DAUGHTER.
OUR BABY GIRL IS CURRENTLY LIVING WITH VICTOR VON DOOM, SO YOU DON'T HAVE TO CONVINCE ME THAT, IN THIS INSTANCE, GOOD PARENTING MEANS CONSTANT SUPERVISION AND COURSE CORRECTING...
BUT FIRST THERE WAS YOUR URGENCY TO CHECK ON FRANKLIN AND THE REST OF THE FOUNDATION KIDS, THEN, IN THE SAME DAY, TO FLY HALF-WAY AROUND THE WORLD TO SEE VAL.
AM I MISSING SOMETHING?
NO, SUSAN...
I'M JUST SEEING ALL OF MY FAMILY TODAY.

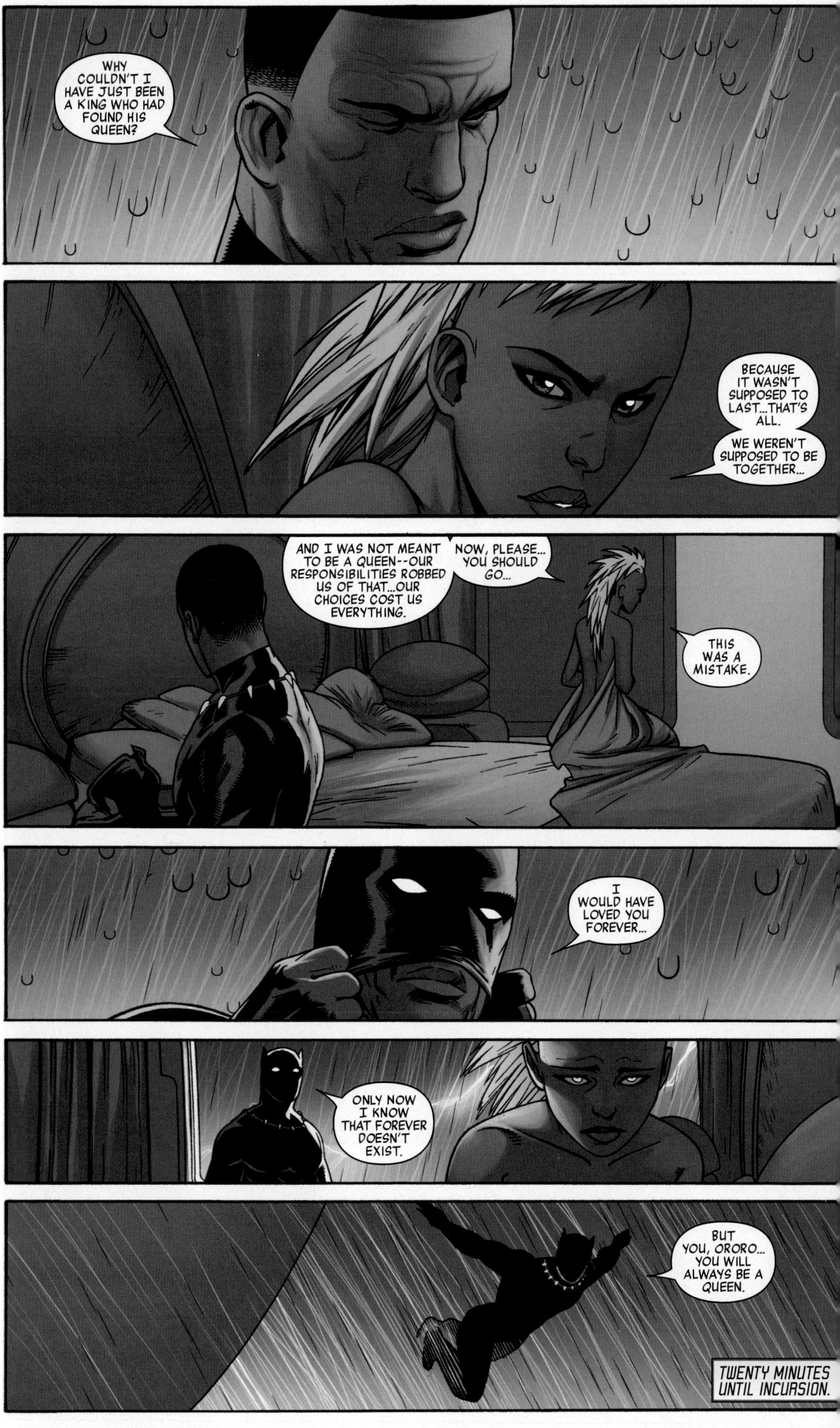
WHY COULDN'T I HAVE JUST BEEN A KING WHO HAD FOUND HIS QUEEN?
BECAUSE IT WASN'T SUPPOSED TO LAST...THAT'S ALL.
WE WEREN'T SUPPOSED TO BE TOGETHER...
AND I WAS NOT MEANT TO BE A QUEEN--OUR RESPONSIBILITIES ROBBED US OF THAT...OUR CHOICES COST US EVERYTHING.
NOW, PLEASE... YOU SHOULD GO...
THIS WAS A MISTAKE.
I WOULD HAVE LOVED YOU FOREVER...
ONLY NOW I KNOW THAT FOREVER DOESN'T EXIST.
BUT YOU, ORORO... YOU WILL ALWAYS BE A QUEEN.
TWENTY MINUTES UNTIL INCURSION.

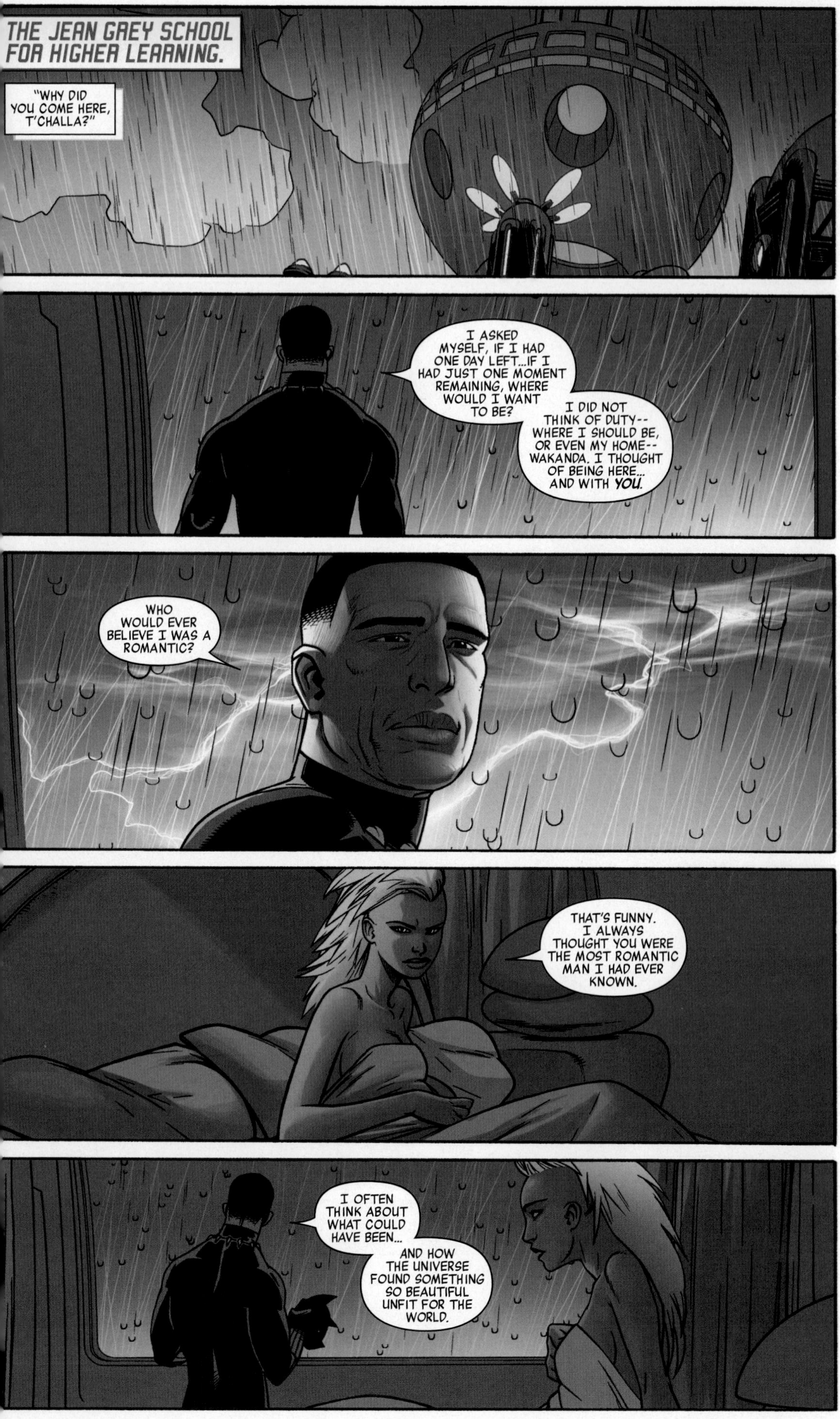
THE JEAN GREY SCHOOL FOR HIGHER LEARNING.
"WHY DID YOU COME HERE, T'CHALLA?"
I ASKED MYSELF, IF I HAD ONE DAY LEFT...IF I HAD JUST ONE MOMENT REMAINING, WHERE WOULD I WANT TO BE?
I DID NOT THINK OF DUTY-- WHERE I SHOULD BE, OR EVEN MY HOME-- WAKANDA. I THOUGHT OF BEING HERE... AND WITH *YOU*.
WHO WOULD EVER BELIEVE I WAS A ROMANTIC?
THAT'S FUNNY. I ALWAYS THOUGHT YOU WERE THE MOST ROMANTIC MAN I HAD EVER KNOWN.
I OFTEN THINK ABOUT WHAT COULD HAVE BEEN...
AND HOW THE UNIVERSE FOUND SOMETHING SO BEAUTIFUL UNFIT FOR THE WORLD.

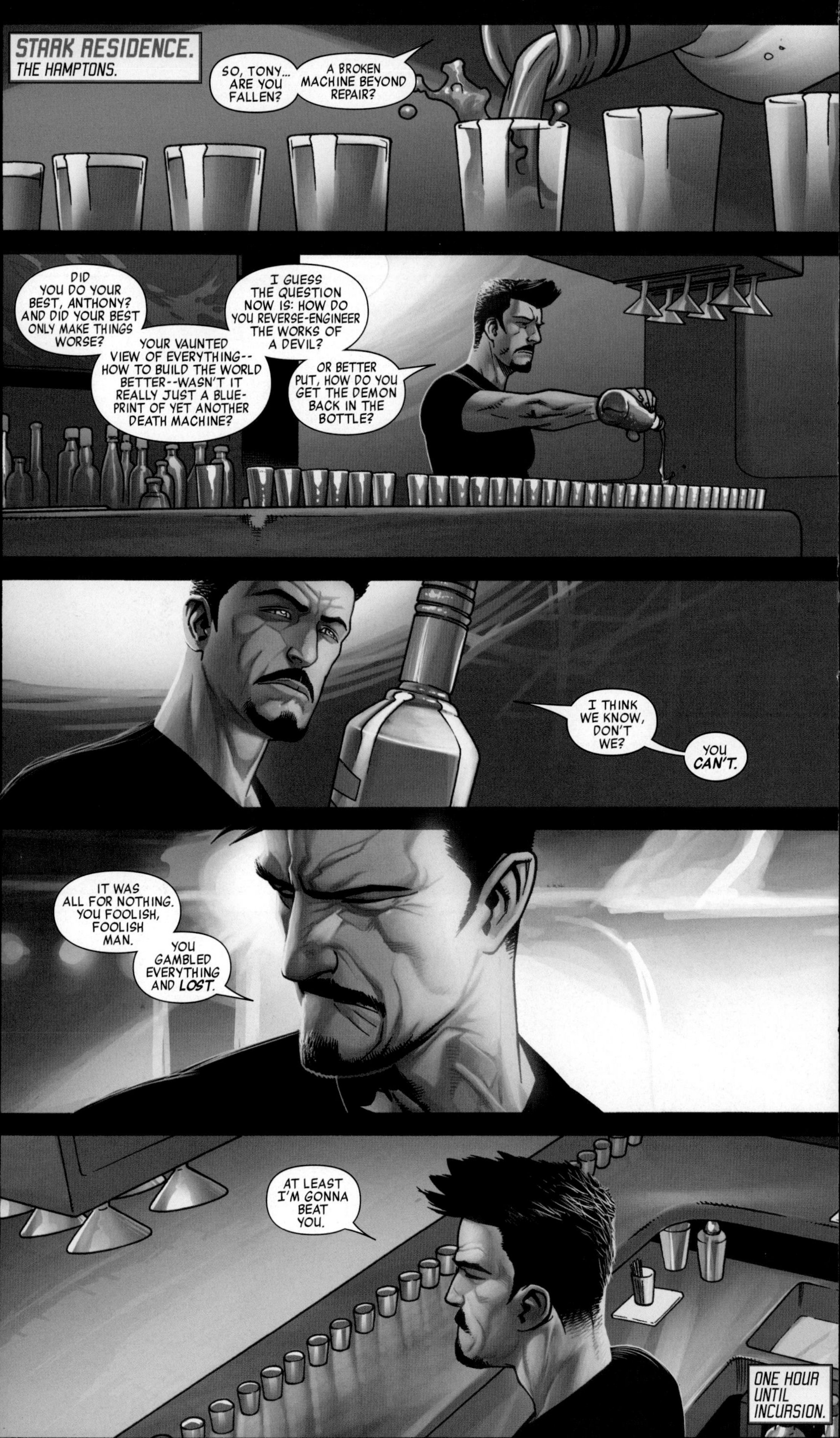
STARK RESIDENCE.
THE HAMPTONS.
SO, TONY... ARE YOU FALLEN?
A BROKEN MACHINE BEYOND REPAIR?
DID YOU DO YOUR BEST, ANTHONY? AND DID YOUR BEST ONLY MAKE THINGS WORSE?
YOUR VAUNTED VIEW OF EVERYTHING--HOW TO BUILD THE WORLD BETTER--WASN'T IT REALLY JUST A BLUE-PRINT OF YET ANOTHER DEATH MACHINE?
I GUESS THE QUESTION NOW IS: HOW DO YOU REVERSE-ENGINEER THE WORKS OF A DEVIL?
OR BETTER PUT, HOW DO YOU GET THE DEMON BACK IN THE BOTTLE?
I THINK WE KNOW, DON'T WE?
YOU ***CAN'T.***
IT WAS ALL FOR NOTHING. YOU FOOLISH, FOOLISH MAN.
YOU GAMBLED EVERYTHING AND ***LOST.***
AT LEAST I'M GONNA BEAT YOU.
ONE HOUR UNTIL INCURSION.

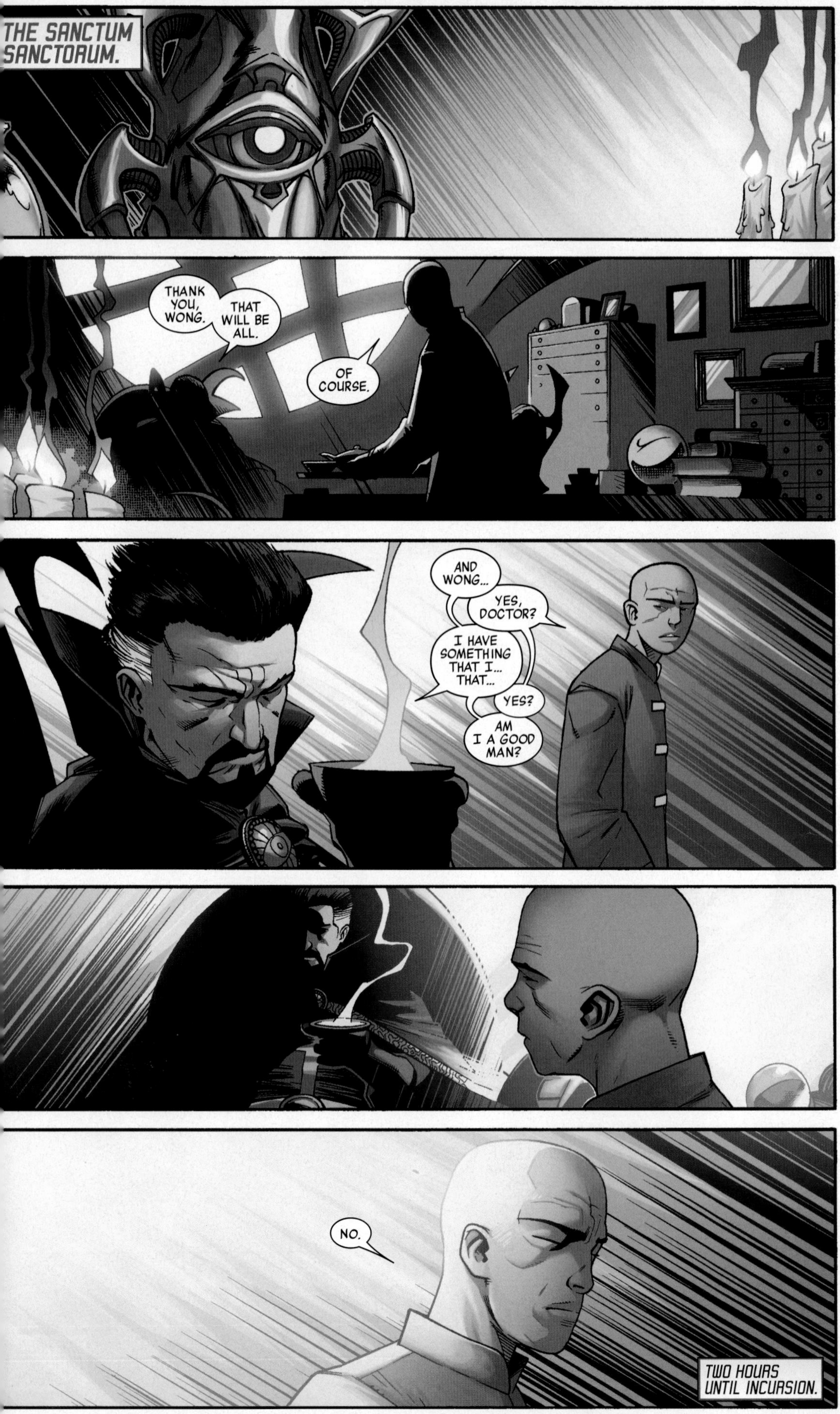
THE SANCTUM SANCTORUM.
THANK YOU, WONG.
THAT WILL BE ALL.
OF COURSE.
AND WONG...
YES, DOCTOR?
I HAVE SOMETHING THAT I... THAT...
YES?
AM I A GOOD MAN?
NO.
TWO HOURS UNTIL INCURSION.

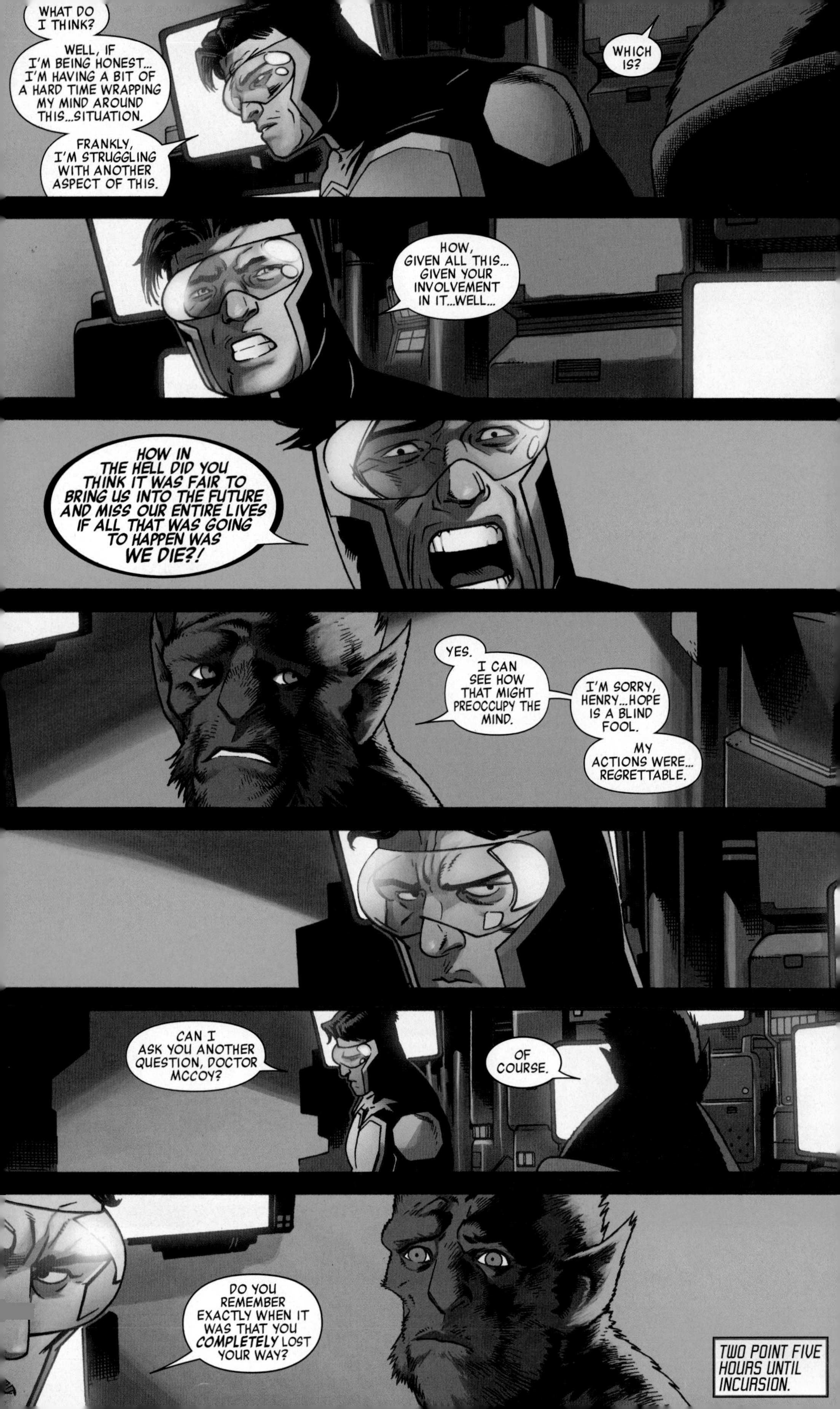
WHAT DO I THINK?
WELL, IF I'M BEING HONEST... I'M HAVING A BIT OF A HARD TIME WRAPPING MY MIND AROUND THIS...SITUATION.
FRANKLY, I'M STRUGGLING WITH ANOTHER ASPECT OF THIS.
WHICH IS?
HOW, GIVEN ALL THIS... GIVEN YOUR INVOLVEMENT IN IT...WELL...
HOW IN THE HELL DID YOU THINK IT WAS FAIR TO BRING US INTO THE FUTURE AND MISS OUR ENTIRE LIVES IF ALL THAT WAS GOING TO HAPPEN WAS WE DIE?!
YES. I CAN SEE HOW THAT MIGHT PREOCCUPY THE MIND.
I'M SORRY, HENRY...HOPE IS A BLIND FOOL.
MY ACTIONS WERE... REGRETTABLE.
CAN I ASK YOU ANOTHER QUESTION, DOCTOR MCCOY?
OF COURSE.
DO YOU REMEMBER EXACTLY WHEN IT WAS THAT YOU COMPLETELY LOST YOUR WAY?
TWO POINT FIVE HOURS UNTIL INCURSION.

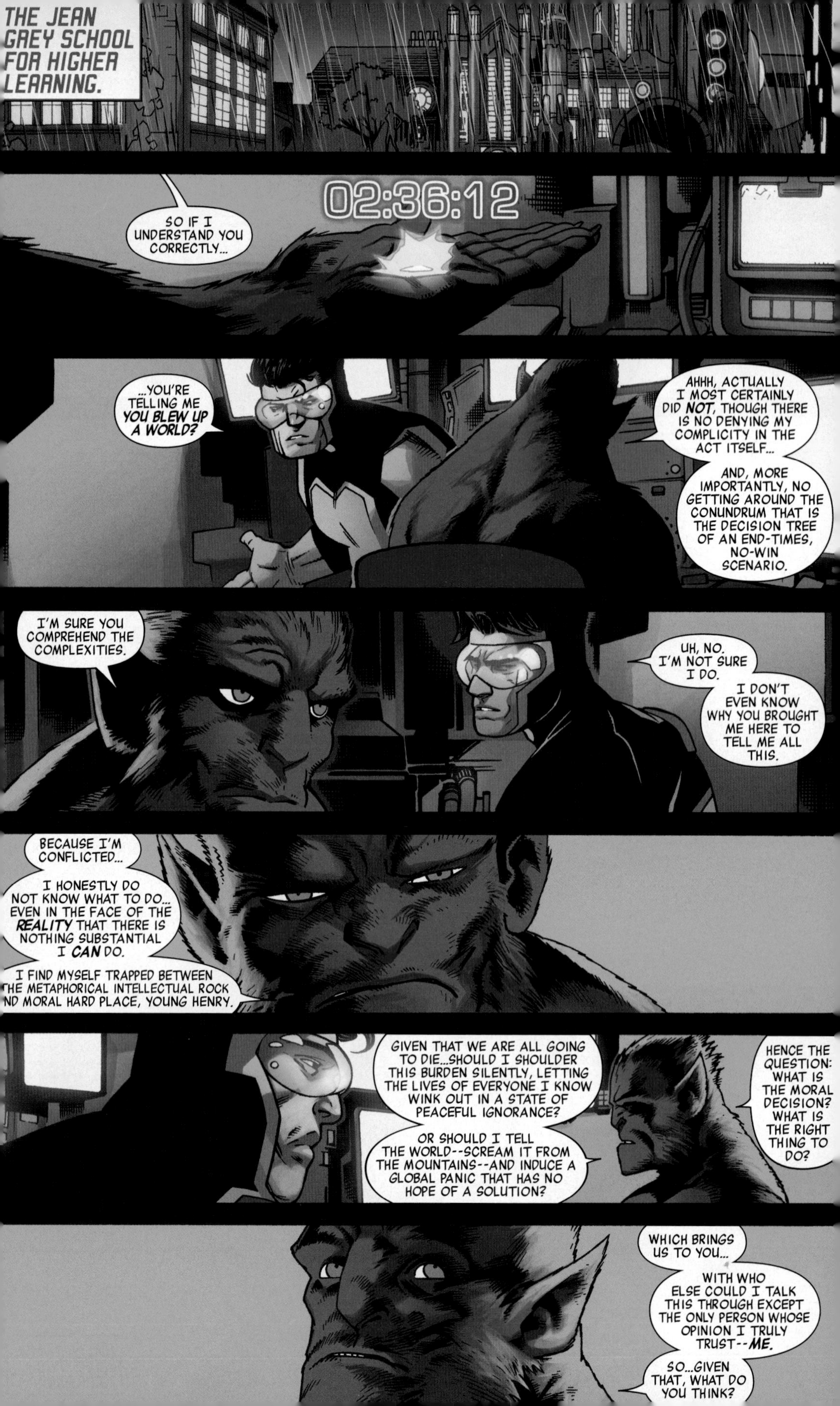
THE JEAN GREY SCHOOL FOR HIGHER LEARNING.
02:36:12
SO IF I UNDERSTAND YOU CORRECTLY...
...YOU'RE TELLING ME *YOU BLEW UP A WORLD?*
AHHH, ACTUALLY I MOST CERTAINLY DID *NOT*, THOUGH THERE IS NO DENYING MY COMPLICITY IN THE ACT ITSELF...
AND, MORE IMPORTANTLY, NO GETTING AROUND THE CONUNDRUM THAT IS THE DECISION TREE OF AN END-TIMES, NO-WIN SCENARIO.
I'M SURE YOU COMPREHEND THE COMPLEXITIES.
UH, NO. I'M NOT SURE I DO.
I DON'T EVEN KNOW WHY YOU BROUGHT ME HERE TO TELL ME ALL THIS.
BECAUSE I'M CONFLICTED...
I HONESTLY DO NOT KNOW WHAT TO DO... EVEN IN THE FACE OF THE *REALITY* THAT THERE IS NOTHING SUBSTANTIAL I *CAN* DO.
I FIND MYSELF TRAPPED BETWEEN THE METAPHORICAL INTELLECTUAL ROCK ND MORAL HARD PLACE, YOUNG HENRY.
GIVEN THAT WE ARE ALL GOING TO DIE...SHOULD I SHOULDER THIS BURDEN SILENTLY, LETTING THE LIVES OF EVERYONE I KNOW WINK OUT IN A STATE OF PEACEFUL IGNORANCE?
OR SHOULD I TELL THE WORLD--SCREAM IT FROM THE MOUNTAINS--AND INDUCE A GLOBAL PANIC THAT HAS NO HOPE OF A SOLUTION?
HENCE THE QUESTION: WHAT IS THE MORAL DECISION? WHAT IS THE RIGHT THING TO DO?
WHICH BRINGS US TO YOU...
WITH WHO ELSE COULD I TALK THIS THROUGH EXCEPT THE ONLY PERSON WHOSE OPINION I TRULY TRUST--*ME.*
SO...GIVEN THAT, WHAT DO YOU THINK?

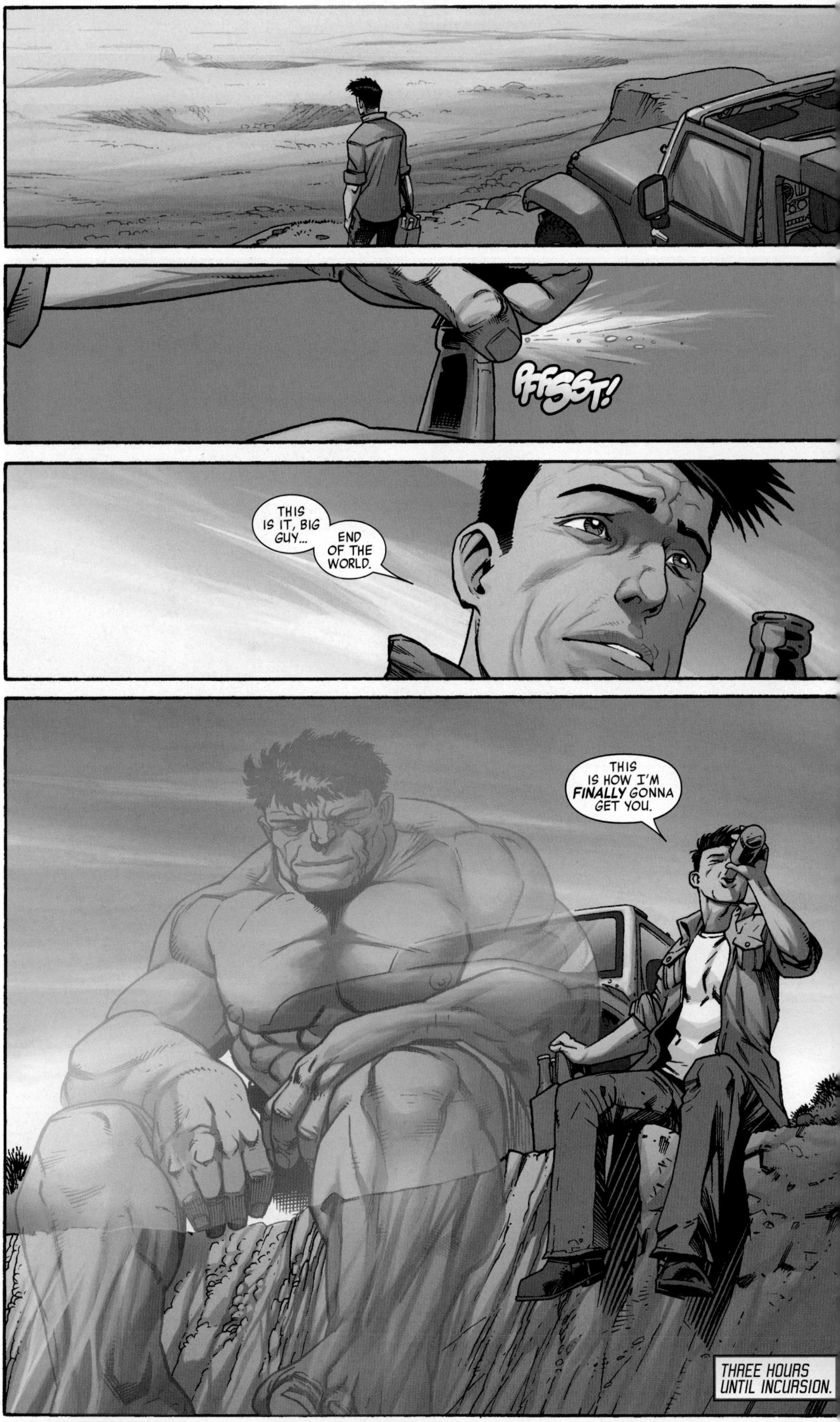
PFFSST!
THIS IS IT, BIG GUY... END OF THE WORLD.
THIS IS HOW I'M **FINALLY** GONNA GET YOU.
THREE HOURS UNTIL INCURSION.

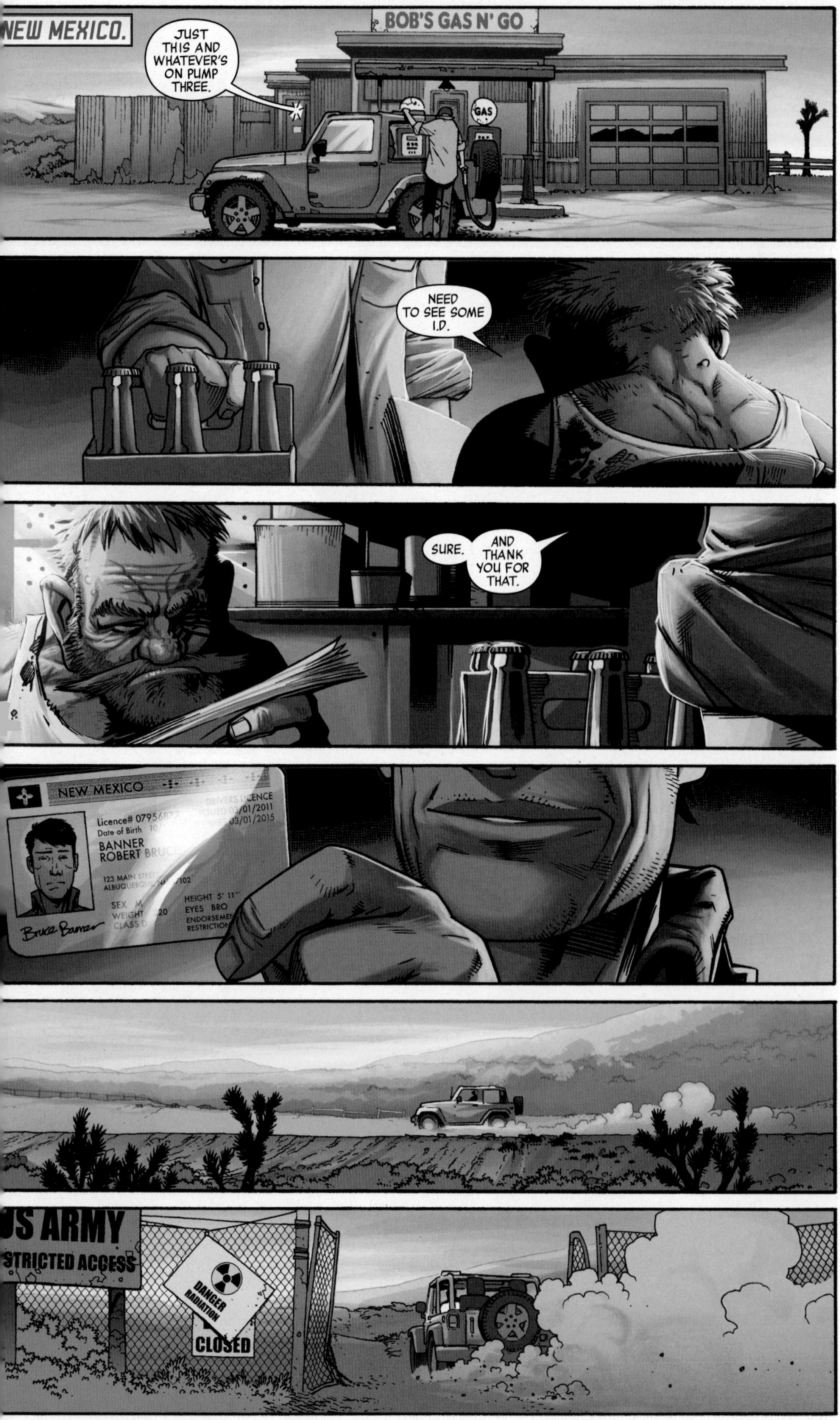
NEW MEXICO.
BOB'S GAS N' GO
JUST THIS AND WHATEVER'S ON PUMP THREE.
GAS
NEED TO SEE SOME I.D.
SURE.
AND THANK YOU FOR THAT.
NEW MEXICO
DRIVERS LICENCE
BANNER
ROBERT BRUCE
US ARMY
STRICTED ACCESS
DANGER RADIATION
CLOSED

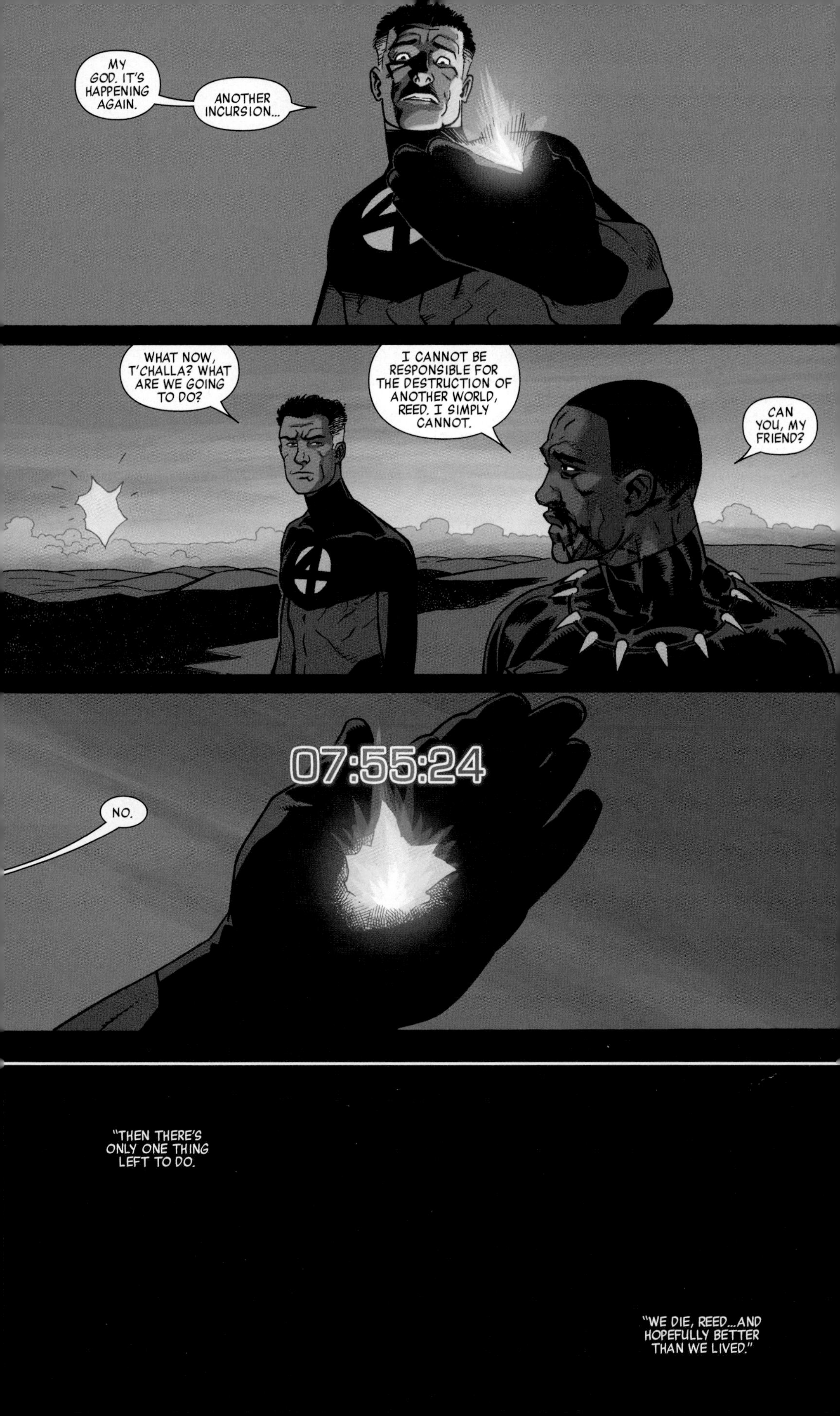

MY GOD. IT'S HAPPENING AGAIN.
ANOTHER INCURSION...
WHAT NOW, T'CHALLA? WHAT ARE WE GOING TO DO?
I CANNOT BE RESPONSIBLE FOR THE DESTRUCTION OF ANOTHER WORLD, REED. I SIMPLY CANNOT.
CAN YOU, MY FRIEND?
07:55:24
NO.
"THEN THERE'S ONLY ONE THING LEFT TO DO.
"WE DIE, REED...AND HOPEFULLY BETTER THAN WE LIVED."

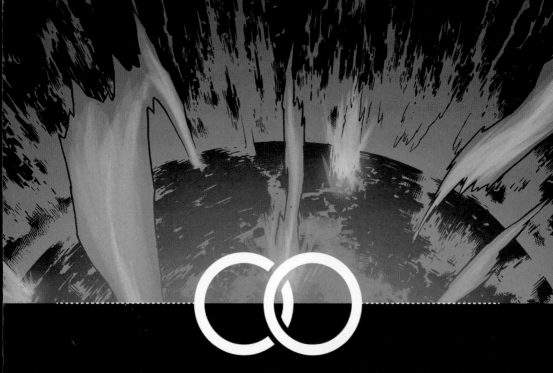

"ALL THE ANGELS HAVE FALLEN"

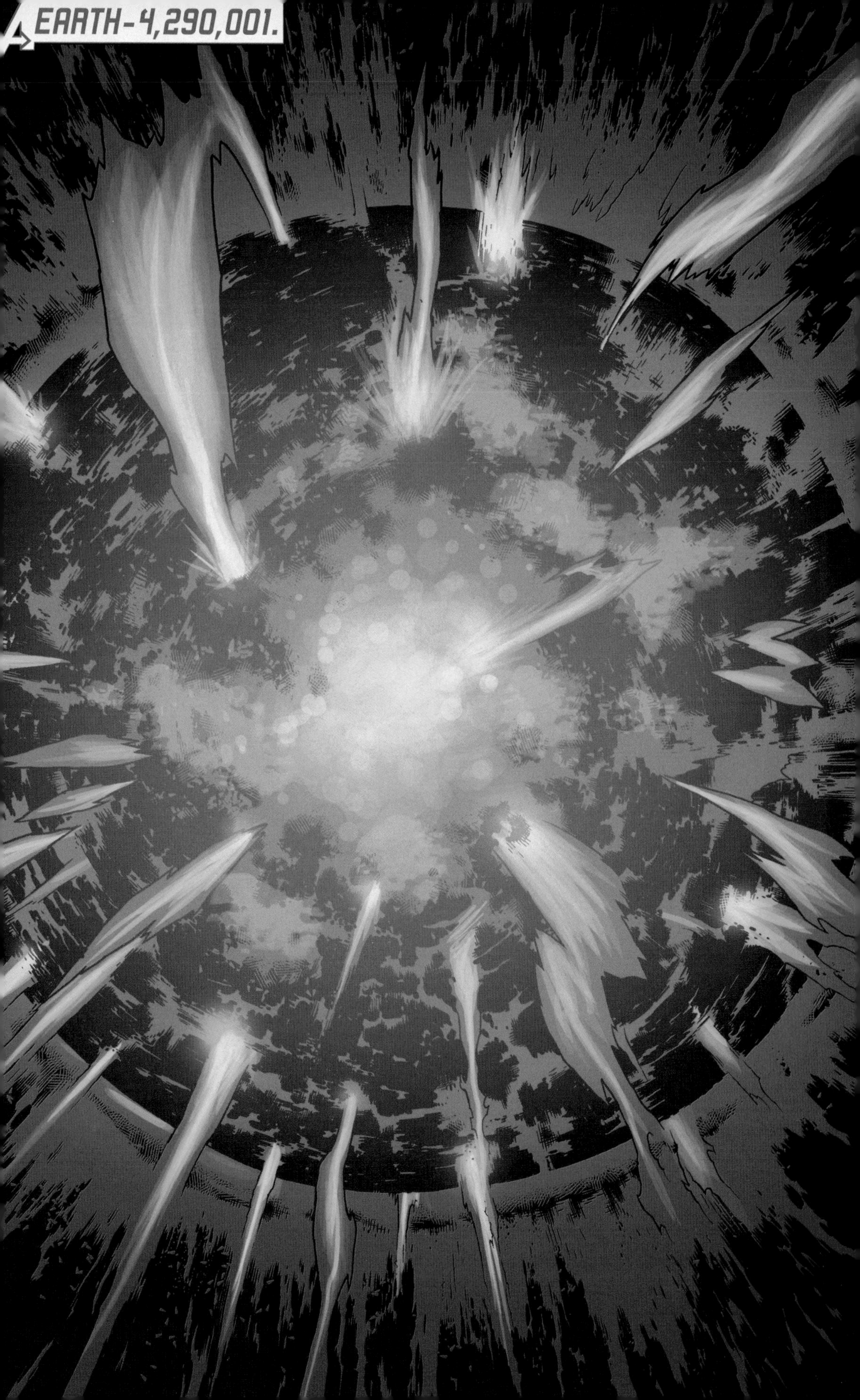
EARTH-4,290,001.

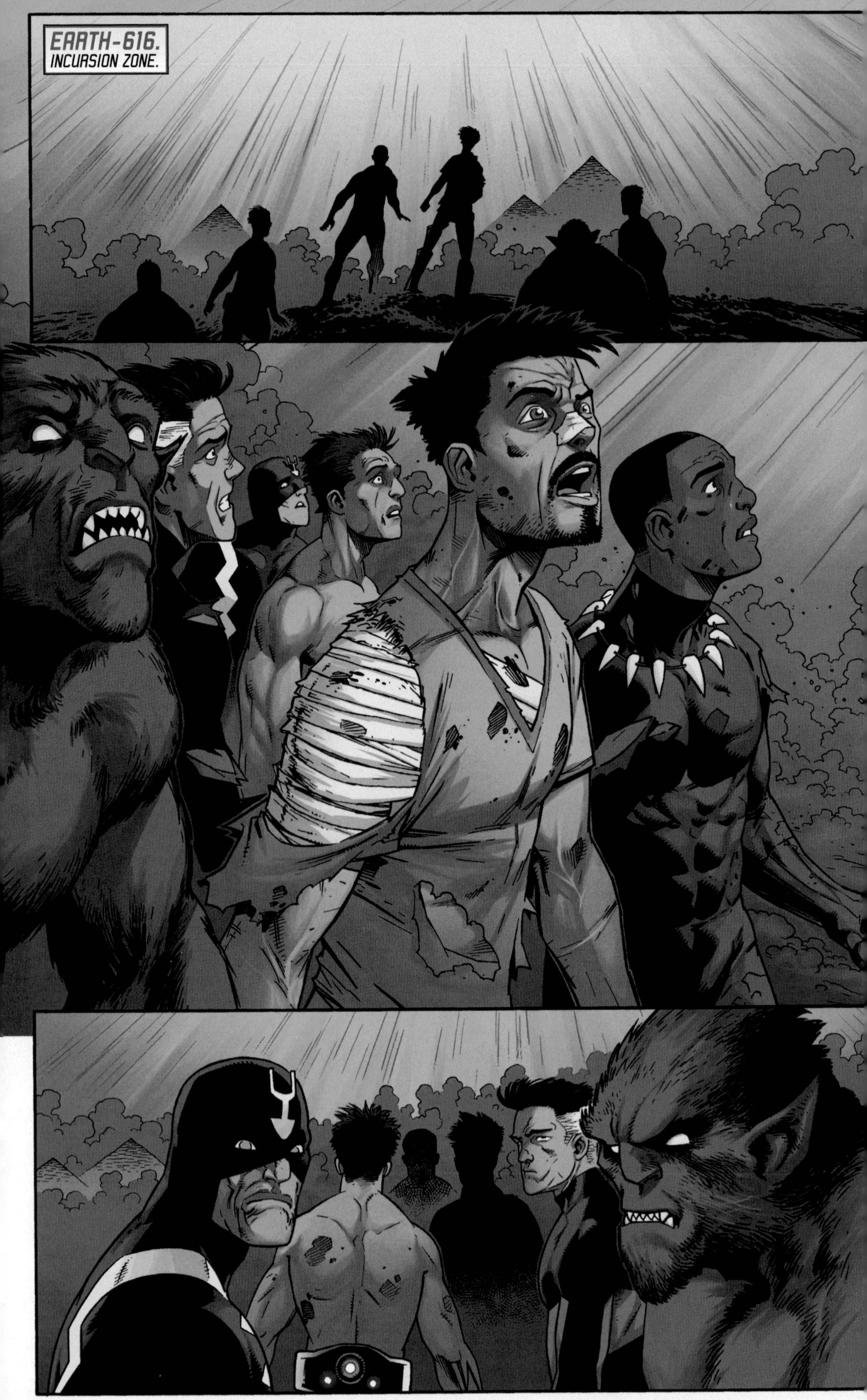
EARTH-616.
INCURSION ZONE.

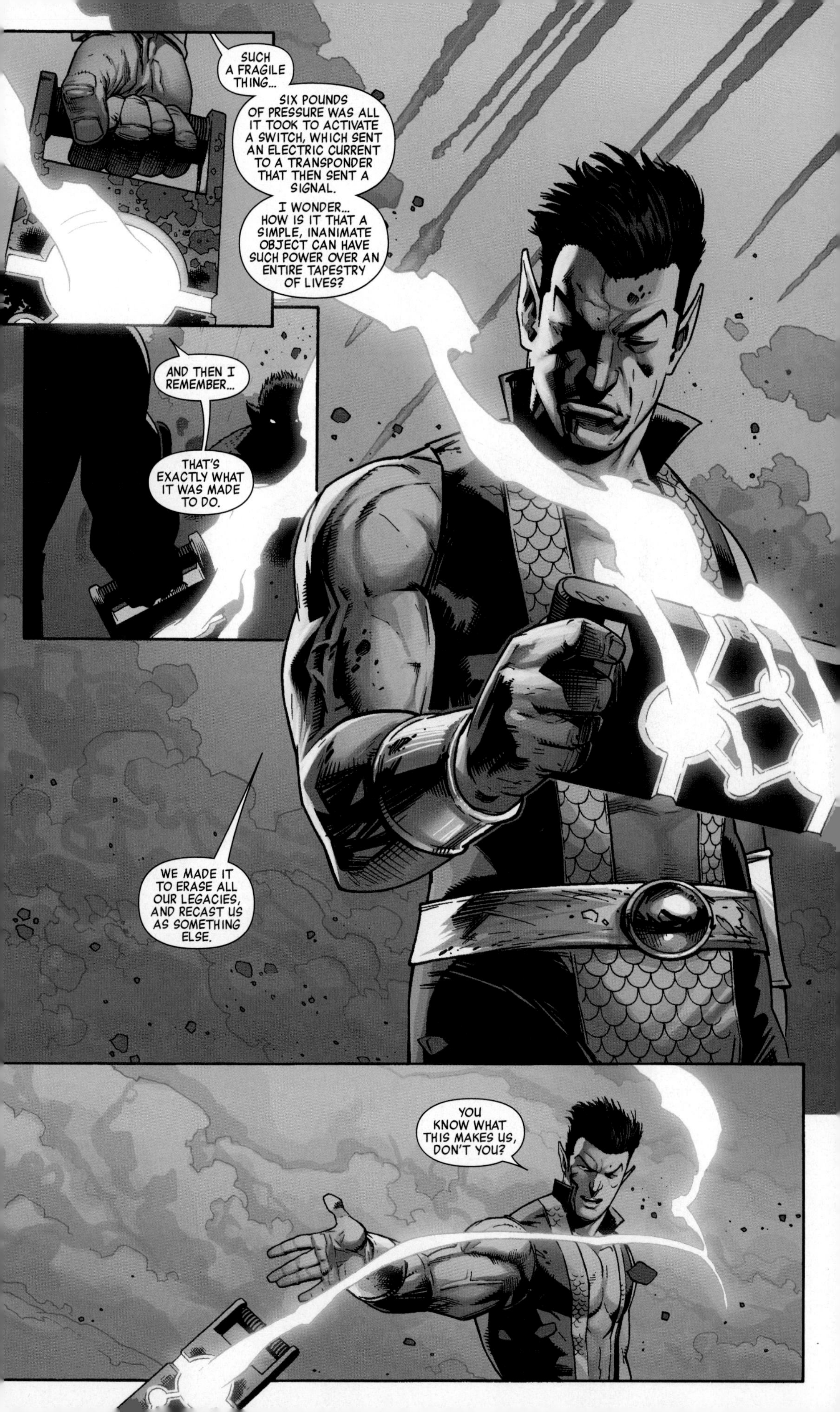
SUCH A FRAGILE THING...
SIX POUNDS OF PRESSURE WAS ALL IT TOOK TO ACTIVATE A SWITCH, WHICH SENT AN ELECTRIC CURRENT TO A TRANSPONDER THAT THEN SENT A SIGNAL.
I WONDER... HOW IS IT THAT A SIMPLE, INANIMATE OBJECT CAN HAVE SUCH POWER OVER AN ENTIRE TAPESTRY OF LIVES?
AND THEN I REMEMBER...
THAT'S EXACTLY WHAT IT WAS MADE TO DO.
WE MADE IT TO ERASE ALL OUR LEGACIES, AND RECAST US AS SOMETHING ELSE.
YOU KNOW WHAT THIS MAKES US, DON'T YOU?

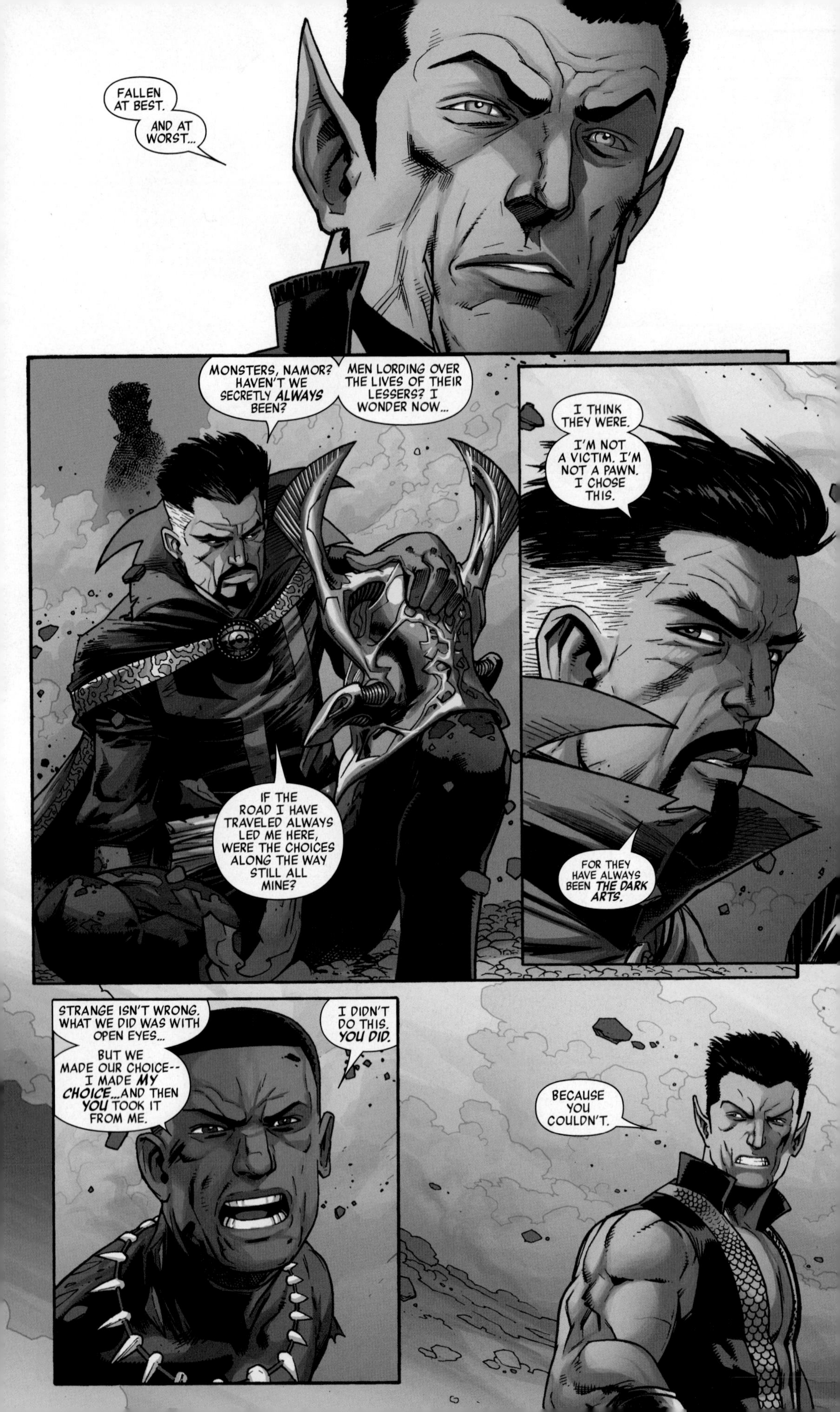
FALLEN AT BEST.
AND AT WORST...
MONSTERS, NAMOR? HAVEN'T WE SECRETLY ALWAYS BEEN?
MEN LORDING OVER THE LIVES OF THEIR LESSERS? I WONDER NOW...
IF THE ROAD I HAVE TRAVELED ALWAYS LED ME HERE, WERE THE CHOICES ALONG THE WAY STILL ALL MINE?
I THINK THEY WERE.
I'M NOT A VICTIM. I'M NOT A PAWN. I CHOSE THIS.
FOR THEY HAVE ALWAYS BEEN THE DARK ARTS.
STRANGE ISN'T WRONG. WHAT WE DID WAS WITH OPEN EYES...
BUT WE MADE OUR CHOICE-- I MADE MY CHOICE...AND THEN YOU TOOK IT FROM ME.
I DIDN'T DO THIS. YOU DID.
BECAUSE YOU COULDN'T.

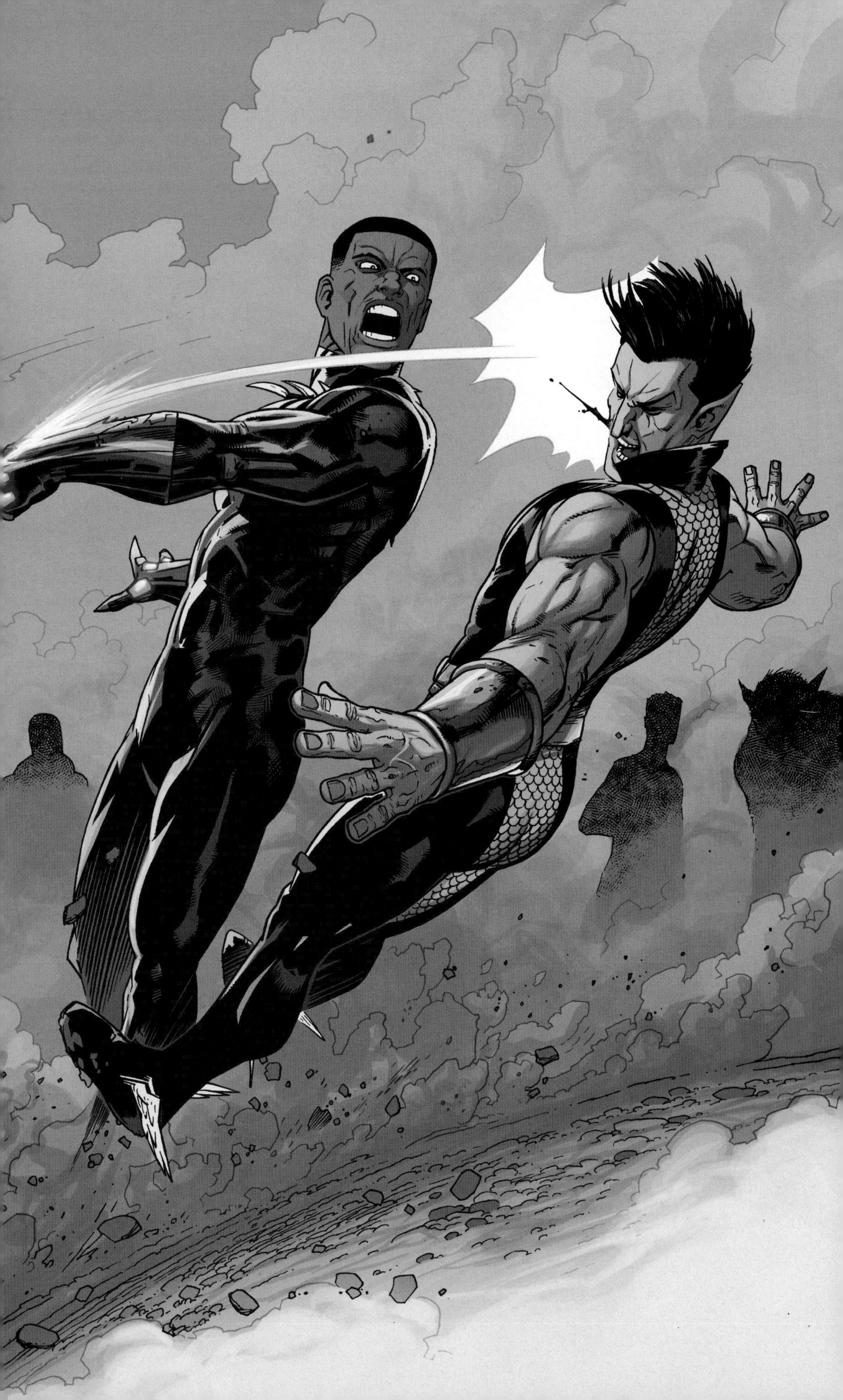

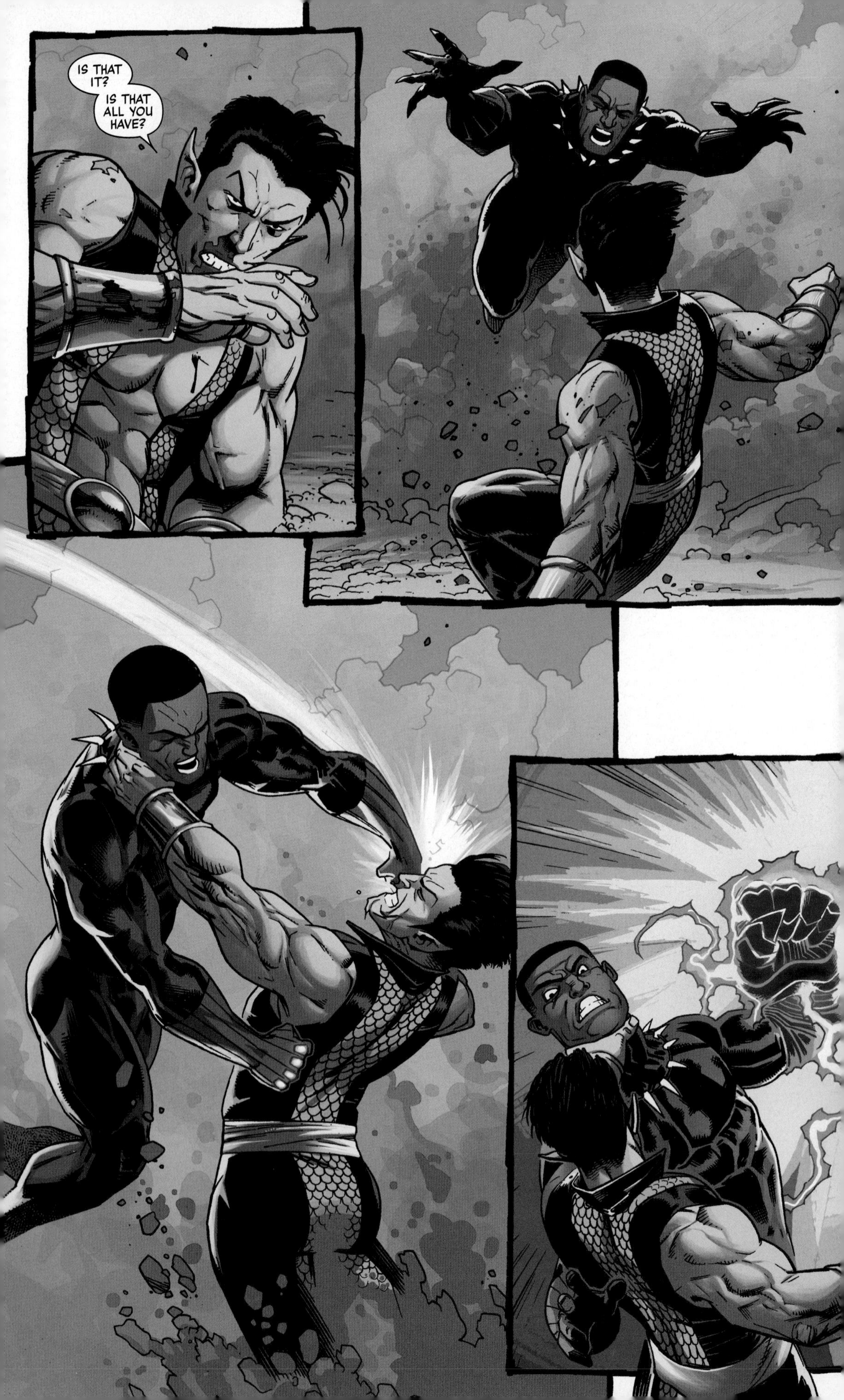
IS THAT IT?
IS THAT ALL YOU HAVE?

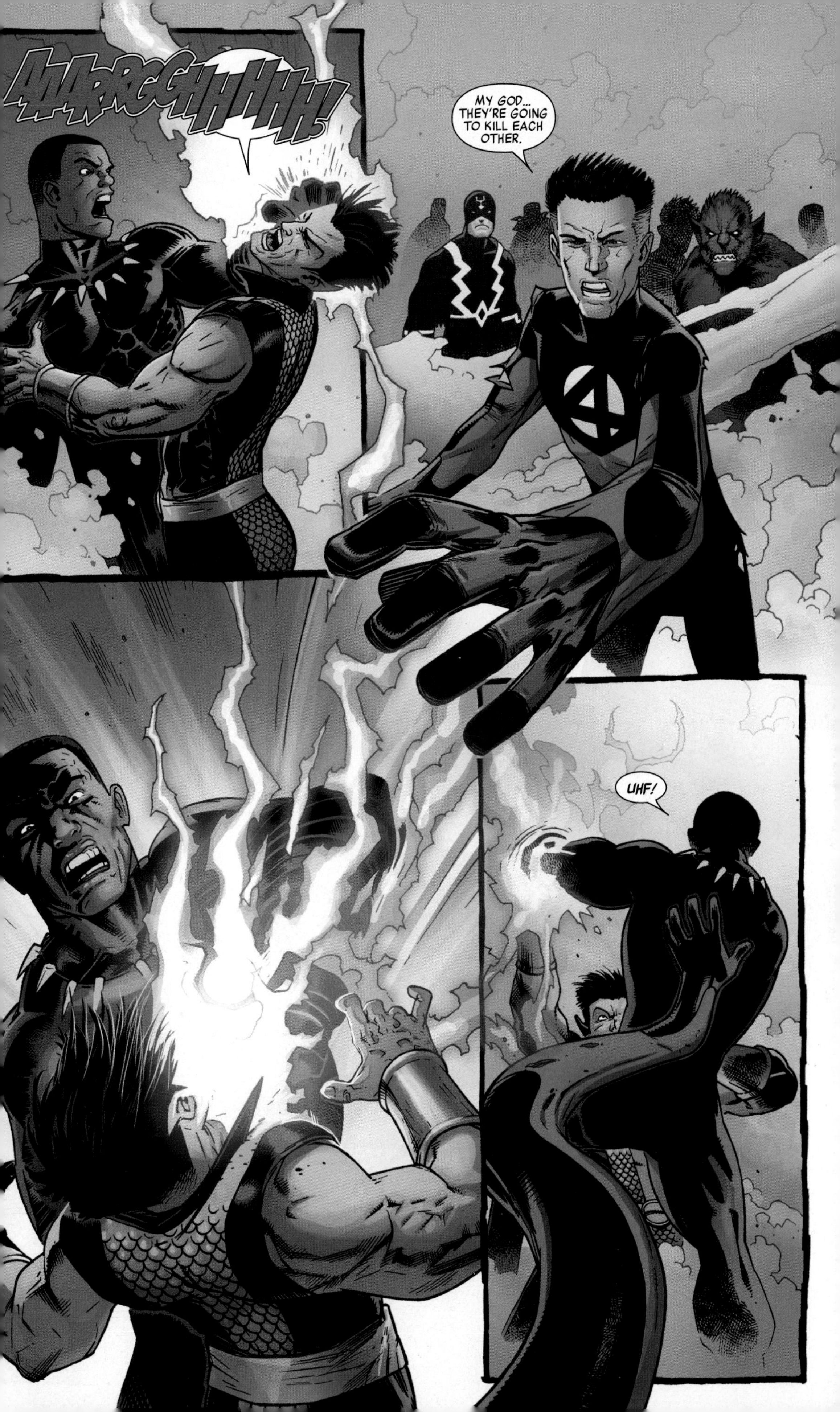
AAARRGGHHHHH!
MY GOD... THEY'RE GOING TO KILL EACH OTHER.
UHF!

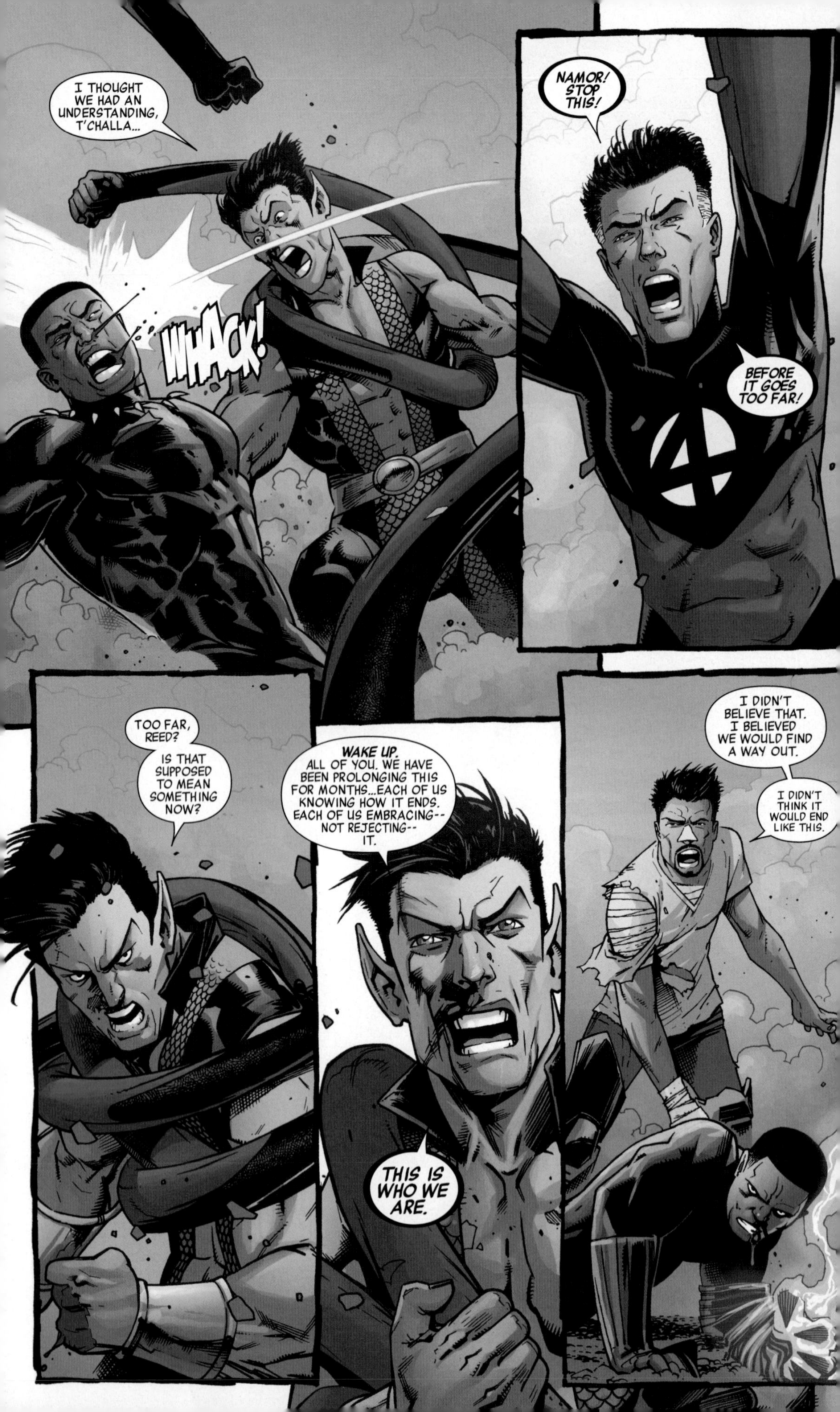
I THOUGHT WE HAD AN UNDERSTANDING, T'CHALLA...
WHACK!
NAMOR! STOP THIS!
BEFORE IT GOES TOO FAR!
TOO FAR, REED?
IS THAT SUPPOSED TO MEAN SOMETHING NOW?
WAKE UP. ALL OF YOU. WE HAVE BEEN PROLONGING THIS FOR MONTHS...EACH OF US KNOWING HOW IT ENDS. EACH OF US EMBRACING-- NOT REJECTING-- IT.
THIS IS WHO WE ARE.
I DIDN'T BELIEVE THAT. I BELIEVED WE WOULD FIND A WAY OUT.
I DIDN'T THINK IT WOULD END LIKE THIS.

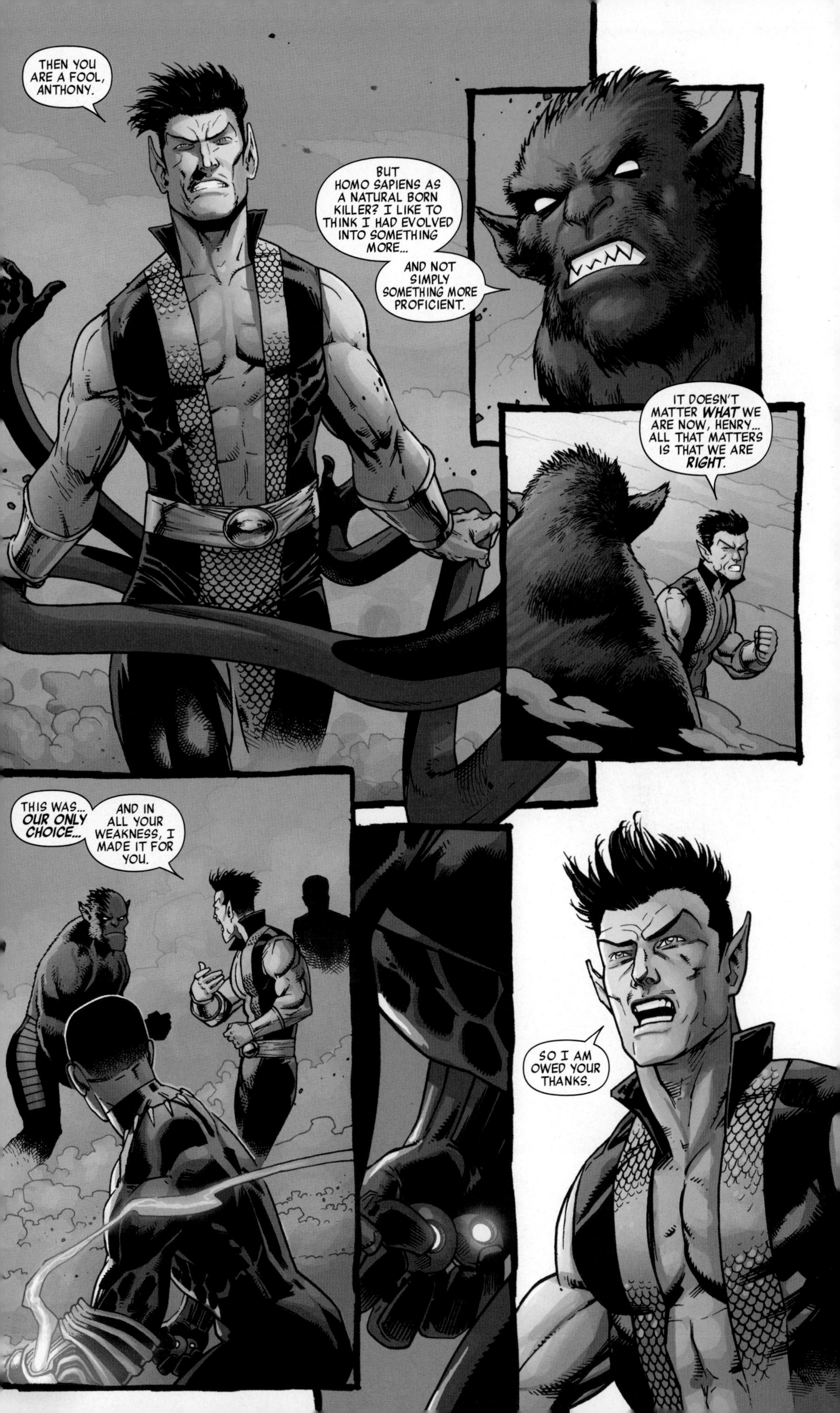
THEN YOU ARE A FOOL, ANTHONY.
BUT HOMO SAPIENS AS A NATURAL BORN KILLER? I LIKE TO THINK I HAD EVOLVED INTO SOMETHING MORE...
AND NOT SIMPLY SOMETHING MORE PROFICIENT.
IT DOESN'T MATTER **WHAT** WE ARE NOW, HENRY... ALL THAT MATTERS IS THAT WE ARE **RIGHT**.
THIS WAS... **OUR ONLY CHOICE...**
AND IN ALL YOUR WEAKNESS, I MADE IT FOR YOU.
SO I AM OWED YOUR THANKS.

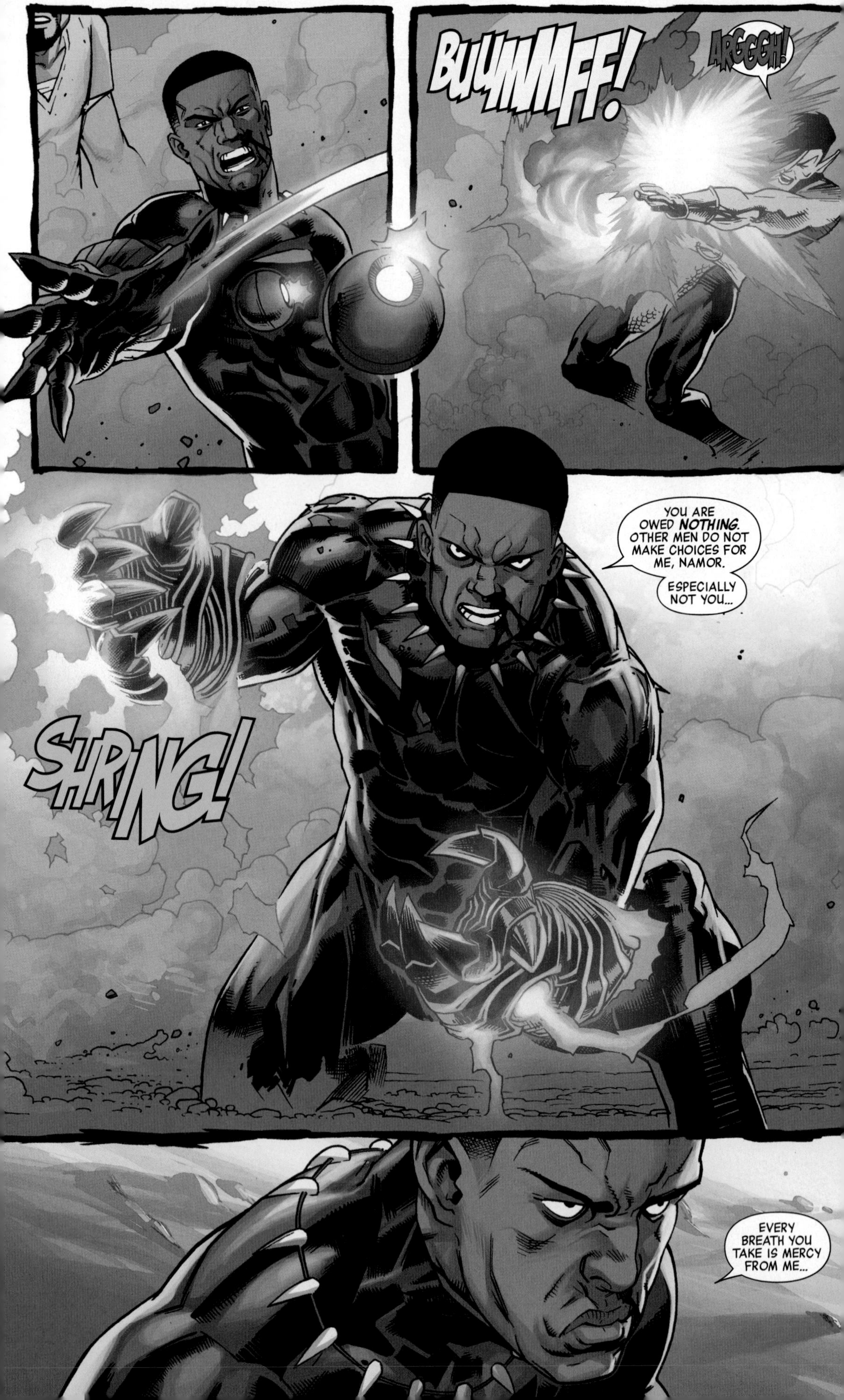
BUUMMFF!
ARGGGH!
YOU ARE OWED NOTHING. OTHER MEN DO NOT MAKE CHOICES FOR ME, NAMOR.
ESPECIALLY NOT YOU...
SHRING!
EVERY BREATH YOU TAKE IS MERCY FROM ME...

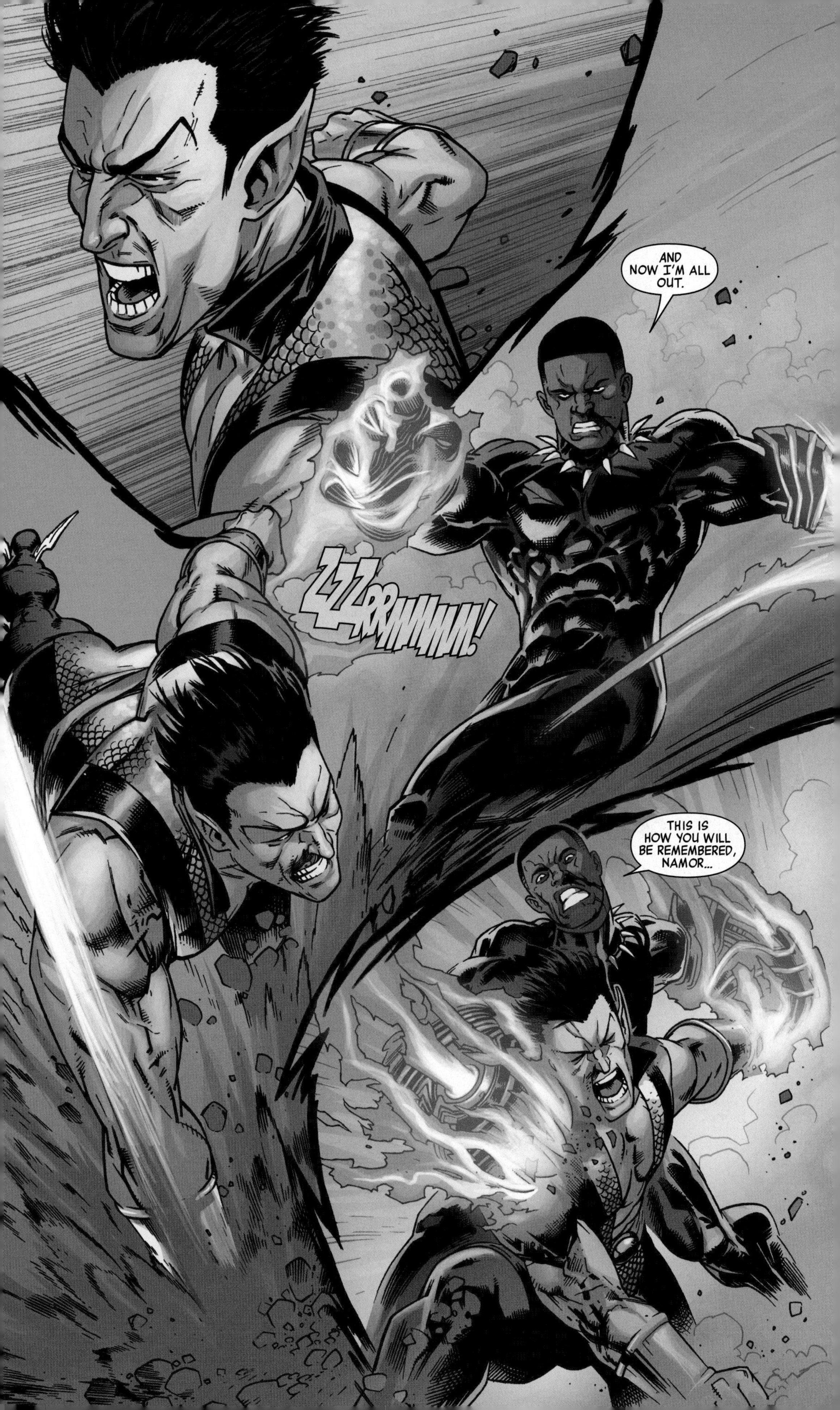
AND NOW I'M ALL OUT.
ZZZRRMMMMM!
THIS IS HOW YOU WILL BE REMEMBERED, NAMOR...

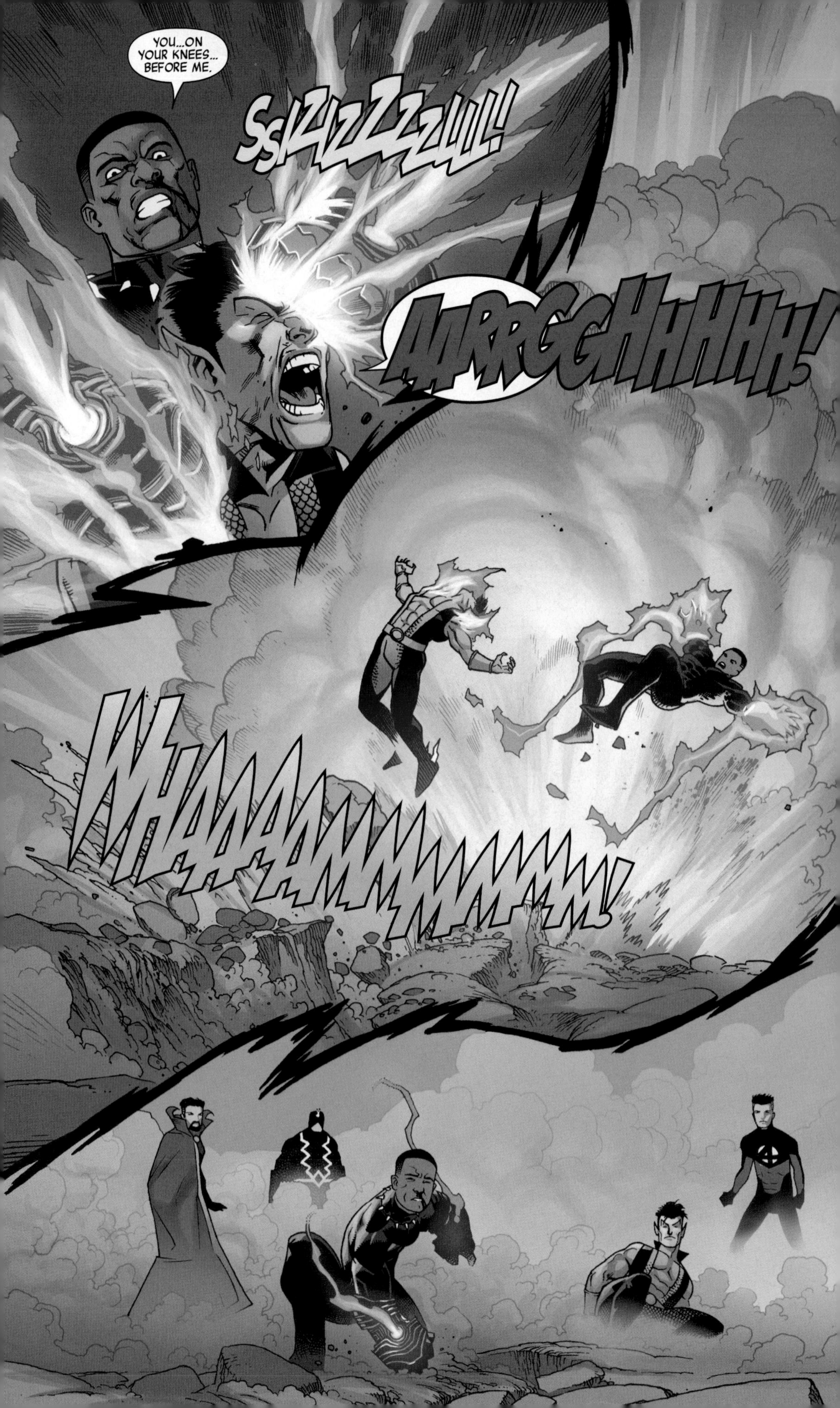
YOU...ON YOUR KNEES... BEFORE ME.
SSIZIZZZZUUL!
AARRGGHHHHH!
WHAAAMMMMMM!

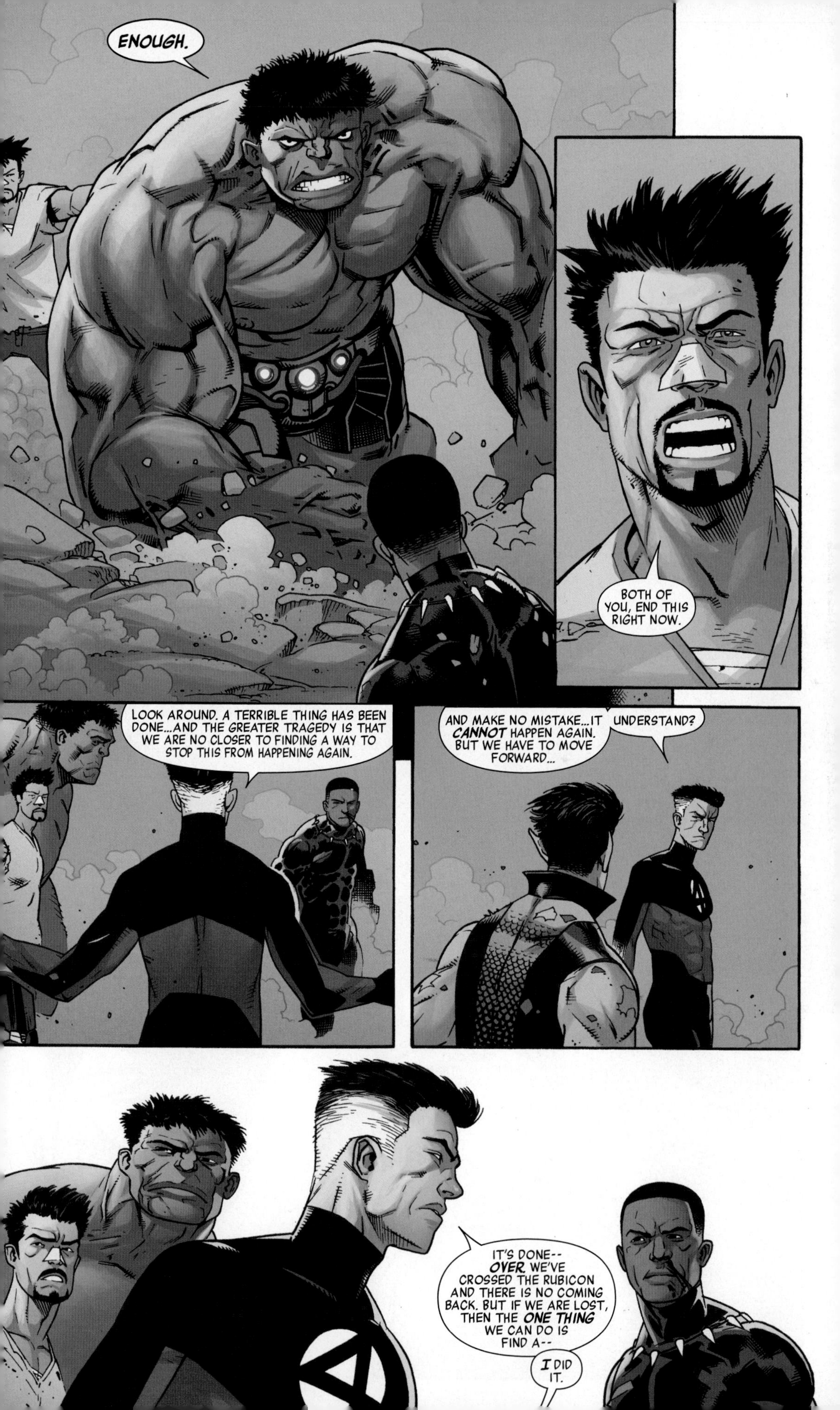
ENOUGH.
BOTH OF YOU, END THIS RIGHT NOW.
LOOK AROUND. A TERRIBLE THING HAS BEEN DONE...AND THE GREATER TRAGEDY IS THAT WE ARE NO CLOSER TO FINDING A WAY TO STOP THIS FROM HAPPENING AGAIN.
AND MAKE NO MISTAKE...IT CANNOT HAPPEN AGAIN. BUT WE HAVE TO MOVE FORWARD...
UNDERSTAND?
IT'S DONE-- OVER. WE'VE CROSSED THE RUBICON AND THERE IS NO COMING BACK. BUT IF WE ARE LOST, THEN THE ONE THING WE CAN DO IS FIND A--
I DID IT.

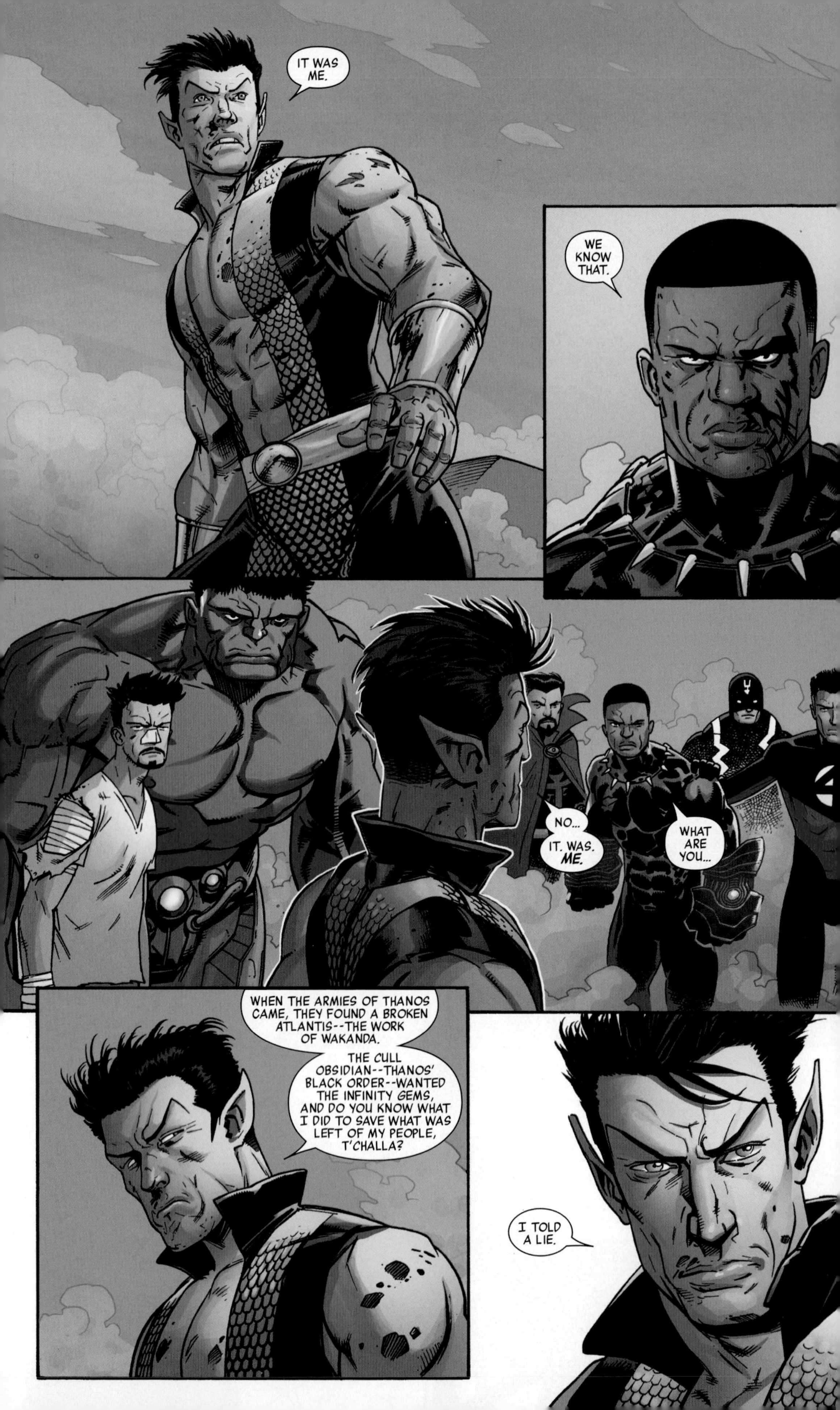
IT WAS ME.
WE KNOW THAT.
NO... IT. WAS. ME.
WHAT ARE YOU...
WHEN THE ARMIES OF THANOS CAME, THEY FOUND A BROKEN ATLANTIS--THE WORK OF WAKANDA.
THE CULL OBSIDIAN--THANOS' BLACK ORDER--WANTED THE INFINITY GEMS, AND DO YOU KNOW WHAT I DID TO SAVE WHAT WAS LEFT OF MY PEOPLE, T'CHALLA?
I TOLD A LIE.

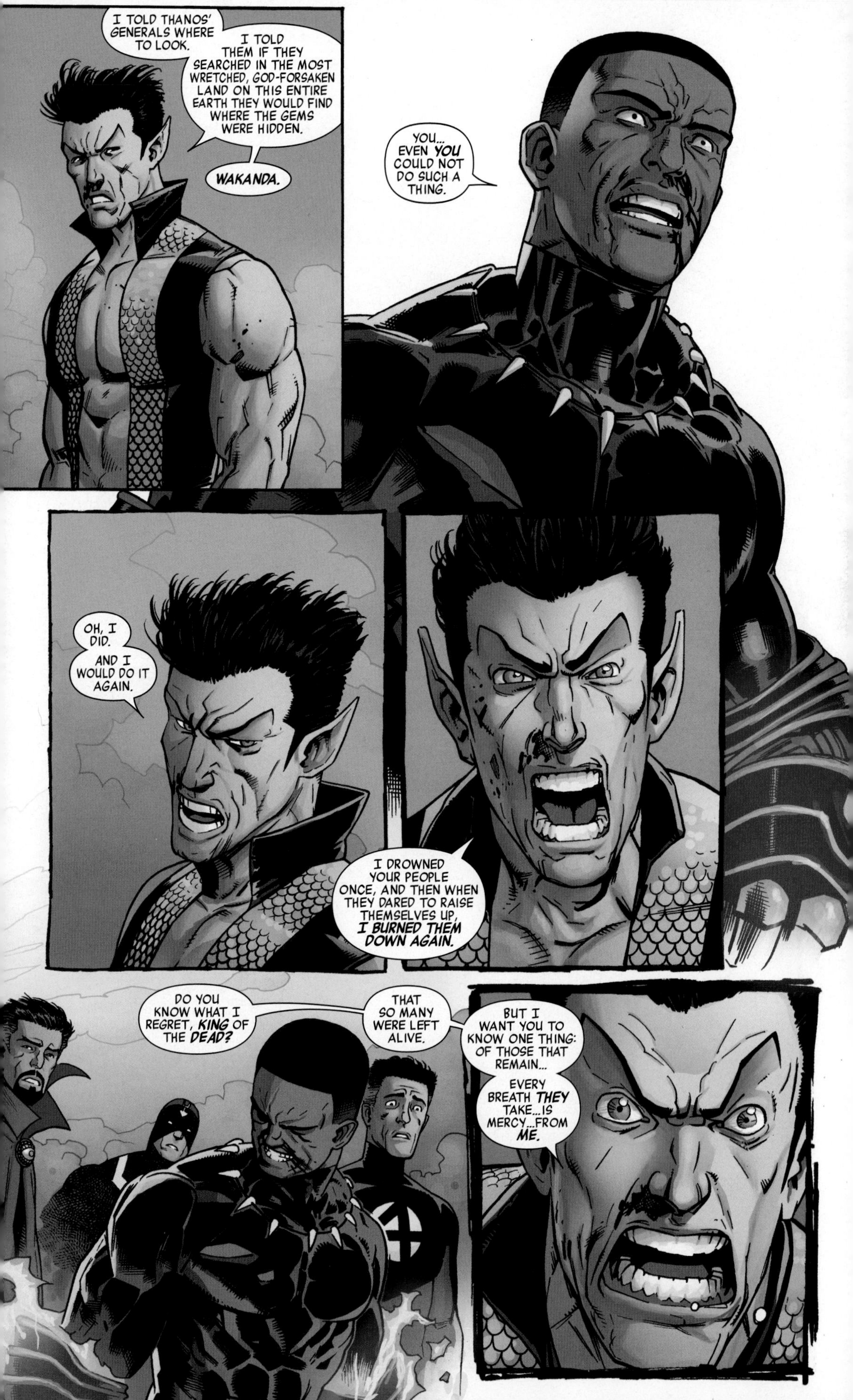
I TOLD THANOS' GENERALS WHERE TO LOOK.
I TOLD THEM IF THEY SEARCHED IN THE MOST WRETCHED, GOD-FORSAKEN LAND ON THIS ENTIRE EARTH THEY WOULD FIND WHERE THE GEMS WERE HIDDEN.
WAKANDA.
YOU... EVEN YOU COULD NOT DO SUCH A THING.
OH, I DID.
AND I WOULD DO IT AGAIN.
I DROWNED YOUR PEOPLE ONCE, AND THEN WHEN THEY DARED TO RAISE THEMSELVES UP, I BURNED THEM DOWN AGAIN.
DO YOU KNOW WHAT I REGRET, KING OF THE DEAD?
THAT SO MANY WERE LEFT ALIVE.
BUT I WANT YOU TO KNOW ONE THING: OF THOSE THAT REMAIN...
EVERY BREATH THEY TAKE...IS MERCY...FROM ME.

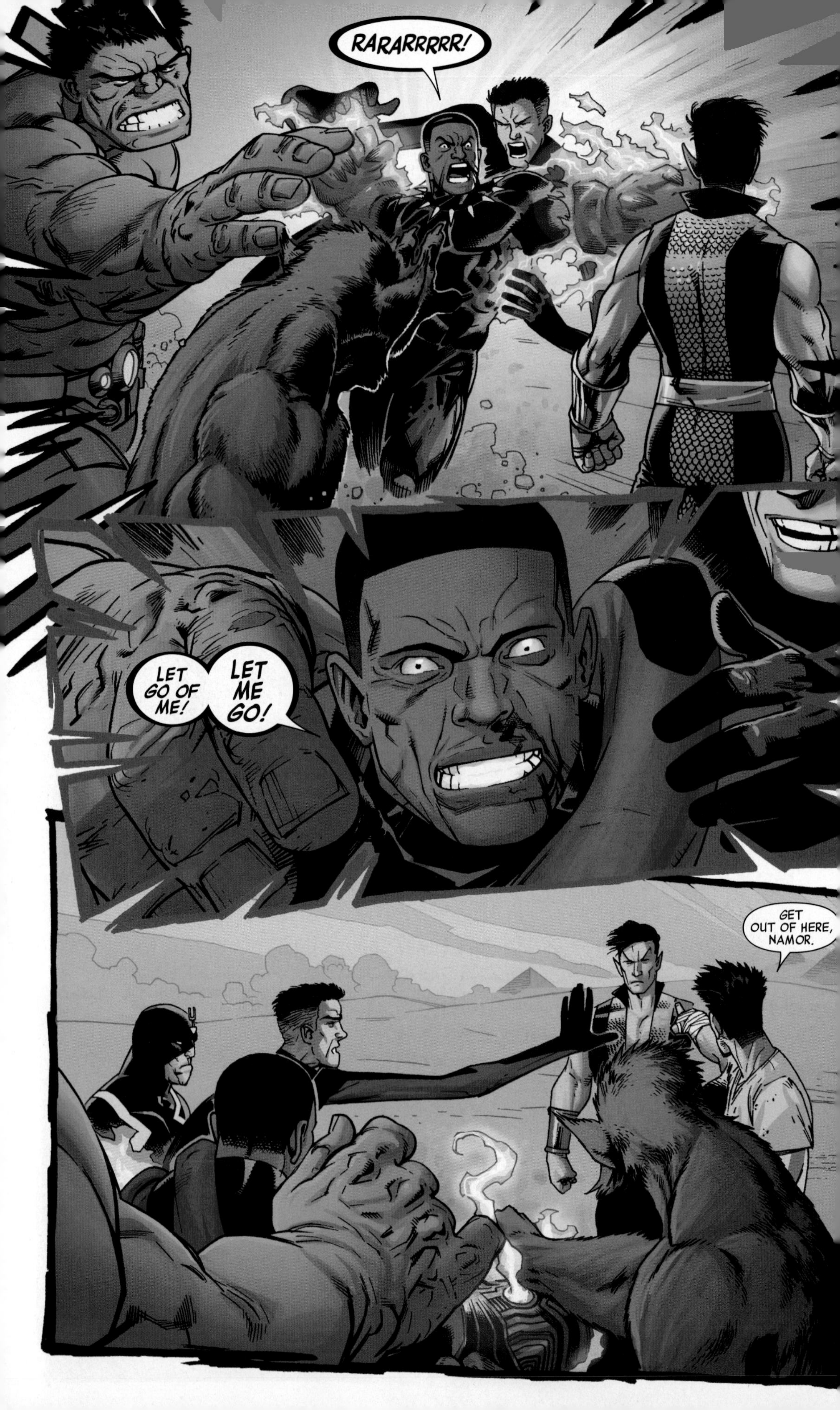
RARARRRRR!
LET GO OF ME!
LET ME GO!
GET OUT OF HERE, NAMOR.

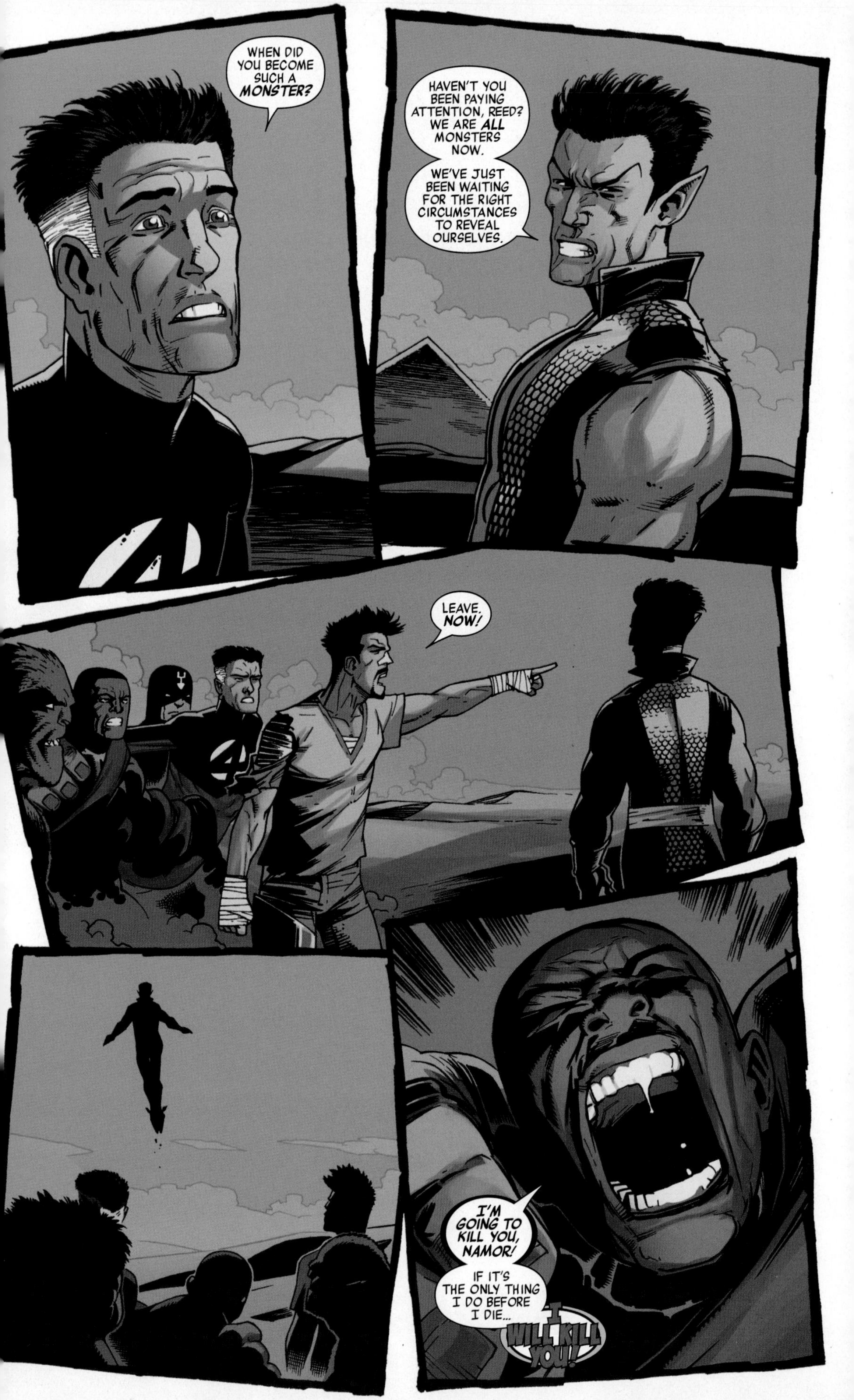
WHEN DID YOU BECOME SUCH A MONSTER?
HAVEN'T YOU BEEN PAYING ATTENTION, REED? WE ARE ALL MONSTERS NOW.
WE'VE JUST BEEN WAITING FOR THE RIGHT CIRCUMSTANCES TO REVEAL OURSELVES.
LEAVE. NOW!
I'M GOING TO KILL YOU, NAMOR!
IF IT'S THE ONLY THING I DO BEFORE I DIE...
I WILL KILL YOU!

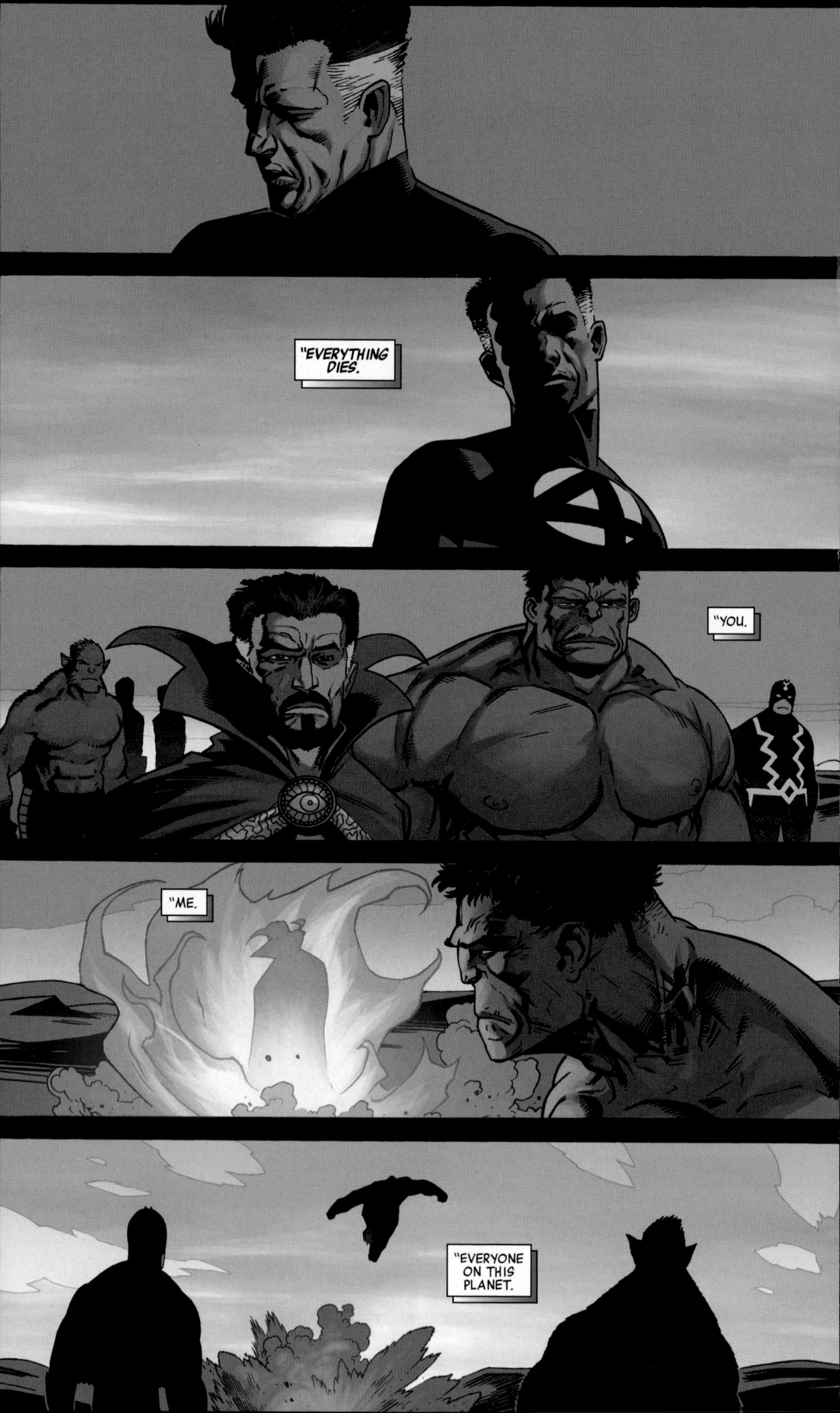
"EVERYTHING DIES.
"YOU.
"ME.
"EVERYONE ON THIS PLANET.

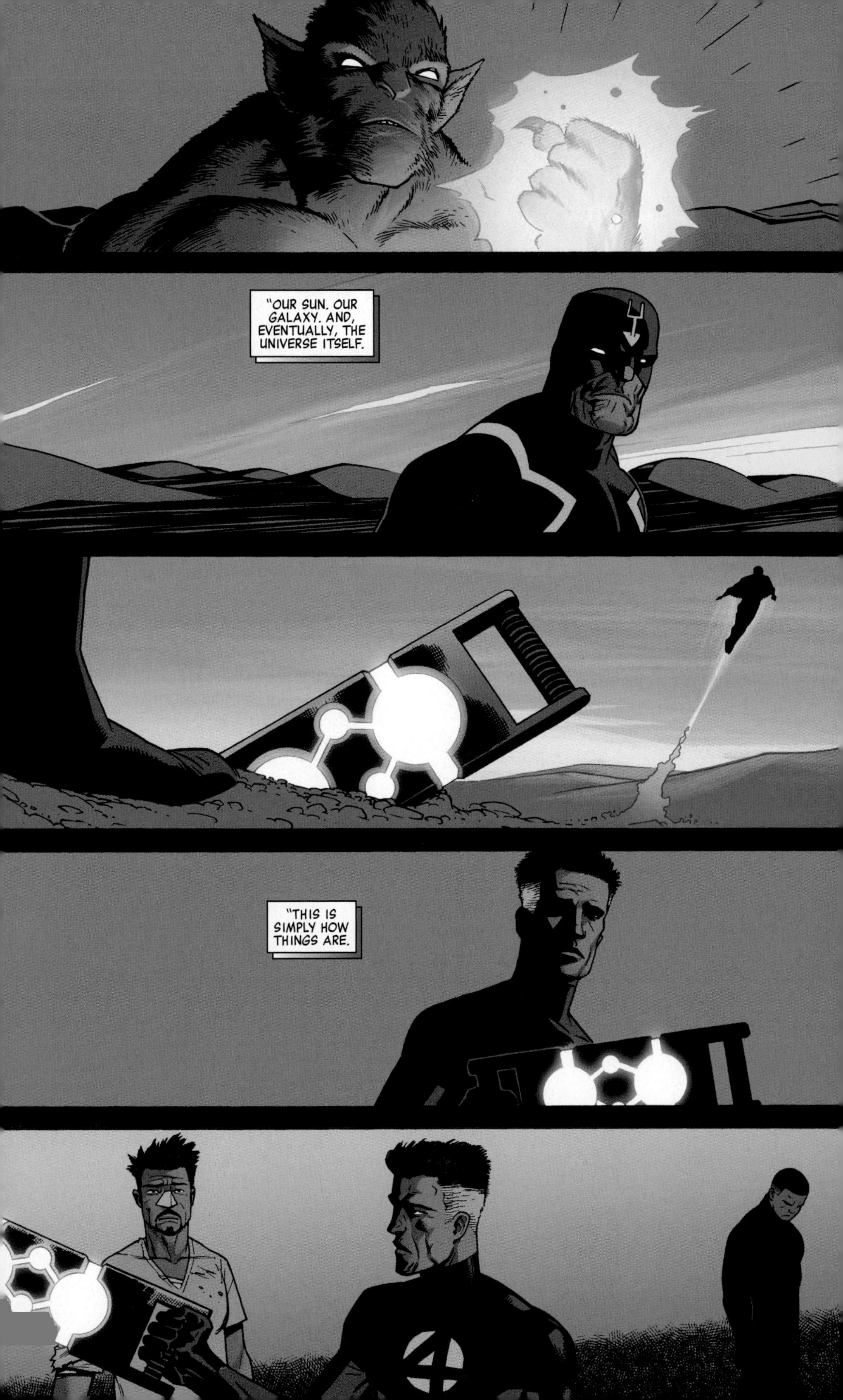
"OUR SUN. OUR GALAXY. AND, EVENTUALLY, THE UNIVERSE ITSELF.
"THIS IS SIMPLY HOW THINGS ARE.

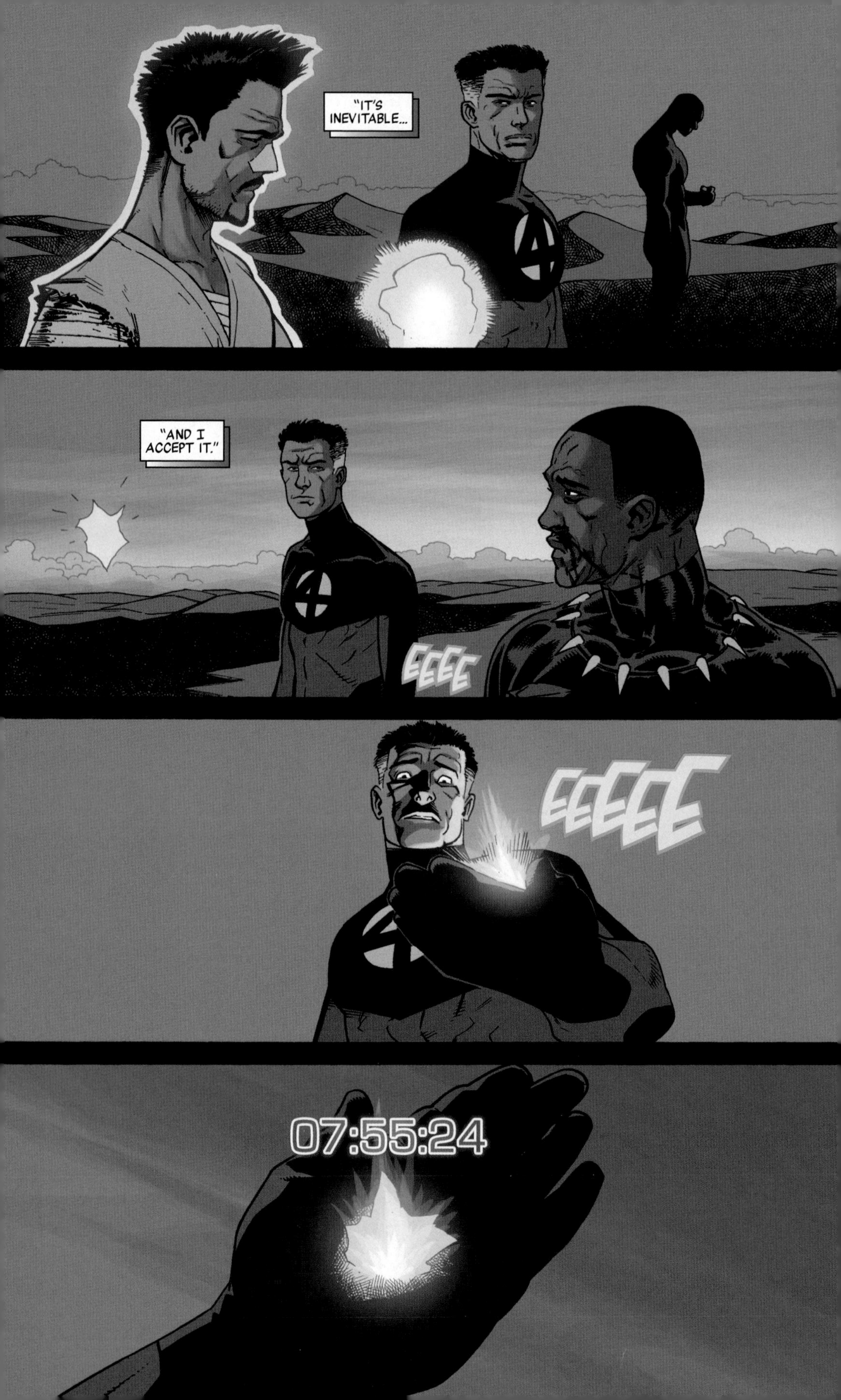

"IT'S INEVITABLE...
"AND I ACCEPT IT."
EEEE
EEEEE
07:55:24

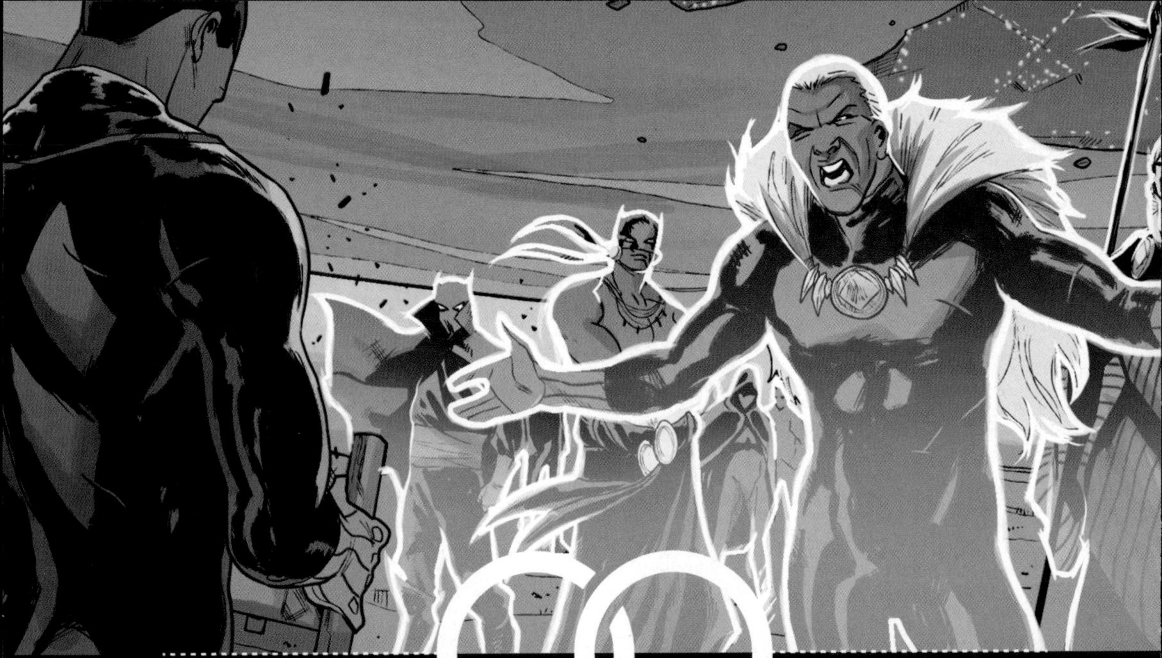

"WE ARE NOT BROTHERS"

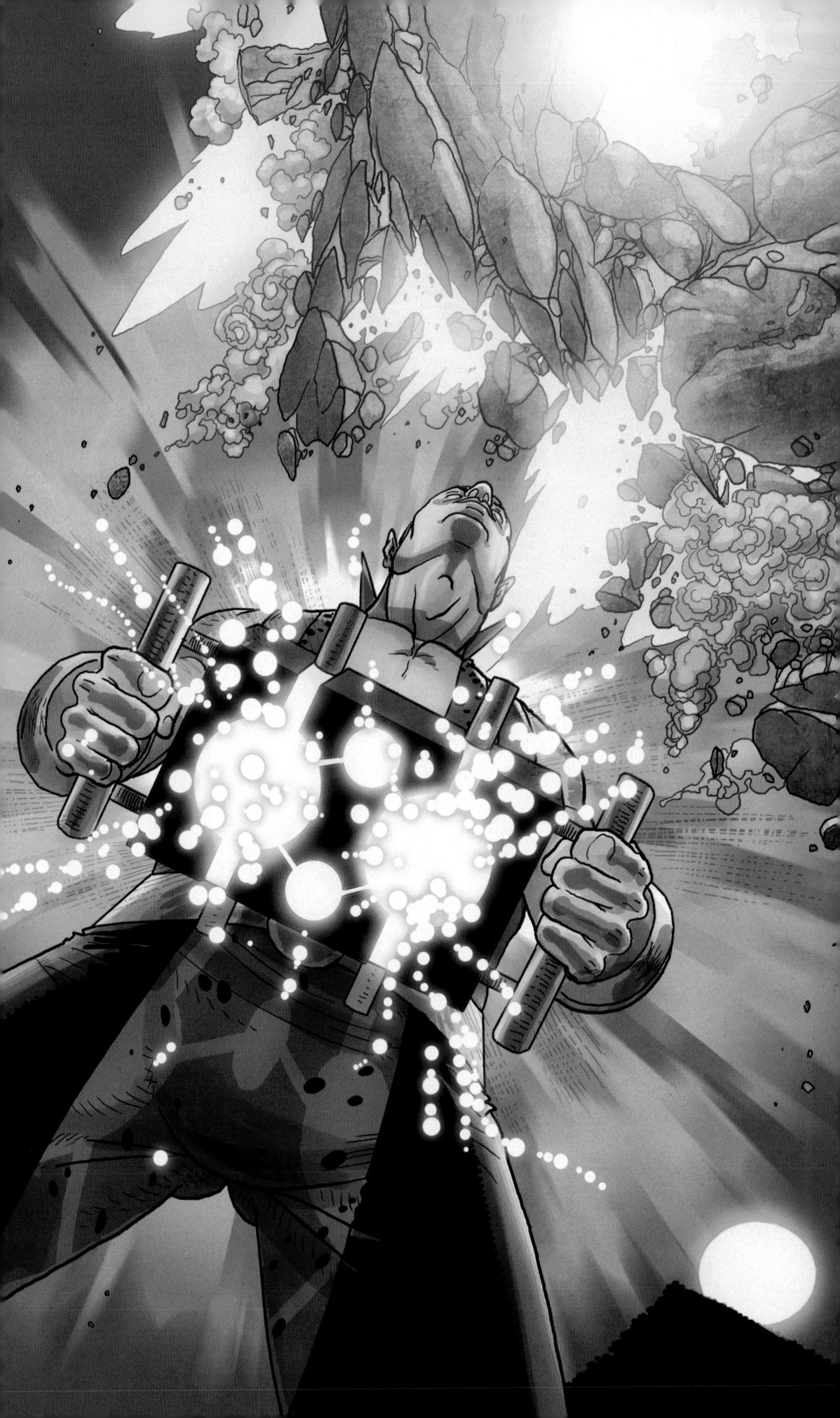

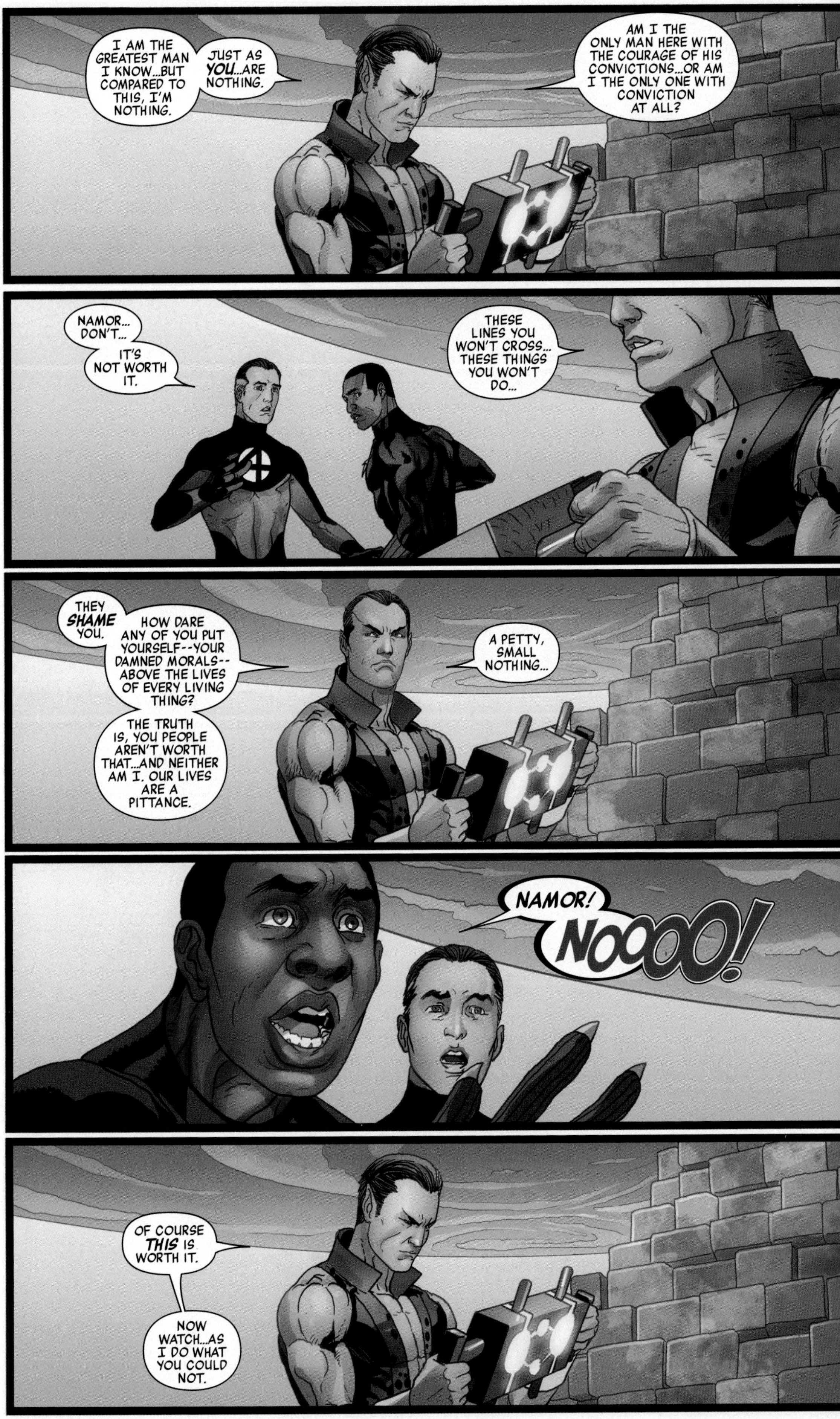
I AM THE GREATEST MAN I KNOW...BUT COMPARED TO THIS, I'M NOTHING.
JUST AS YOU...ARE NOTHING.
AM I THE ONLY MAN HERE WITH THE COURAGE OF HIS CONVICTIONS...OR AM I THE ONLY ONE WITH CONVICTION AT ALL?
NAMOR... DON'T...
IT'S NOT WORTH IT.
THESE LINES YOU WON'T CROSS... THESE THINGS YOU WON'T DO...
THEY SHAME YOU.
HOW DARE ANY OF YOU PUT YOURSELF--YOUR DAMNED MORALS--ABOVE THE LIVES OF EVERY LIVING THING?
THE TRUTH IS, YOU PEOPLE AREN'T WORTH THAT...AND NEITHER AM I. OUR LIVES ARE A PITTANCE.
A PETTY, SMALL NOTHING...
NAMOR! NOOOO!
OF COURSE THIS IS WORTH IT.
NOW WATCH...AS I DO WHAT YOU COULD NOT.

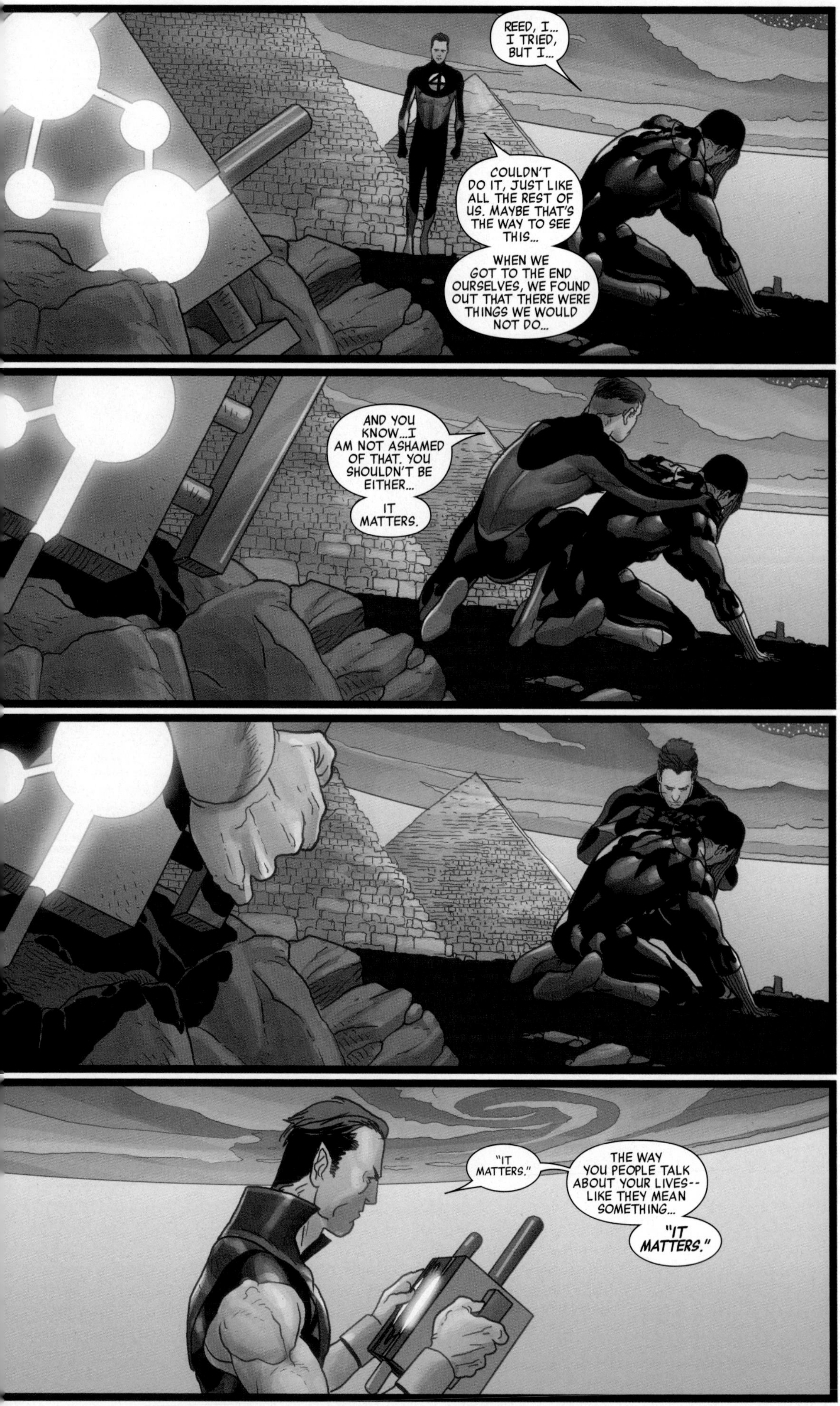

REED, I... I TRIED, BUT I...
COULDN'T DO IT, JUST LIKE ALL THE REST OF US. MAYBE THAT'S THE WAY TO SEE THIS...
WHEN WE GOT TO THE END OURSELVES, WE FOUND OUT THAT THERE WERE THINGS WE WOULD NOT DO...
AND YOU KNOW...I AM NOT ASHAMED OF THAT. YOU SHOULDN'T BE EITHER...
IT MATTERS.
"IT MATTERS."
THE WAY YOU PEOPLE TALK ABOUT YOUR LIVES--LIKE THEY MEAN SOMETHING...
"IT MATTERS."

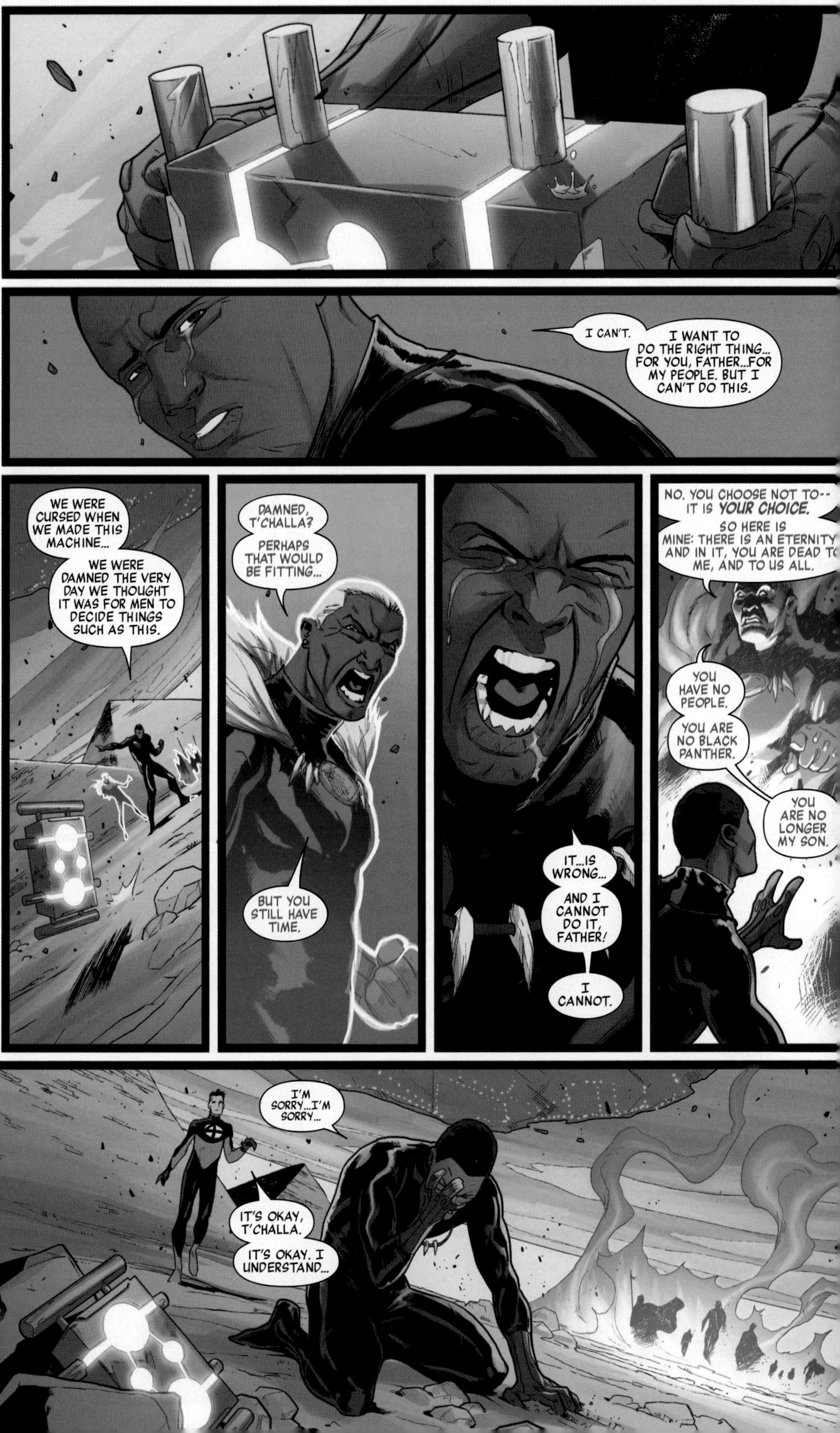
I CAN'T.
I WANT TO DO THE RIGHT THING... FOR YOU, FATHER...FOR MY PEOPLE. BUT I CAN'T DO THIS.
WE WERE CURSED WHEN WE MADE THIS MACHINE...
WE WERE DAMNED THE VERY DAY WE THOUGHT IT WAS FOR MEN TO DECIDE THINGS SUCH AS THIS.
DAMNED, T'CHALLA?
PERHAPS THAT WOULD BE FITTING...
BUT YOU STILL HAVE TIME.
IT...IS WRONG...
AND I CANNOT DO IT, FATHER!
I CANNOT.
NO. YOU CHOOSE NOT TO-- IT IS YOUR CHOICE.
SO HERE IS MINE: THERE IS AN ETERNITY AND IN IT, YOU ARE DEAD TO ME, AND TO US ALL.
YOU HAVE NO PEOPLE.
YOU ARE NO BLACK PANTHER.
YOU ARE NO LONGER MY SON.
I'M SORRY...I'M SORRY...
IT'S OKAY, T'CHALLA.
IT'S OKAY. I UNDERSTAND...

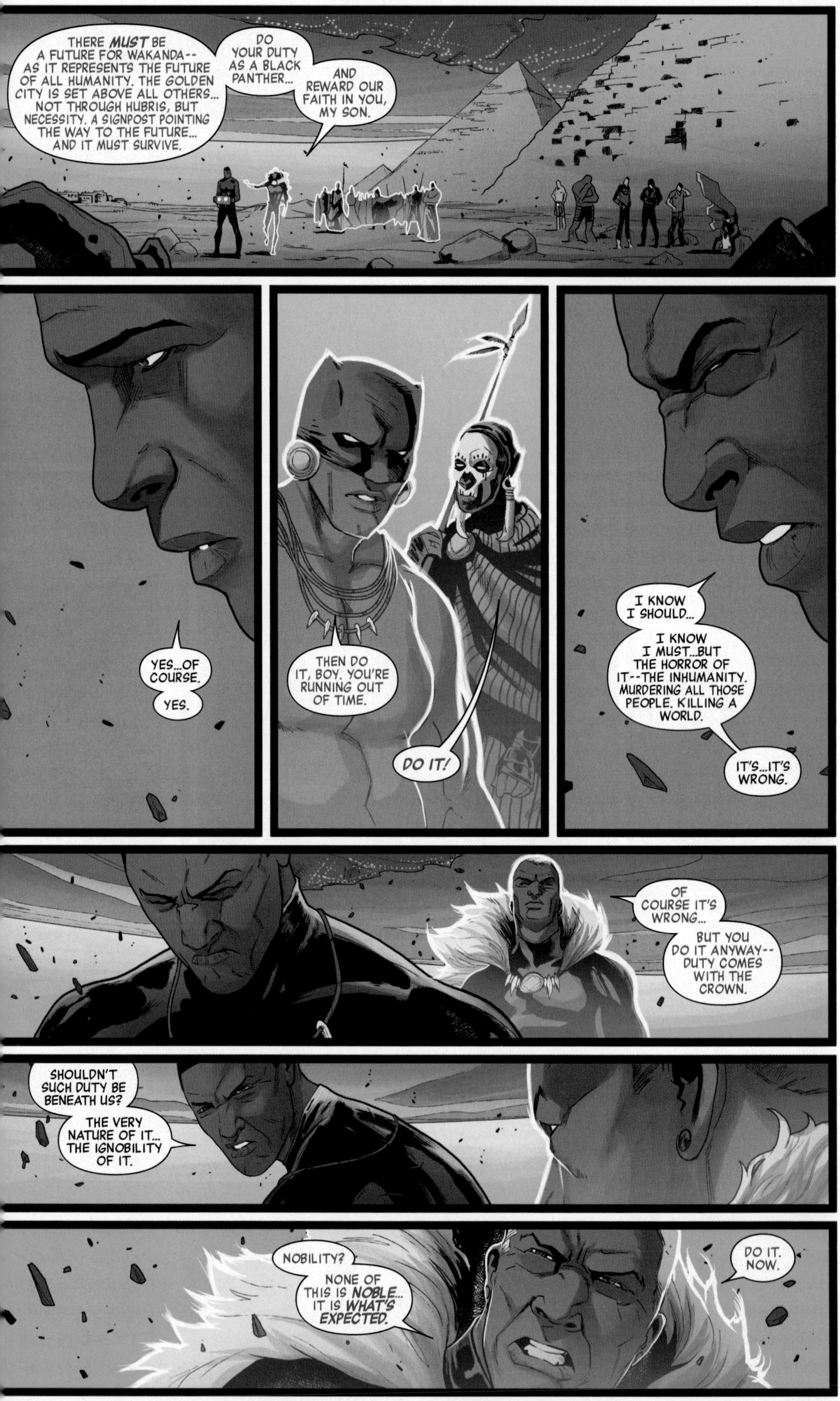
THERE MUST BE A FUTURE FOR WAKANDA-- AS IT REPRESENTS THE FUTURE OF ALL HUMANITY. THE GOLDEN CITY IS SET ABOVE ALL OTHERS... NOT THROUGH HUBRIS, BUT NECESSITY. A SIGNPOST POINTING THE WAY TO THE FUTURE... AND IT MUST SURVIVE.
DO YOUR DUTY AS A BLACK PANTHER...
AND REWARD OUR FAITH IN YOU, MY SON.
YES...OF COURSE.
YES.
THEN DO IT, BOY. YOU'RE RUNNING OUT OF TIME.
DO IT!
I KNOW I SHOULD...
I KNOW I MUST...BUT THE HORROR OF IT--THE INHUMANITY. MURDERING ALL THOSE PEOPLE. KILLING A WORLD.
IT'S...IT'S WRONG.
OF COURSE IT'S WRONG...
BUT YOU DO IT ANYWAY-- DUTY COMES WITH THE CROWN.
SHOULDN'T SUCH DUTY BE BENEATH US?
THE VERY NATURE OF IT... THE IGNOBILITY OF IT.
NOBILITY?
NONE OF THIS IS NOBLE... IT IS WHAT'S EXPECTED.
DO IT. NOW.

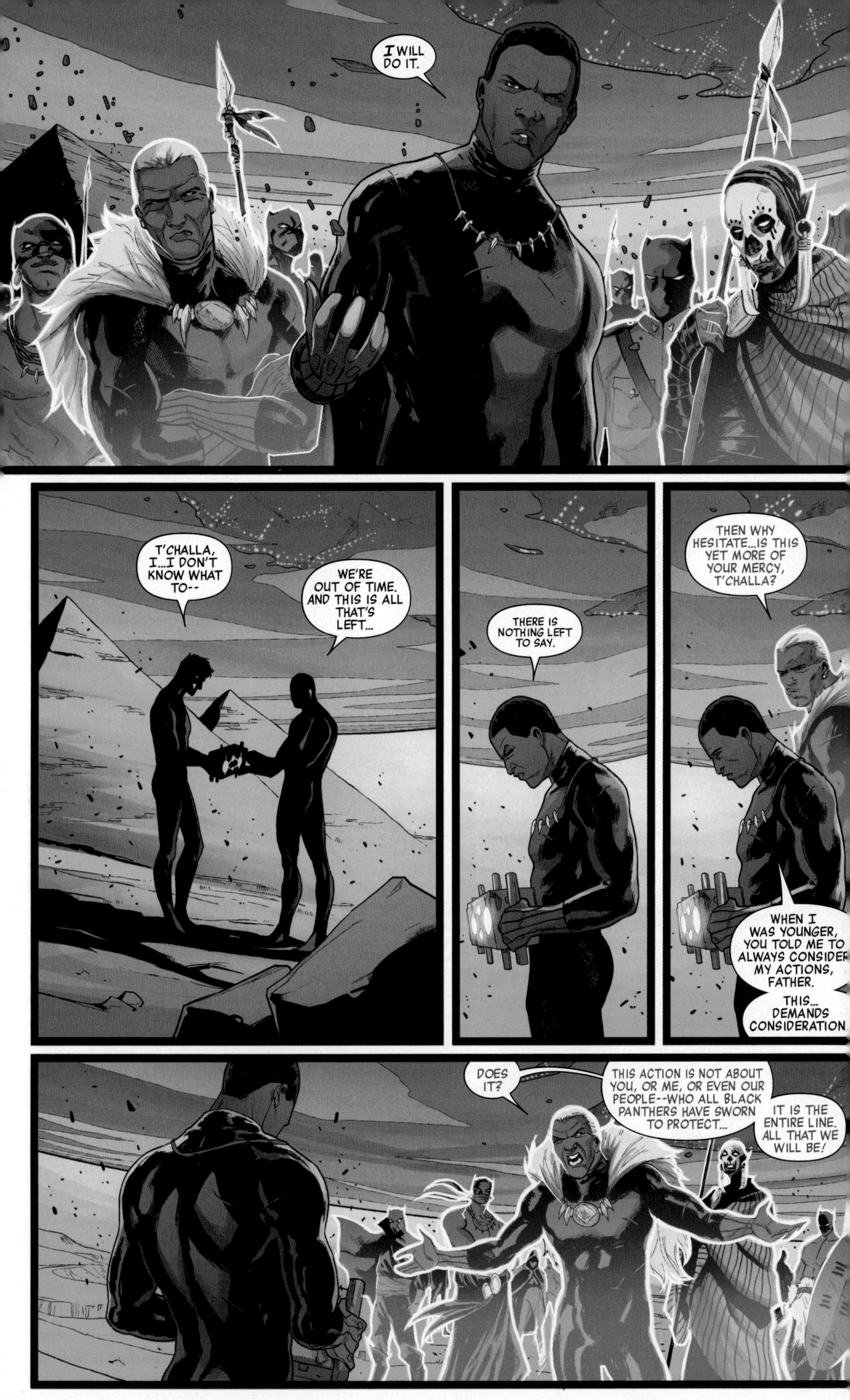

I WILL DO IT.
T'CHALLA, I...I DON'T KNOW WHAT TO--
WE'RE OUT OF TIME. AND THIS IS ALL THAT'S LEFT...
THERE IS NOTHING LEFT TO SAY.
THEN WHY HESITATE...IS THIS YET MORE OF YOUR MERCY, T'CHALLA?
WHEN I WAS YOUNGER, YOU TOLD ME TO ALWAYS CONSIDER MY ACTIONS, FATHER.
THIS... DEMANDS CONSIDERATION
DOES IT?
THIS ACTION IS NOT ABOUT YOU, OR ME, OR EVEN OUR PEOPLE--WHO ALL BLACK PANTHERS HAVE SWORN TO PROTECT...
IT IS THE ENTIRE LINE. ALL THAT WE WILL BE!

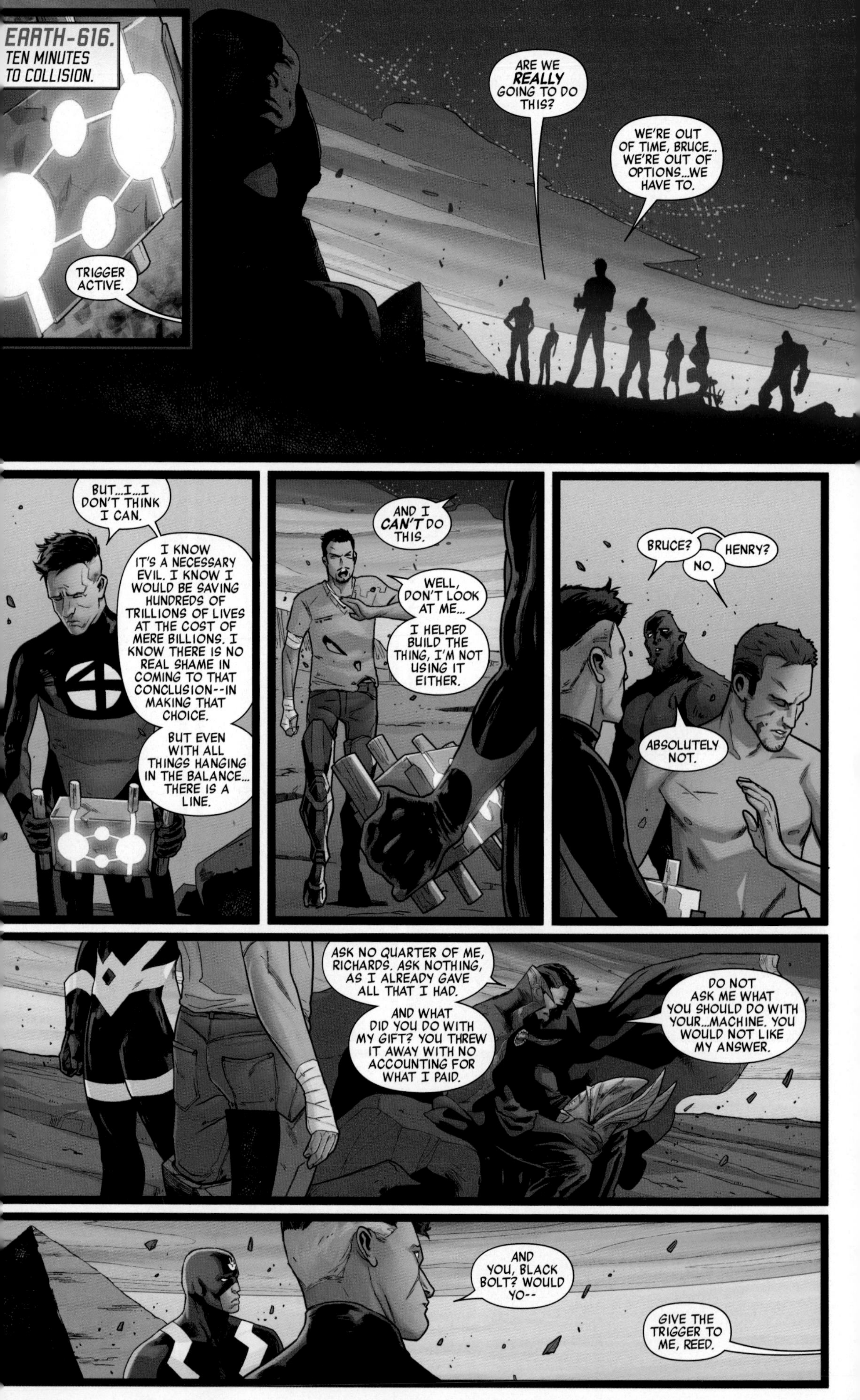
EARTH-616. TEN MINUTES TO COLLISION.
TRIGGER ACTIVE.
ARE WE *REALLY* GOING TO DO THIS?
WE'RE OUT OF TIME, BRUCE... WE'RE OUT OF OPTIONS...WE HAVE TO.
BUT...I...I DON'T THINK I CAN.
I KNOW IT'S A NECESSARY EVIL. I KNOW I WOULD BE SAVING HUNDREDS OF TRILLIONS OF LIVES AT THE COST OF MERE BILLIONS. I KNOW THERE IS NO REAL SHAME IN COMING TO THAT CONCLUSION--IN MAKING THAT CHOICE.
BUT EVEN WITH ALL THINGS HANGING IN THE BALANCE... THERE IS A LINE.
AND I *CAN'T* DO THIS.
WELL, DON'T LOOK AT ME...
I HELPED BUILD THE THING, I'M NOT USING IT EITHER.
BRUCE?
NO.
HENRY?
ABSOLUTELY NOT.
ASK NO QUARTER OF ME, RICHARDS. ASK NOTHING, AS I ALREADY GAVE ALL THAT I HAD.
AND WHAT DID YOU DO WITH MY GIFT? YOU THREW IT AWAY WITH NO ACCOUNTING FOR WHAT I PAID.
DO NOT ASK ME WHAT YOU SHOULD DO WITH YOUR...MACHINE. YOU WOULD NOT LIKE MY ANSWER.
AND YOU, BLACK BOLT? WOULD YO--
GIVE THE TRIGGER TO ME, REED.

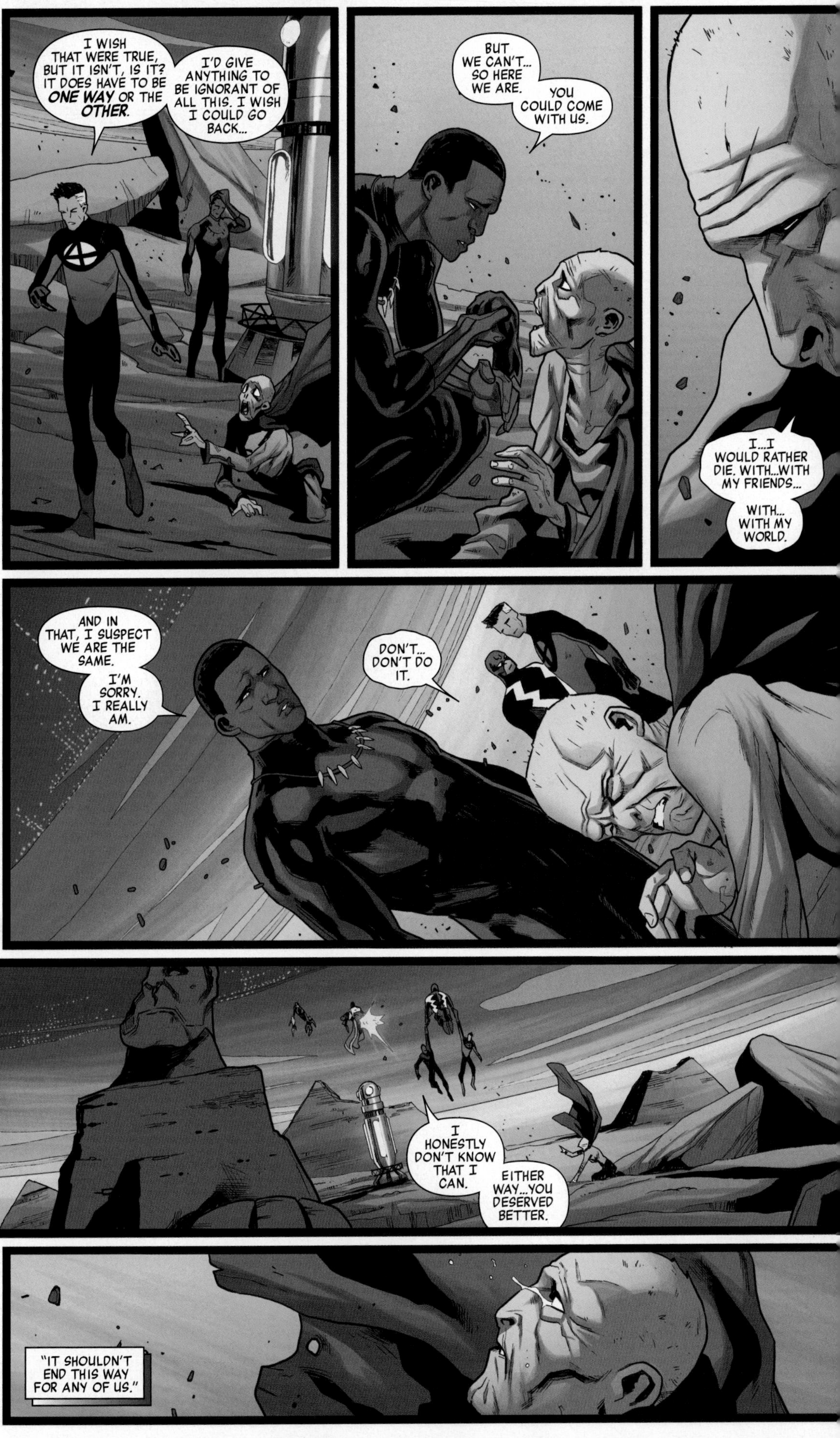

I WISH THAT WERE TRUE, BUT IT ISN'T, IS IT? IT DOES HAVE TO BE **ONE WAY** OR THE **OTHER**.
I'D GIVE ANYTHING TO BE IGNORANT OF ALL THIS. I WISH I COULD GO BACK...
BUT WE CAN'T... SO HERE WE ARE.
YOU COULD COME WITH US.
I...I WOULD RATHER DIE. WITH...WITH MY FRIENDS...
WITH... WITH MY WORLD.
AND IN THAT, I SUSPECT WE ARE THE SAME.
I'M SORRY. I REALLY AM.
DON'T... DON'T DO IT.
I HONESTLY DON'T KNOW THAT I CAN.
EITHER WAY...YOU DESERVED BETTER.
"IT SHOULDN'T END THIS WAY FOR ANY OF US."

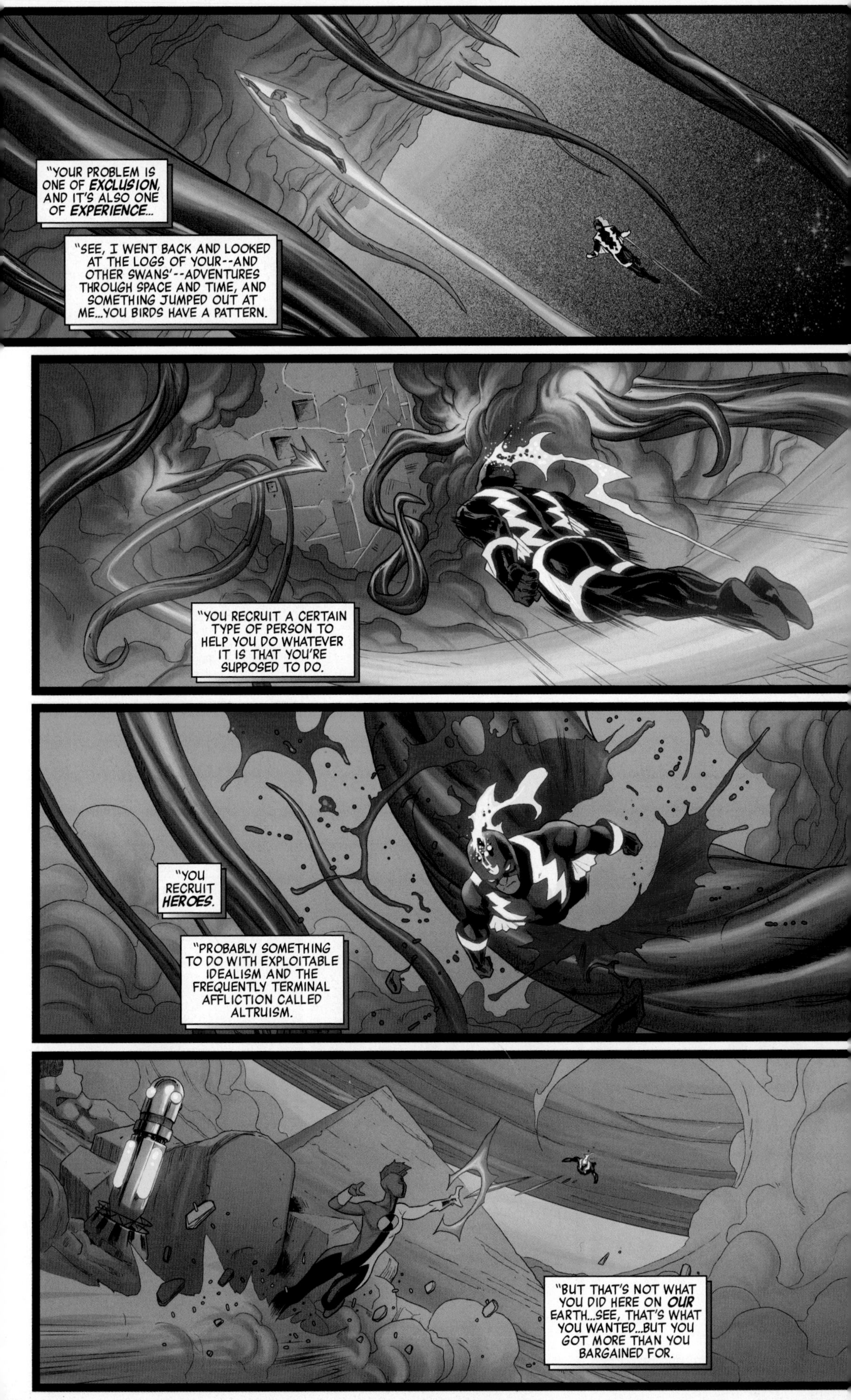
"YOUR PROBLEM IS ONE OF EXCLUSION, AND IT'S ALSO ONE OF EXPERIENCE...
"SEE, I WENT BACK AND LOOKED AT THE LOGS OF YOUR--AND OTHER SWANS'--ADVENTURES THROUGH SPACE AND TIME, AND SOMETHING JUMPED OUT AT ME...YOU BIRDS HAVE A PATTERN.
"YOU RECRUIT A CERTAIN TYPE OF PERSON TO HELP YOU DO WHATEVER IT IS THAT YOU'RE SUPPOSED TO DO.
"YOU RECRUIT HEROES.
"PROBABLY SOMETHING TO DO WITH EXPLOITABLE IDEALISM AND THE FREQUENTLY TERMINAL AFFLICTION CALLED ALTRUISM.
"BUT THAT'S NOT WHAT YOU DID HERE ON OUR EARTH...SEE, THAT'S WHAT YOU WANTED...BUT YOU GOT MORE THAN YOU BARGAINED FOR.

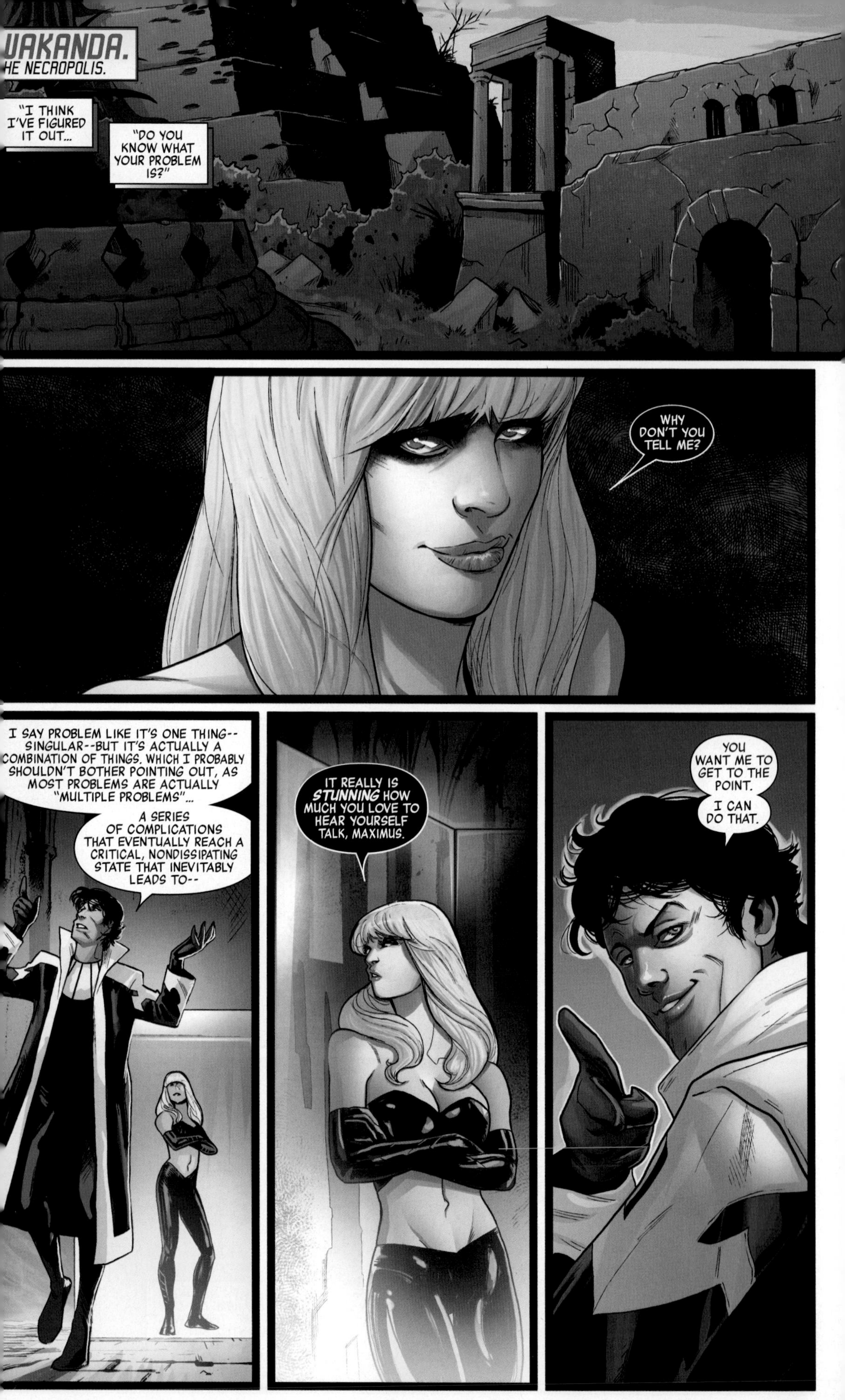

UAKANDA.
HE NECROPOLIS.
"I THINK I'VE FIGURED IT OUT...
"DO YOU KNOW WHAT YOUR PROBLEM IS?"
WHY DON'T YOU TELL ME?
I SAY PROBLEM LIKE IT'S ONE THING-- SINGULAR--BUT IT'S ACTUALLY A COMBINATION OF THINGS. WHICH I PROBABLY SHOULDN'T BOTHER POINTING OUT, AS MOST PROBLEMS ARE ACTUALLY "MULTIPLE PROBLEMS"...
A SERIES OF COMPLICATIONS THAT EVENTUALLY REACH A CRITICAL, NONDISSIPATING STATE THAT INEVITABLY LEADS TO--
IT REALLY IS STUNNING HOW MUCH YOU LOVE TO HEAR YOURSELF TALK, MAXIMUS.
YOU WANT ME TO GET TO THE POINT.
I CAN DO THAT.

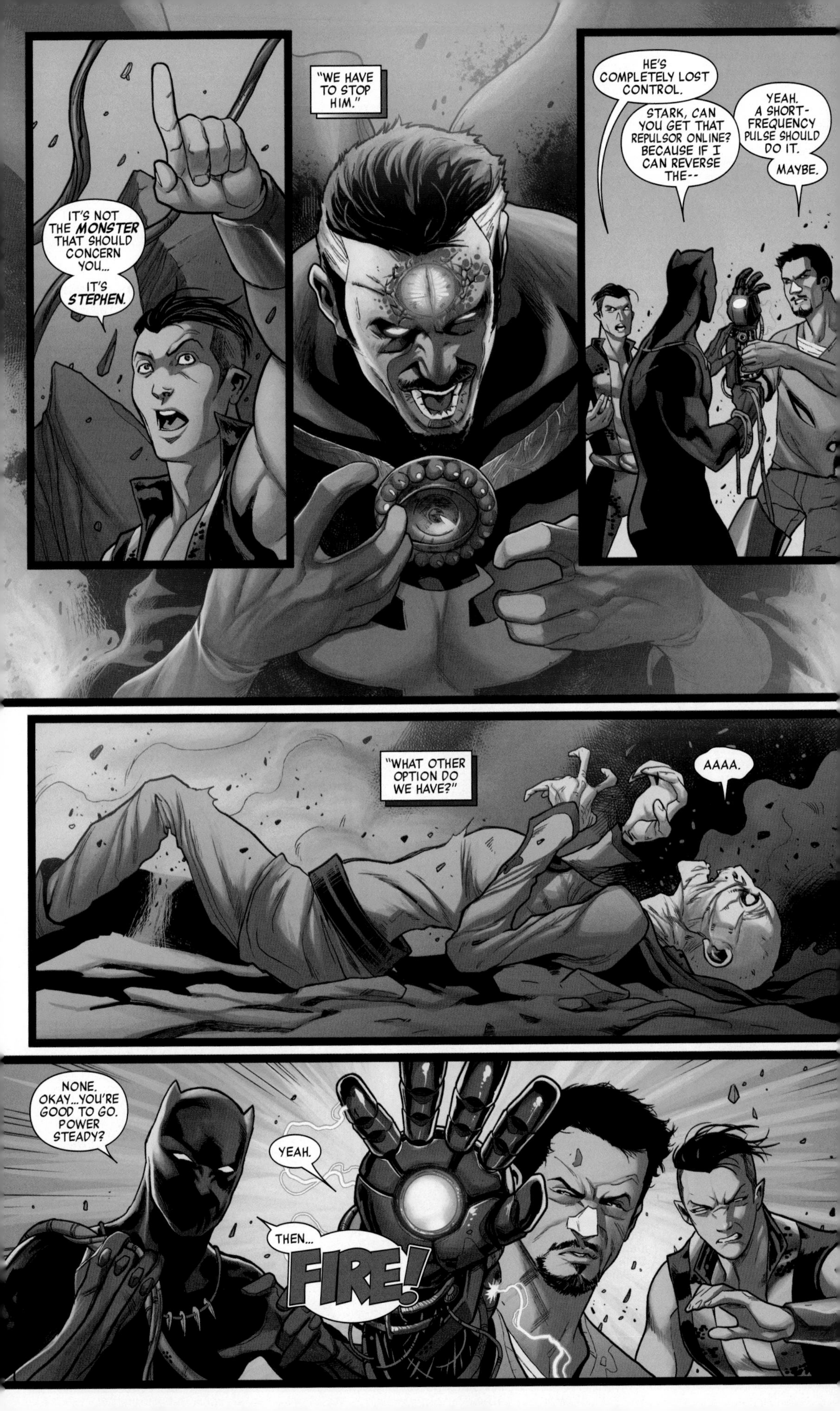

IT'S NOT THE **MONSTER** THAT SHOULD CONCERN YOU...
IT'S **STEPHEN.**
"WE HAVE TO STOP HIM."
HE'S COMPLETELY LOST CONTROL.
STARK, CAN YOU GET THAT REPULSOR ONLINE? BECAUSE IF I CAN REVERSE THE--
YEAH. A SHORT-FREQUENCY PULSE SHOULD DO IT.
MAYBE.
"WHAT OTHER OPTION DO WE HAVE?"
AAAA.
NONE. OKAY...YOU'RE GOOD TO GO. POWER STEADY?
YEAH.
THEN...
FIRE!

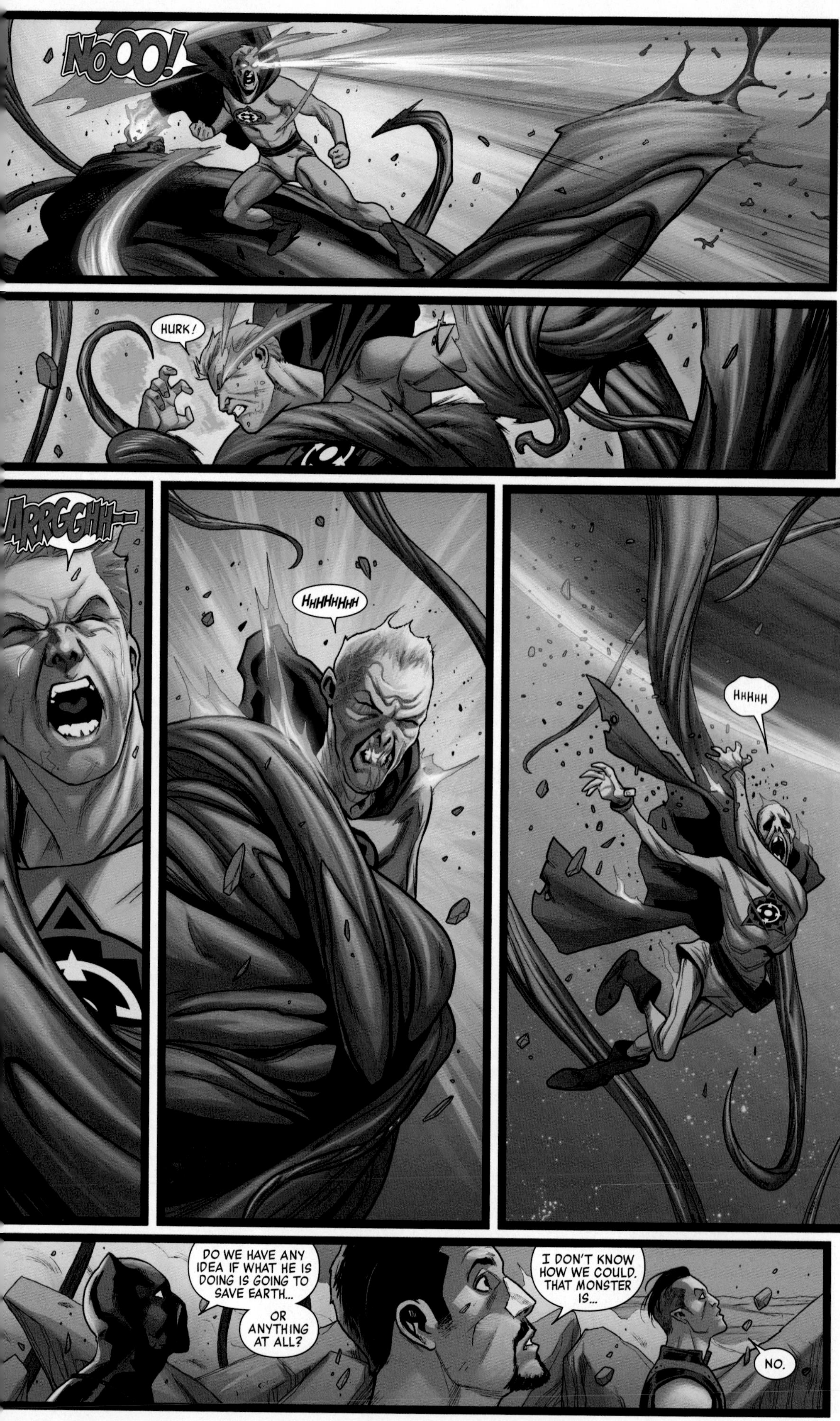
NOOO!
HURK!
ARRGGHH--
HHHHHHHH
HHHHH
DO WE HAVE ANY IDEA IF WHAT HE IS DOING IS GOING TO SAVE EARTH...
OR ANYTHING AT ALL?
I DON'T KNOW HOW WE COULD. THAT MONSTER IS...
NO.

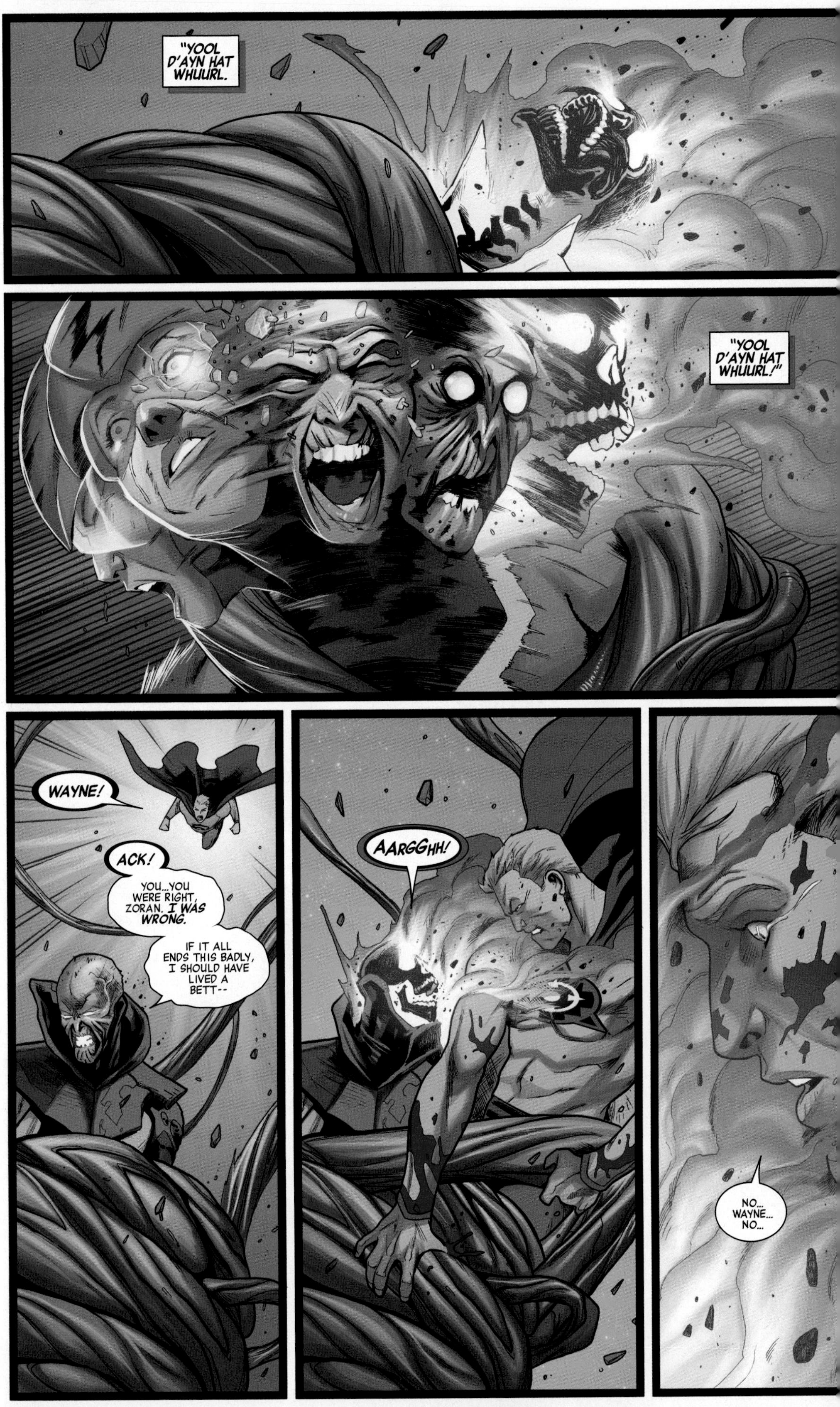
"YOOL D'AYN HAT WHUURL.
"YOOL D'AYN HAT WHUURL!"
WAYNE!
ACK!
YOU...YOU WERE RIGHT, ZORAN. I WAS WRONG.
IF IT ALL ENDS THIS BADLY, I SHOULD HAVE LIVED A BETT--
AARGGHH!
NO... WAYNE... NO...

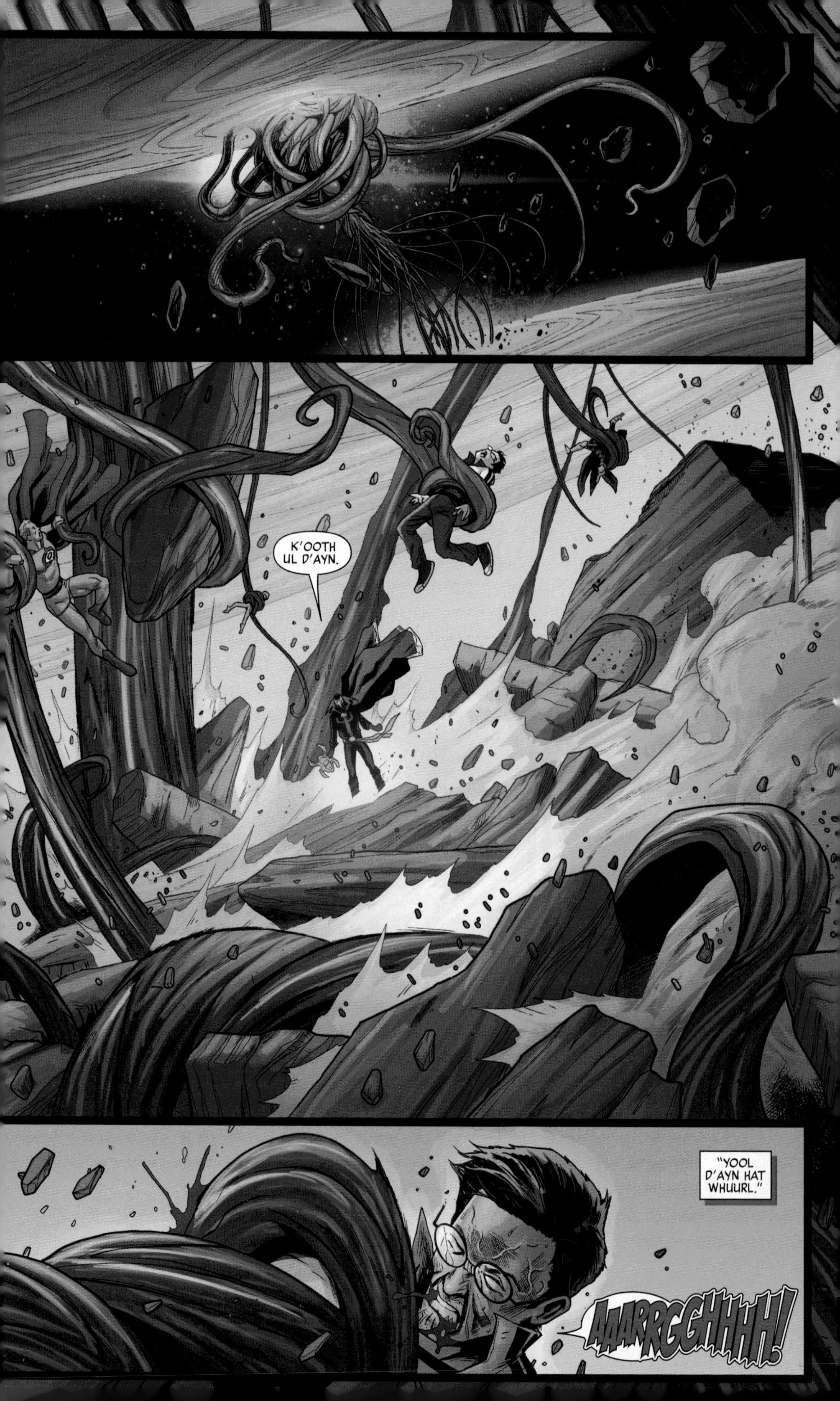
K'OOTH UL D'AYN.
"YOOL D'AYN HAT WHUURL."
AAARRGGHHHH!

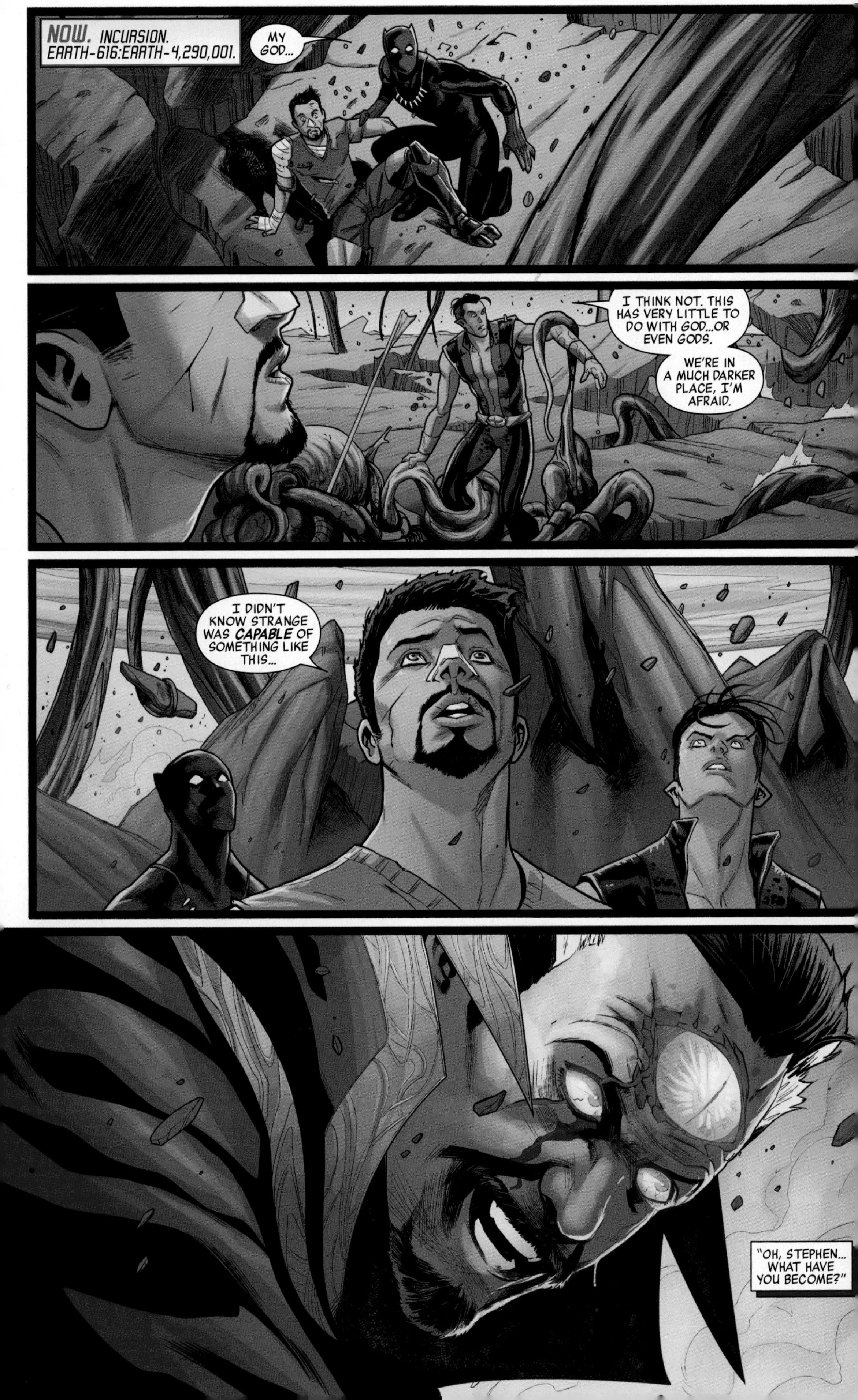
NOW. INCURSION.
EARTH-616:EARTH-4,290,001.
MY GOD...
I THINK NOT. THIS HAS VERY LITTLE TO DO WITH GOD...OR EVEN GODS.
WE'RE IN A MUCH DARKER PLACE, I'M AFRAID.
I DIDN'T KNOW STRANGE WAS CAPABLE OF SOMETHING LIKE THIS...
"OH, STEPHEN... WHAT HAVE YOU BECOME?"

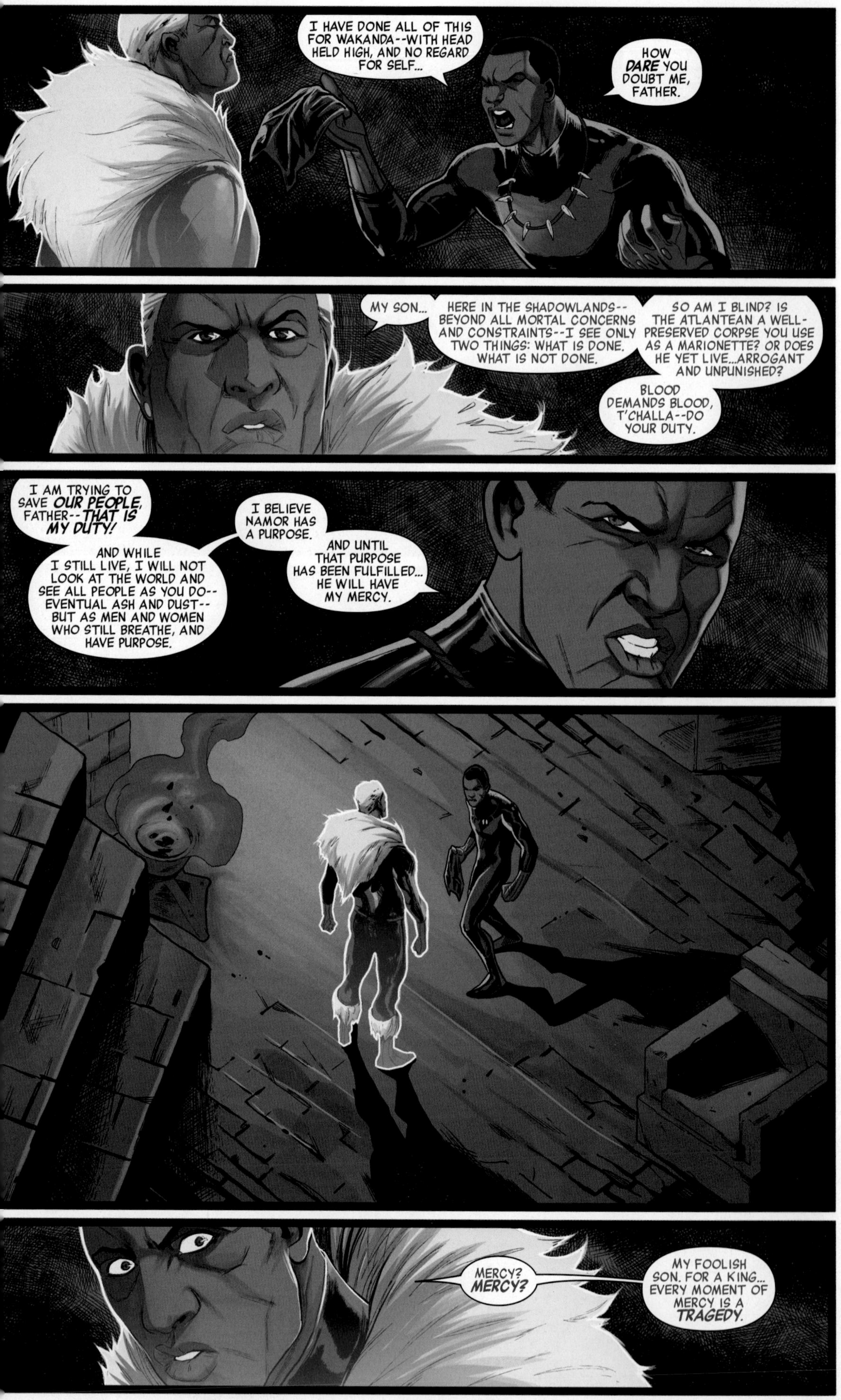
I HAVE DONE ALL OF THIS FOR WAKANDA--WITH HEAD HELD HIGH, AND NO REGARD FOR SELF...
HOW DARE YOU DOUBT ME, FATHER.
MY SON...
HERE IN THE SHADOWLANDS--BEYOND ALL MORTAL CONCERNS AND CONSTRAINTS--I SEE ONLY TWO THINGS: WHAT IS DONE. WHAT IS NOT DONE.
SO AM I BLIND? IS THE ATLANTEAN A WELL-PRESERVED CORPSE YOU USE AS A MARIONETTE? OR DOES HE YET LIVE...ARROGANT AND UNPUNISHED?
BLOOD DEMANDS BLOOD, T'CHALLA--DO YOUR DUTY.
I AM TRYING TO SAVE OUR PEOPLE, FATHER--THAT IS MY DUTY!
AND WHILE I STILL LIVE, I WILL NOT LOOK AT THE WORLD AND SEE ALL PEOPLE AS YOU DO--EVENTUAL ASH AND DUST--BUT AS MEN AND WOMEN WHO STILL BREATHE, AND HAVE PURPOSE.
I BELIEVE NAMOR HAS A PURPOSE.
AND UNTIL THAT PURPOSE HAS BEEN FULFILLED... HE WILL HAVE MY MERCY.
MERCY? MERCY?
MY FOOLISH SON. FOR A KING... EVERY MOMENT OF MERCY IS A TRAGEDY.

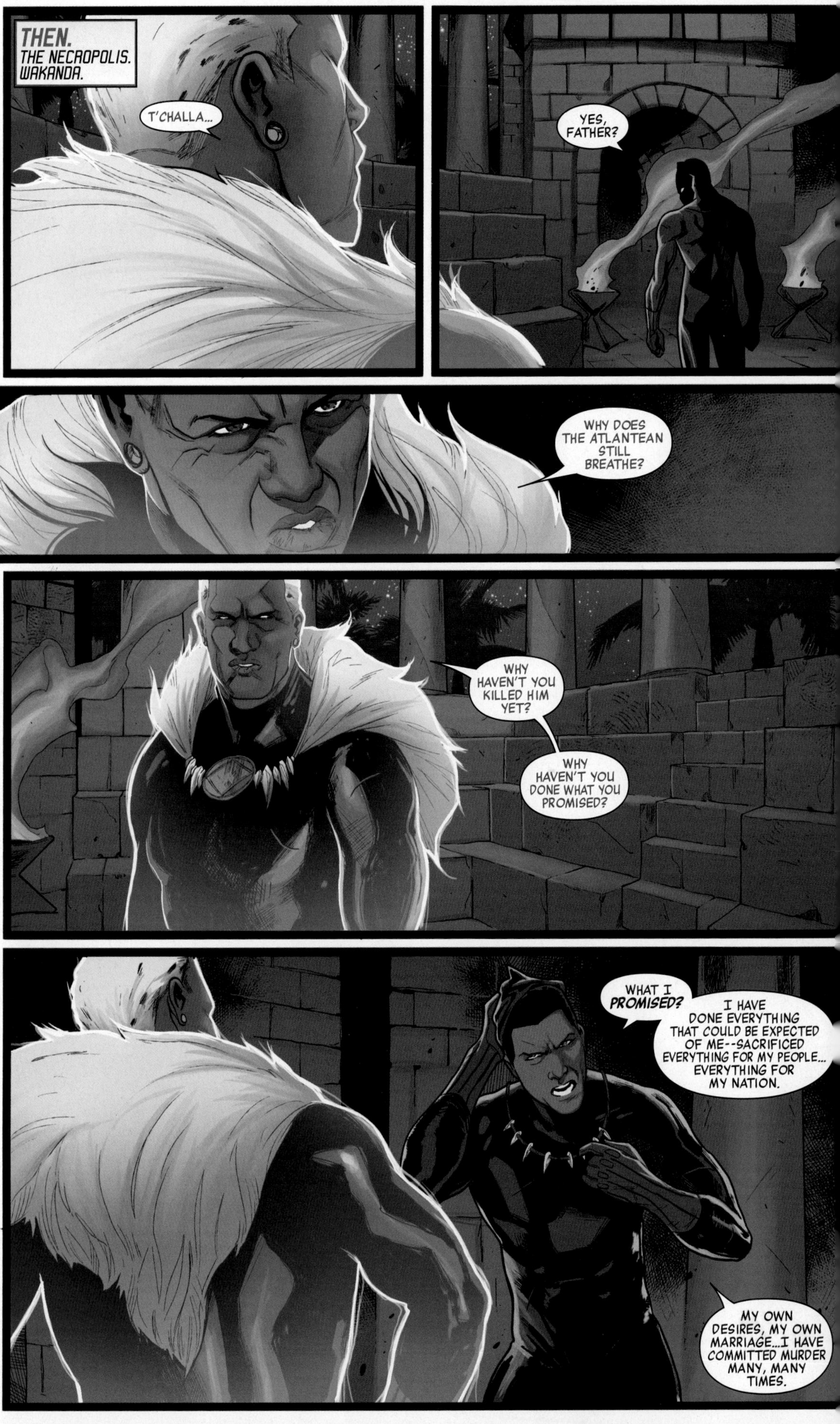
THEN.
THE NECROPOLIS.
WAKANDA.
T'CHALLA...
YES, FATHER?
WHY DOES THE ATLANTEAN STILL BREATHE?
WHY HAVEN'T YOU KILLED HIM YET?
WHY HAVEN'T YOU DONE WHAT YOU PROMISED?
WHAT I *PROMISED?*
I HAVE DONE EVERYTHING THAT COULD BE EXPECTED OF ME--SACRIFICED EVERYTHING FOR MY PEOPLE... EVERYTHING FOR MY NATION.
MY OWN DESIRES, MY OWN MARRIAGE...I HAVE COMMITTED MURDER MANY, MANY TIMES.

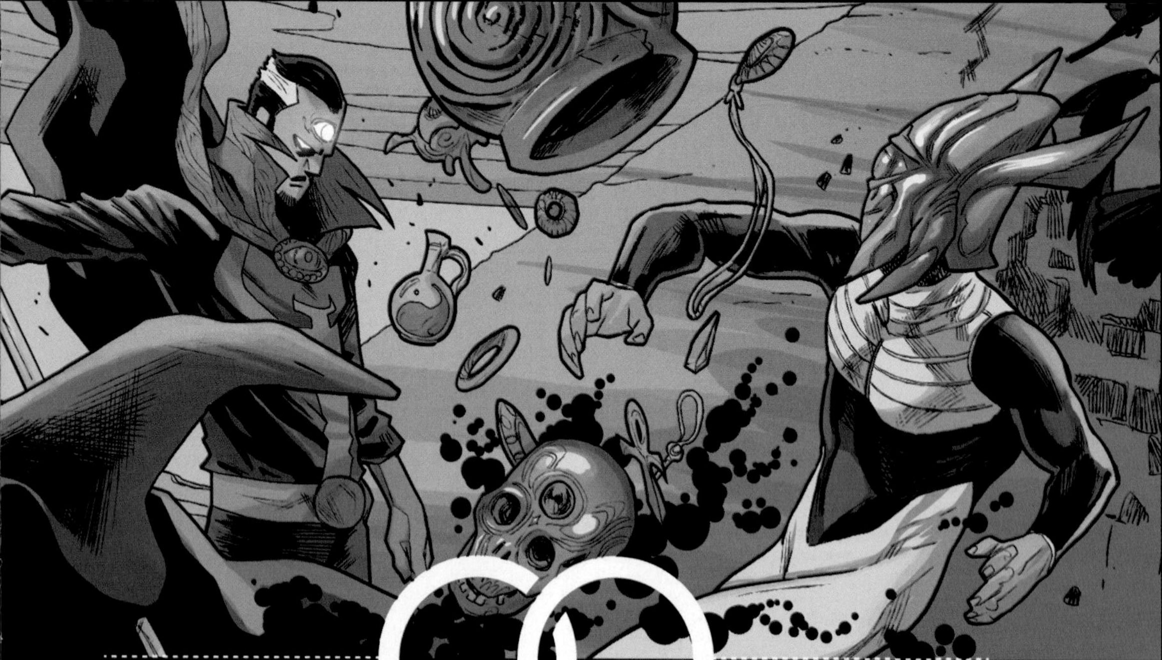

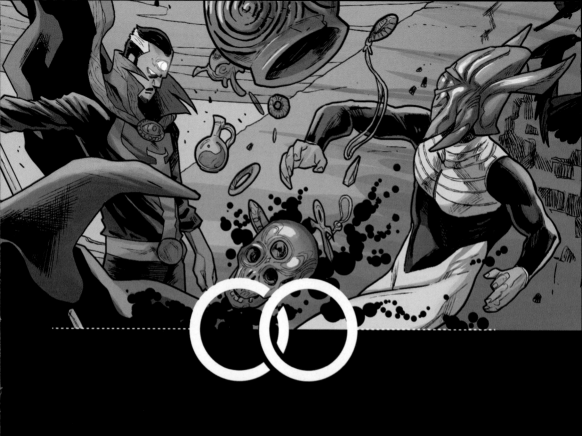

"THE BOMB"

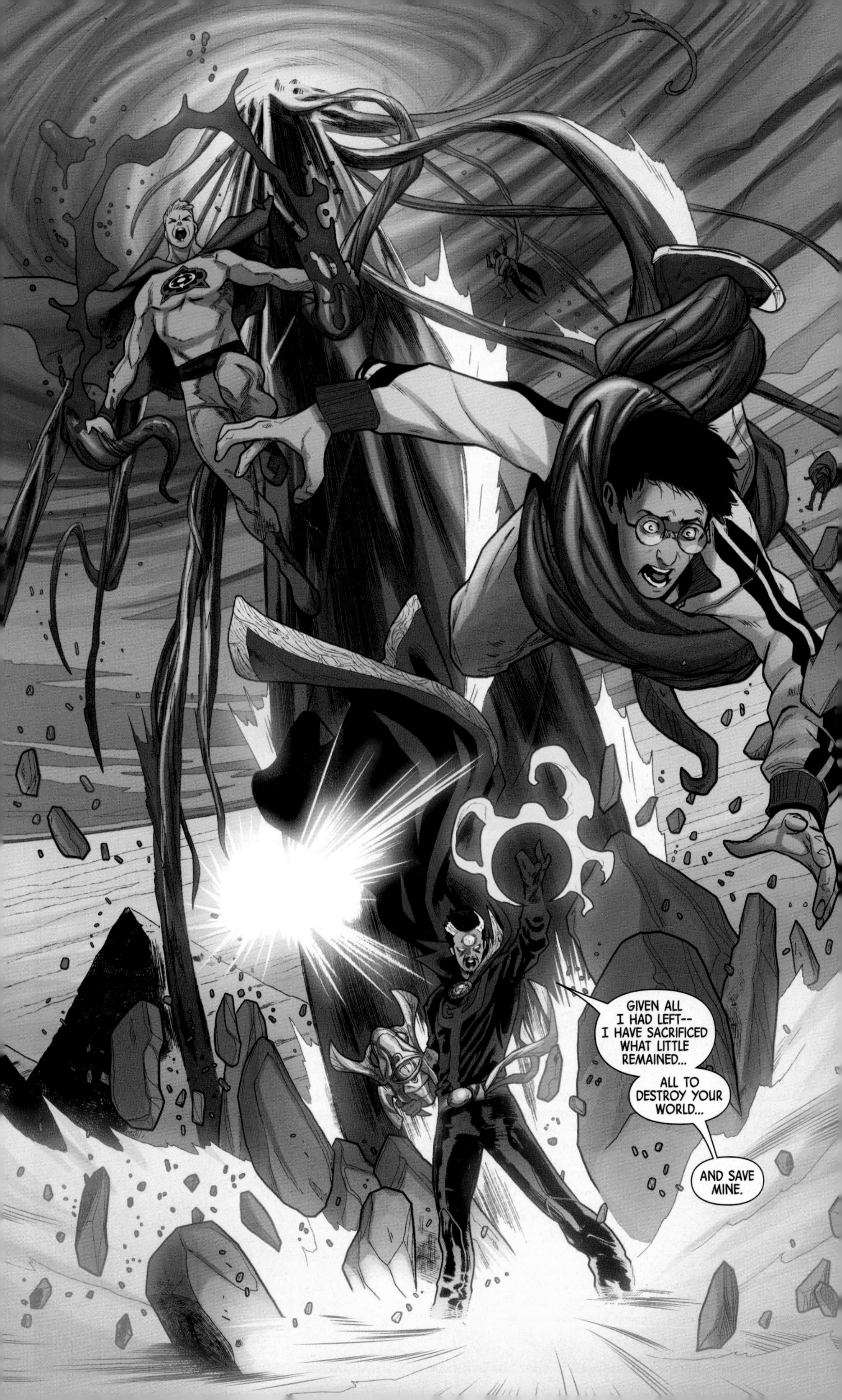
GIVEN ALL I HAD LEFT-- I HAVE SACRIFICED WHAT LITTLE REMAINED...
ALL TO DESTROY YOUR WORLD...
AND SAVE MINE.

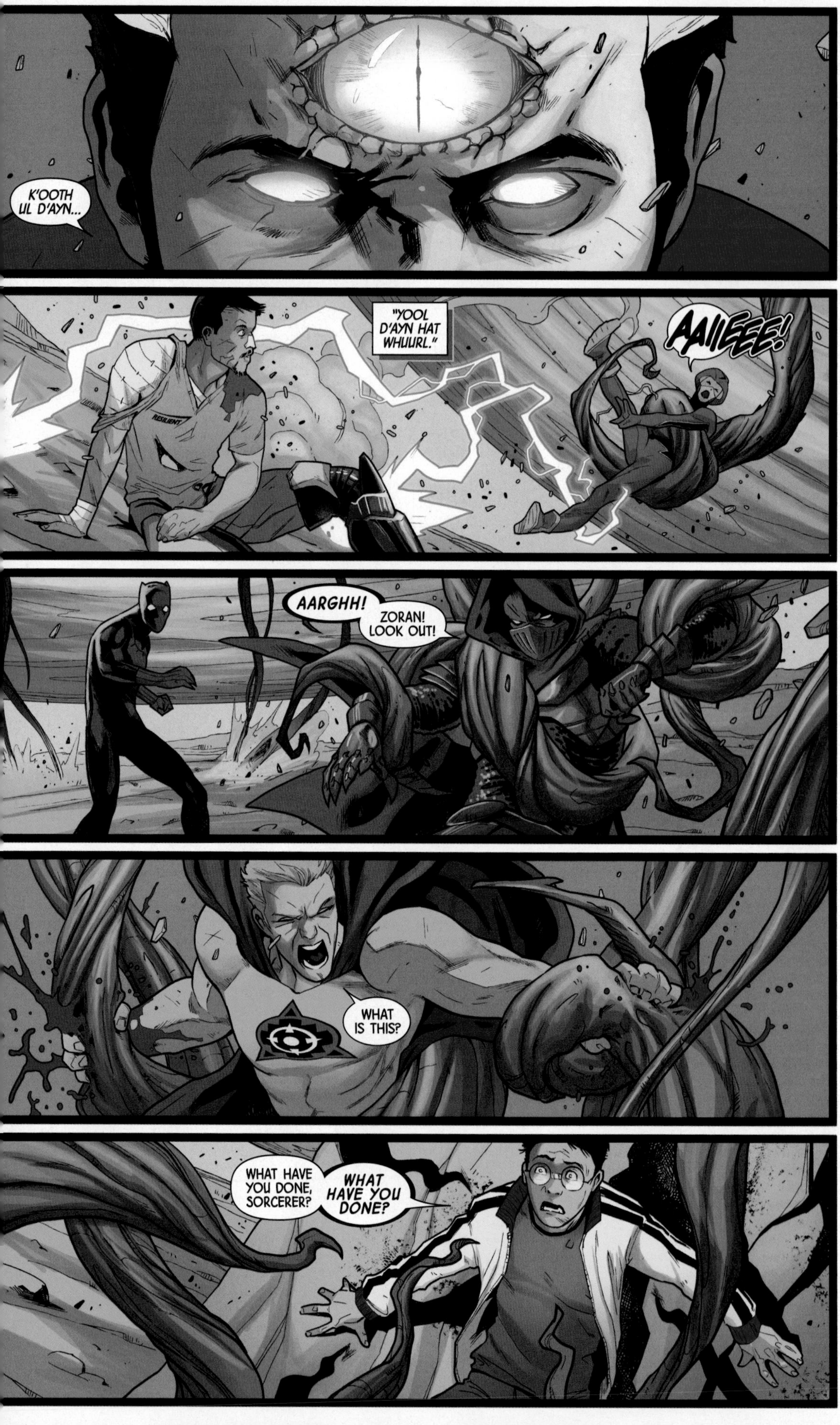
K'OOTH UL D'AYN...
"YOOL D'AYN HAT WHUURL."
AAIIEEE!
RESILIENT
AARGHH!
ZORAN! LOOK OUT!
WHAT IS THIS?
WHAT HAVE YOU DONE, SORCERER?
WHAT HAVE YOU DONE?

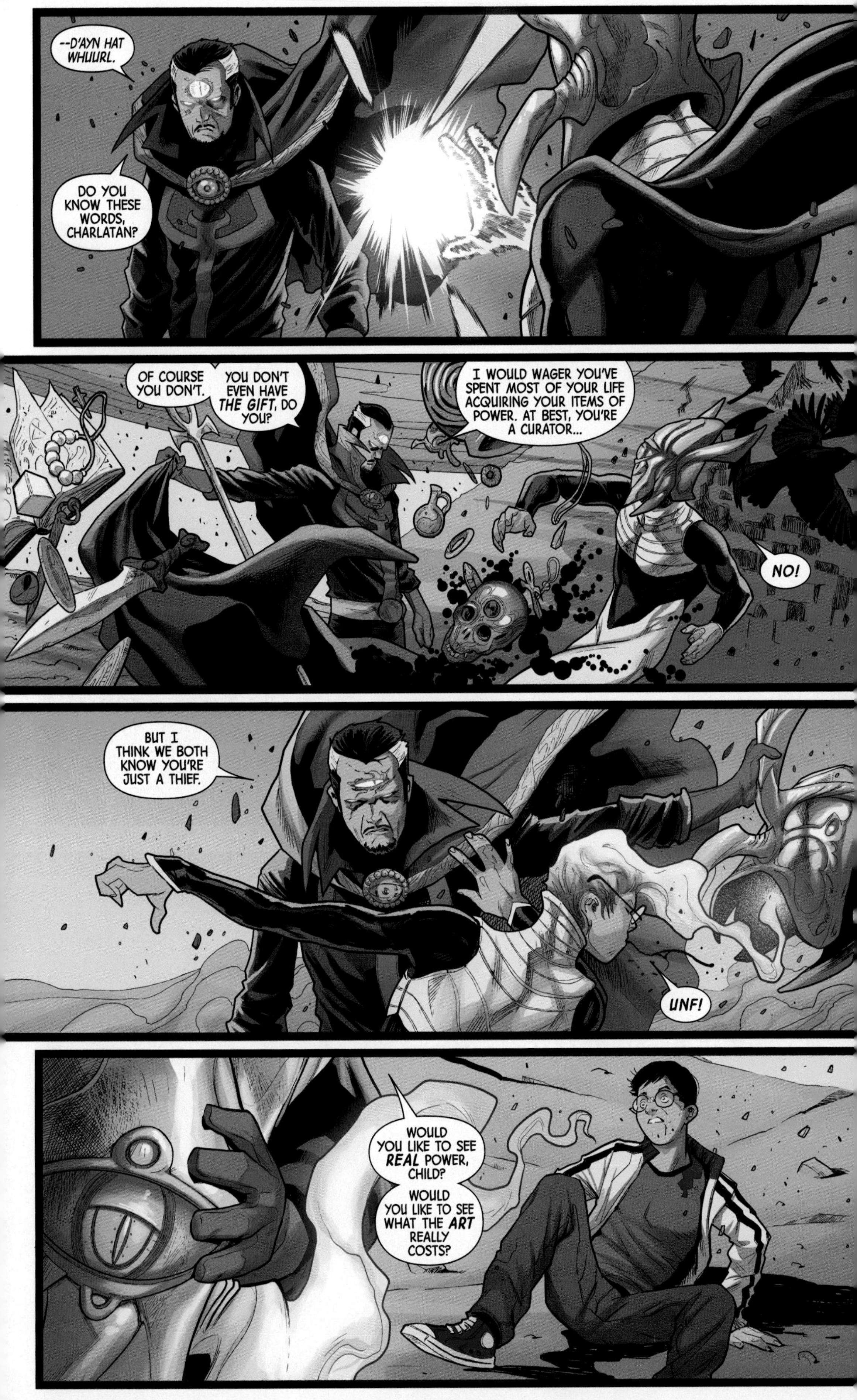
--D'AYN HAT WHUURL.
DO YOU KNOW THESE WORDS, CHARLATAN?
OF COURSE YOU DON'T.
YOU DON'T EVEN HAVE THE GIFT, DO YOU?
I WOULD WAGER YOU'VE SPENT MOST OF YOUR LIFE ACQUIRING YOUR ITEMS OF POWER. AT BEST, YOU'RE A CURATOR...
NO!
BUT I THINK WE BOTH KNOW YOU'RE JUST A THIEF.
UNF!
WOULD YOU LIKE TO SEE REAL POWER, CHILD?
WOULD YOU LIKE TO SEE WHAT THE ART REALLY COSTS?

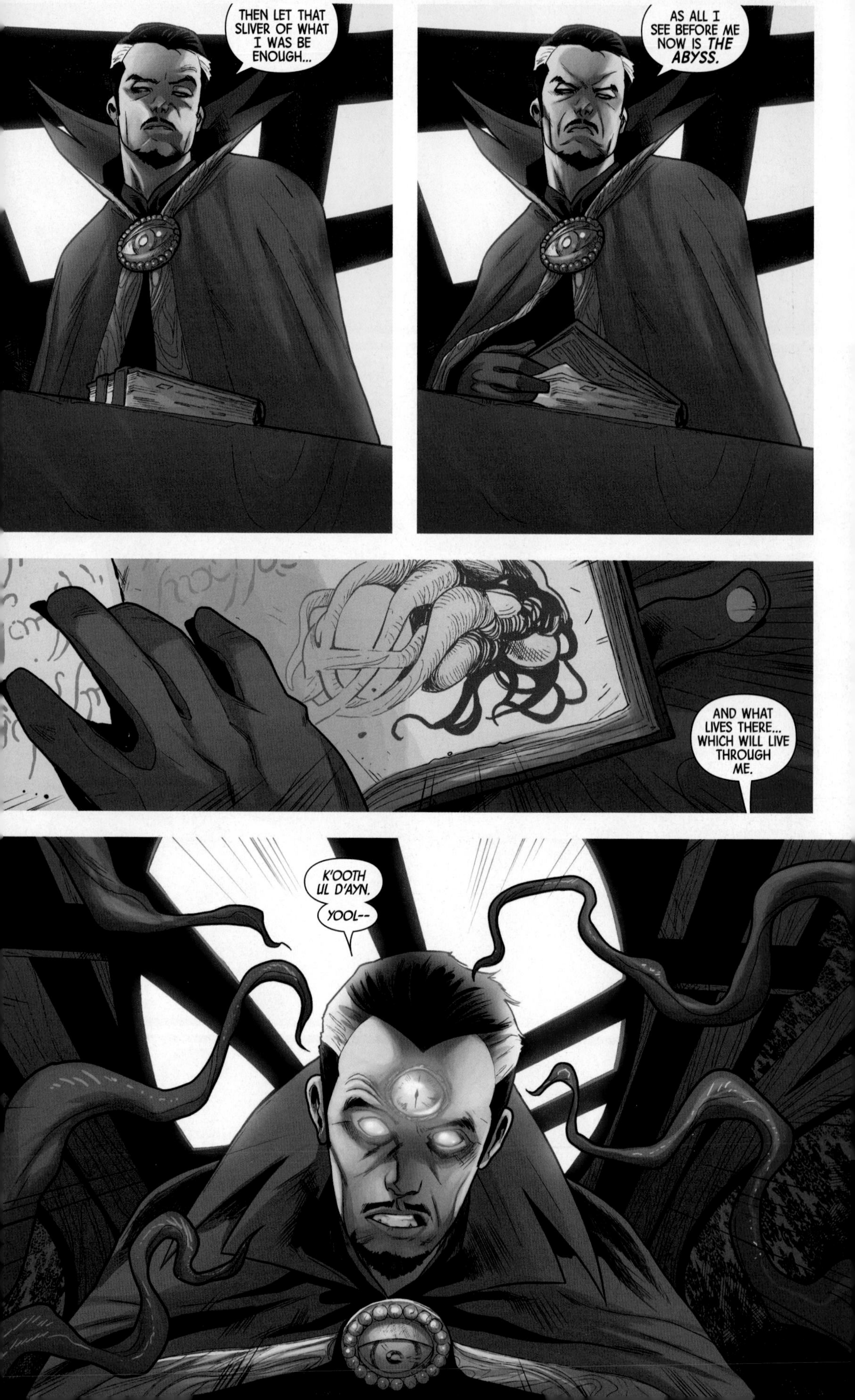
THEN LET THAT SLIVER OF WHAT I WAS BE ENOUGH...
AS ALL I SEE BEFORE ME NOW IS *THE ABYSS.*
AND WHAT LIVES THERE... WHICH WILL LIVE THROUGH ME.
K'OOTH UL D'AYN.
YOOL--

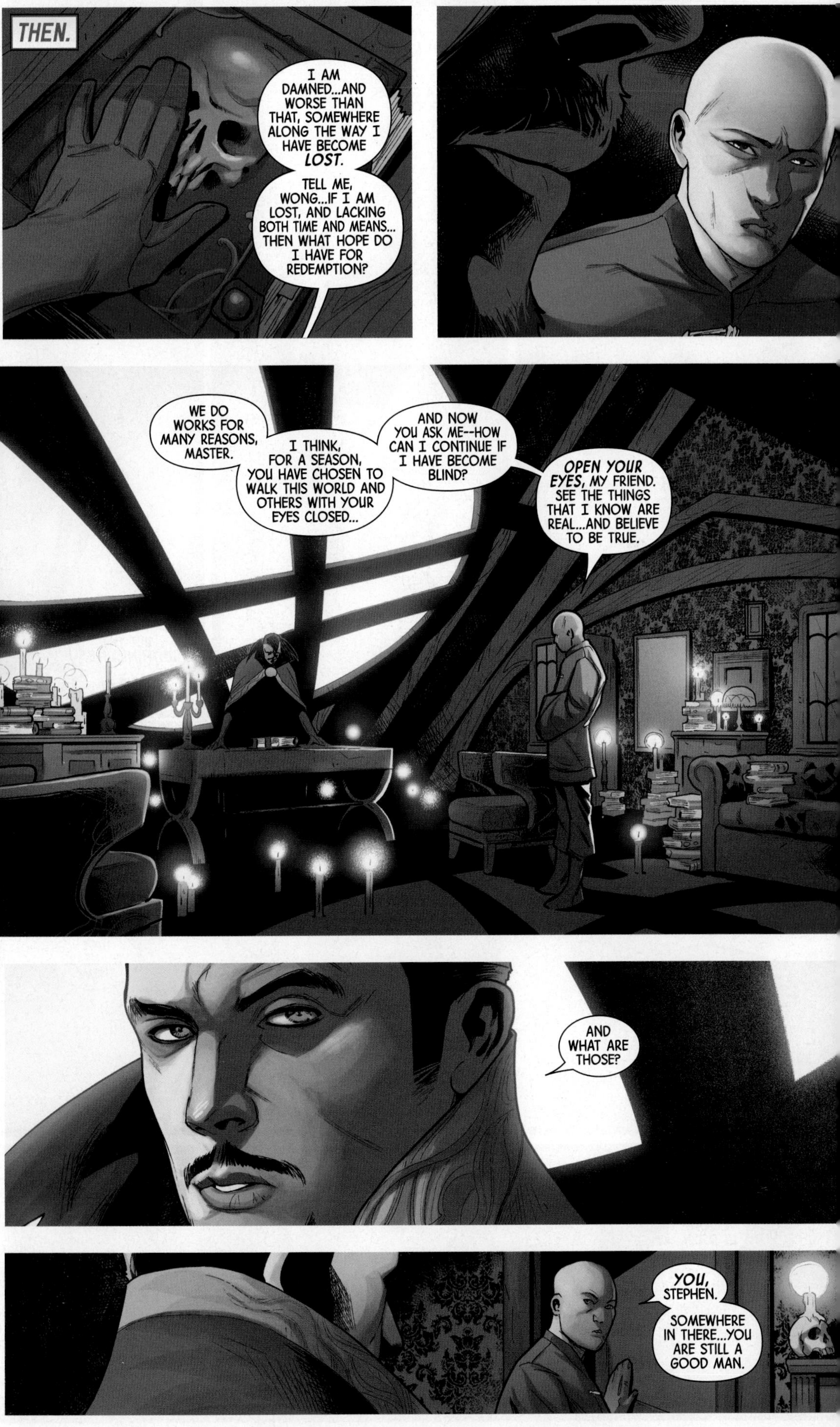
THEN.
I AM DAMNED...AND WORSE THAN THAT, SOMEWHERE ALONG THE WAY I HAVE BECOME LOST.
TELL ME, WONG...IF I AM LOST, AND LACKING BOTH TIME AND MEANS... THEN WHAT HOPE DO I HAVE FOR REDEMPTION?
WE DO WORKS FOR MANY REASONS, MASTER.
I THINK, FOR A SEASON, YOU HAVE CHOSEN TO WALK THIS WORLD AND OTHERS WITH YOUR EYES CLOSED...
AND NOW YOU ASK ME--HOW CAN I CONTINUE IF I HAVE BECOME BLIND?
OPEN YOUR EYES, MY FRIEND. SEE THE THINGS THAT I KNOW ARE REAL...AND BELIEVE TO BE TRUE.
AND WHAT ARE THOSE?
YOU, STEPHEN.
SOMEWHERE IN THERE...YOU ARE STILL A GOOD MAN.

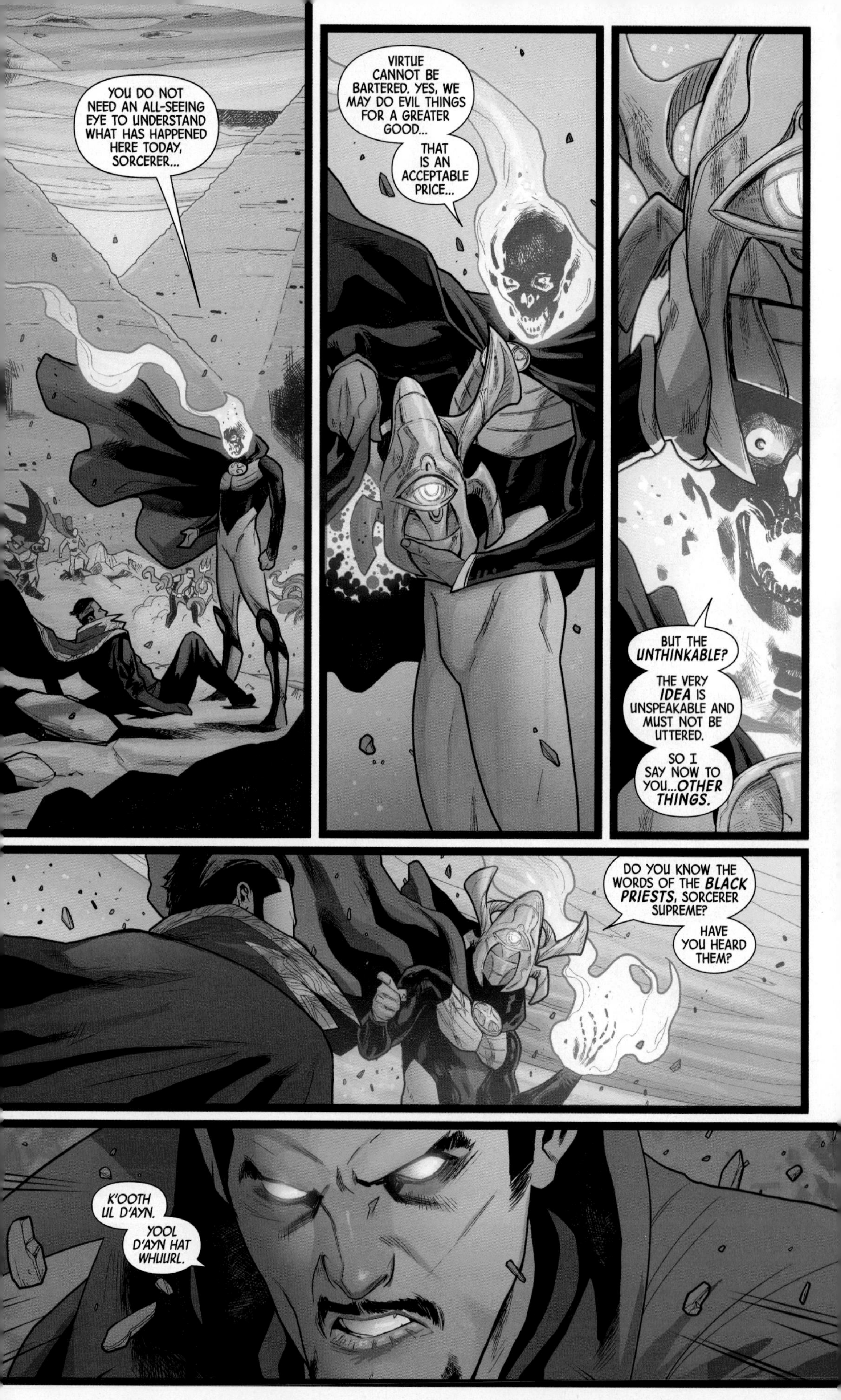
YOU DO NOT NEED AN ALL-SEEING EYE TO UNDERSTAND WHAT HAS HAPPENED HERE TODAY, SORCERER...
VIRTUE CANNOT BE BARTERED. YES, WE MAY DO EVIL THINGS FOR A GREATER GOOD...
THAT IS AN ACCEPTABLE PRICE...
BUT THE *UNTHINKABLE?*
THE VERY *IDEA* IS UNSPEAKABLE AND MUST NOT BE UTTERED.
SO I SAY NOW TO YOU...*OTHER THINGS.*
DO YOU KNOW THE WORDS OF THE *BLACK PRIESTS*, SORCERER SUPREME?
HAVE YOU HEARD THEM?
K'OOTH UL D'AYN.
YOOL D'AYN HAT WHUURL.

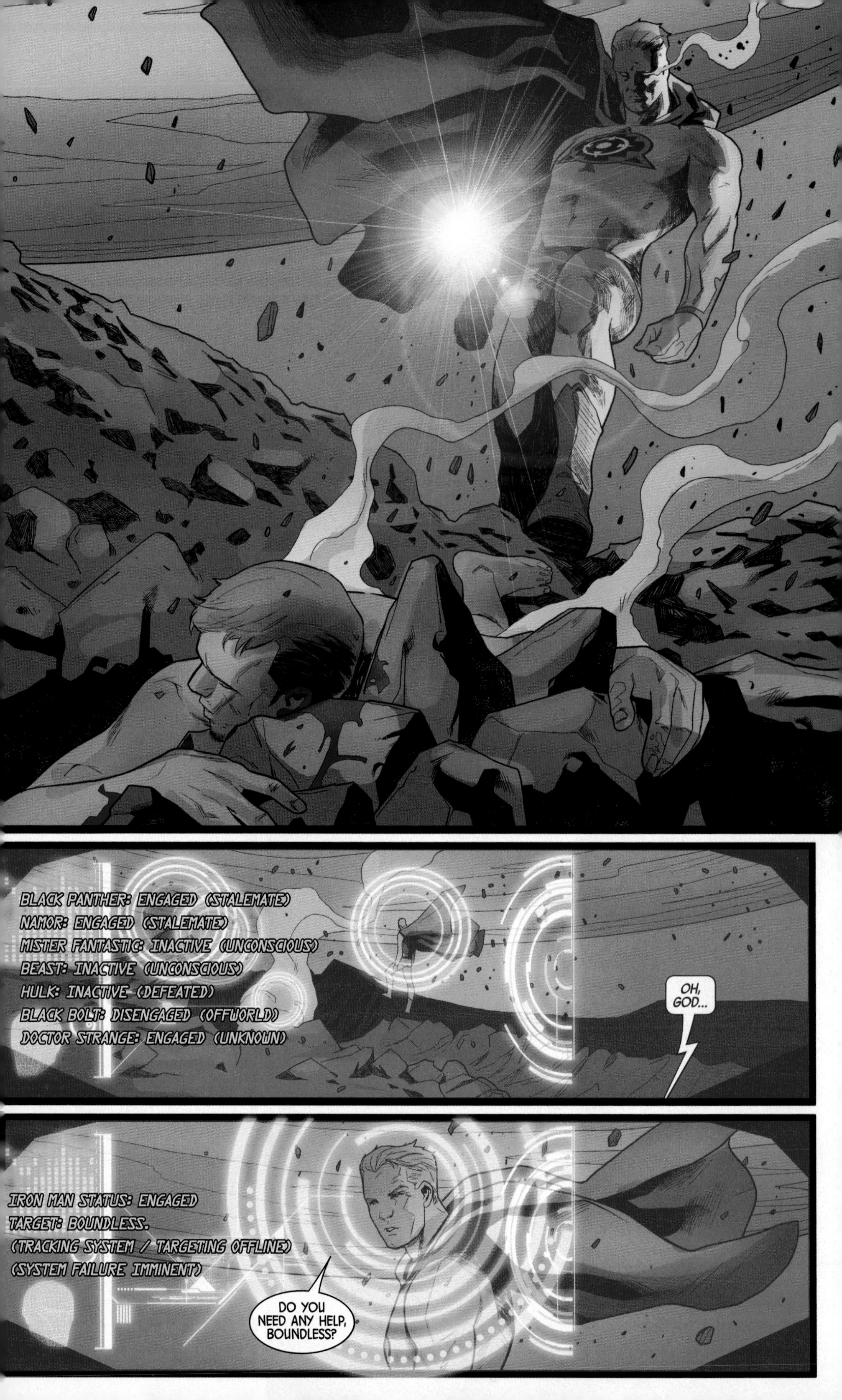
BLACK PANTHER: ENGAGED (STALEMATE)
NAMOR: ENGAGED (STALEMATE)
MISTER FANTASTIC: INACTIVE (UNCONSCIOUS)
BEAST: INACTIVE (UNCONSCIOUS)
HULK: INACTIVE (DEFEATED)
BLACK BOLT: DISENGAGED (OFFWORLD)
DOCTOR STRANGE: ENGAGED (UNKNOWN)
OH, GOD...
IRON MAN STATUS: ENGAGED
TARGET: BOUNDLESS.
(TRACKING SYSTEM / TARGETING OFFLINE)
(SYSTEM FAILURE IMMINENT)
DO YOU NEED ANY HELP, BOUNDLESS?

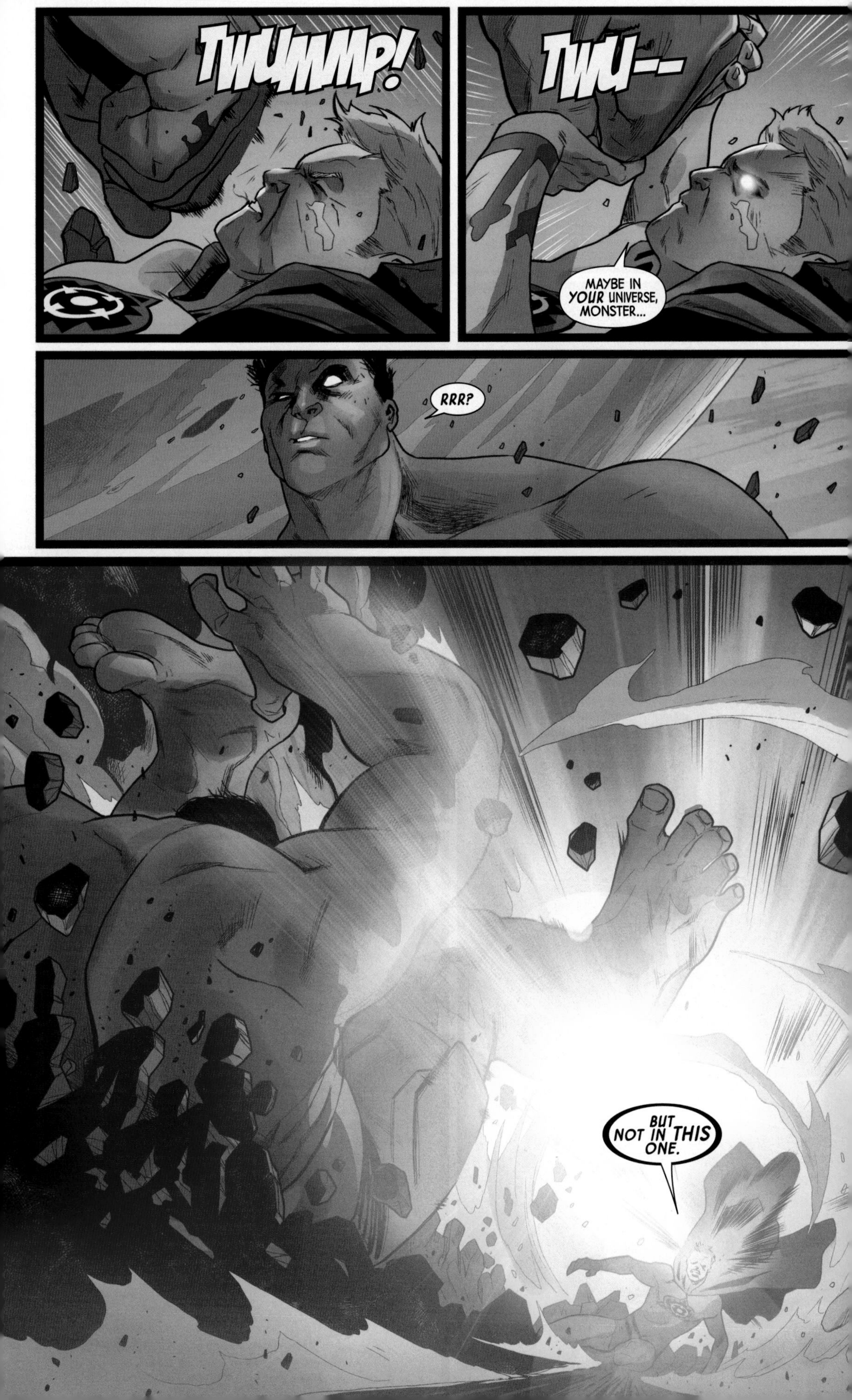
TWUMMP!
TWU--
MAYBE IN YOUR UNIVERSE, MONSTER...
RRR?
BUT NOT IN THIS ONE.

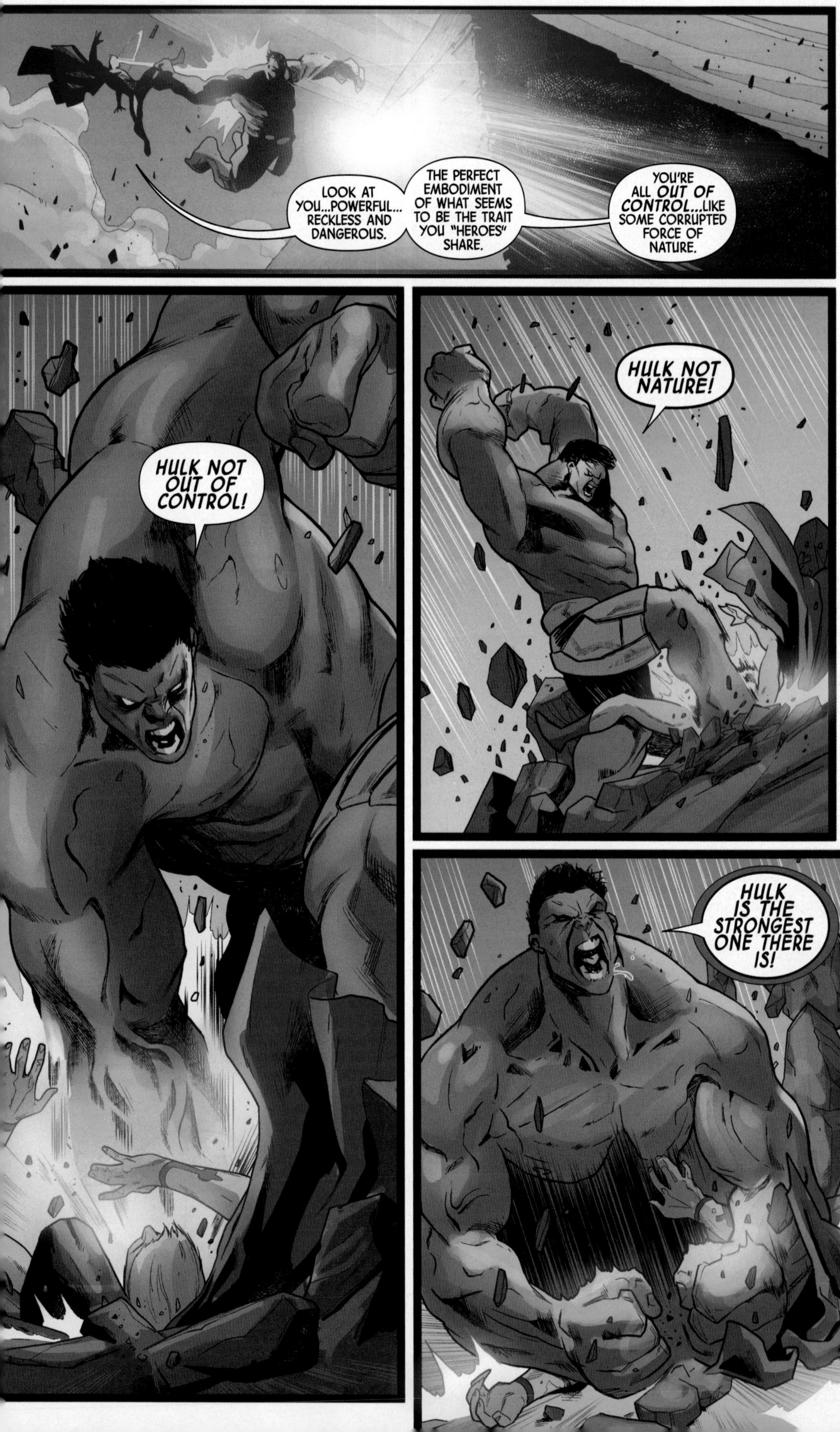
LOOK AT YOU...POWERFUL... RECKLESS AND DANGEROUS.
THE PERFECT EMBODIMENT OF WHAT SEEMS TO BE THE TRAIT YOU "HEROES" SHARE.
YOU'RE ALL *OUT OF CONTROL*...LIKE SOME CORRUPTED FORCE OF NATURE.
HULK NOT OUT OF CONTROL!
HULK NOT NATURE!
HULK IS THE STRONGEST ONE THERE IS!

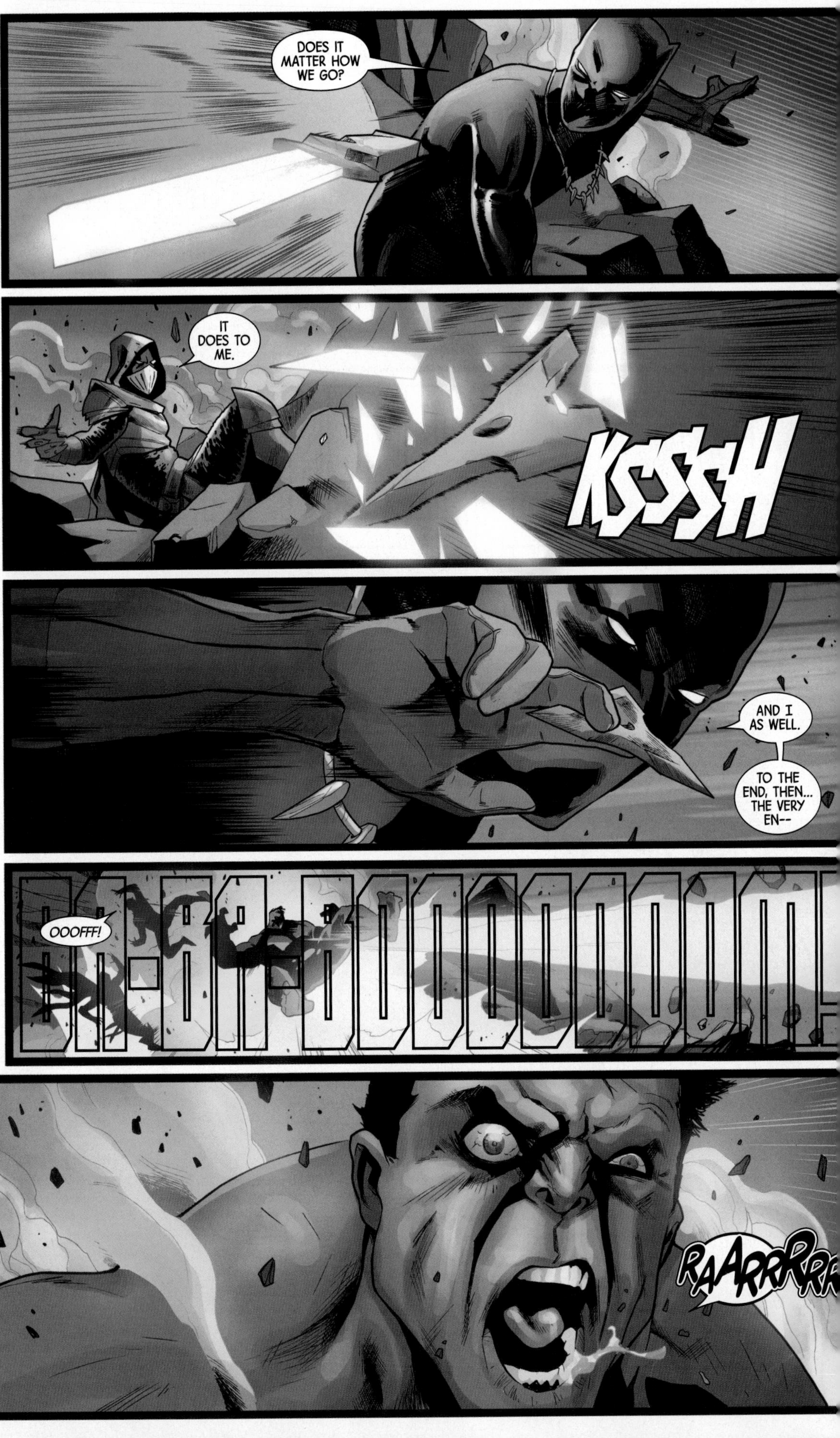

DOES IT MATTER HOW WE GO?
IT DOES TO ME.
KSSSH
AND I AS WELL.
TO THE END, THEN... THE VERY EN--
OOOFFF!
RAARRRRR

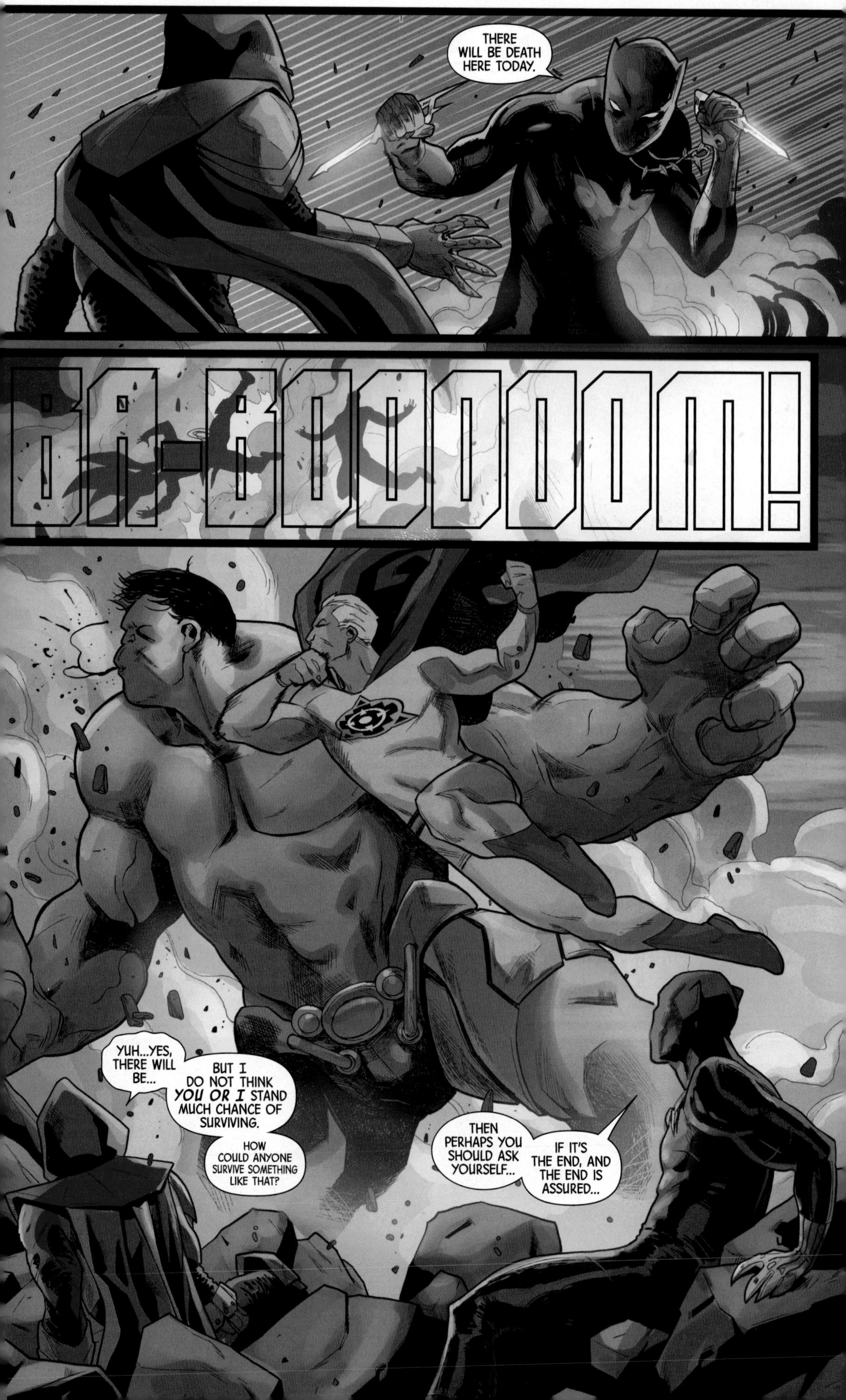
THERE WILL BE DEATH HERE TODAY.
BA-BOOOOOM!
YUH...YES, THERE WILL BE...
BUT I DO NOT THINK YOU OR I STAND MUCH CHANCE OF SURVIVING.
HOW COULD ANYONE SURVIVE SOMETHING LIKE THAT?
THEN PERHAPS YOU SHOULD ASK YOURSELF...
IF IT'S THE END, AND THE END IS ASSURED...

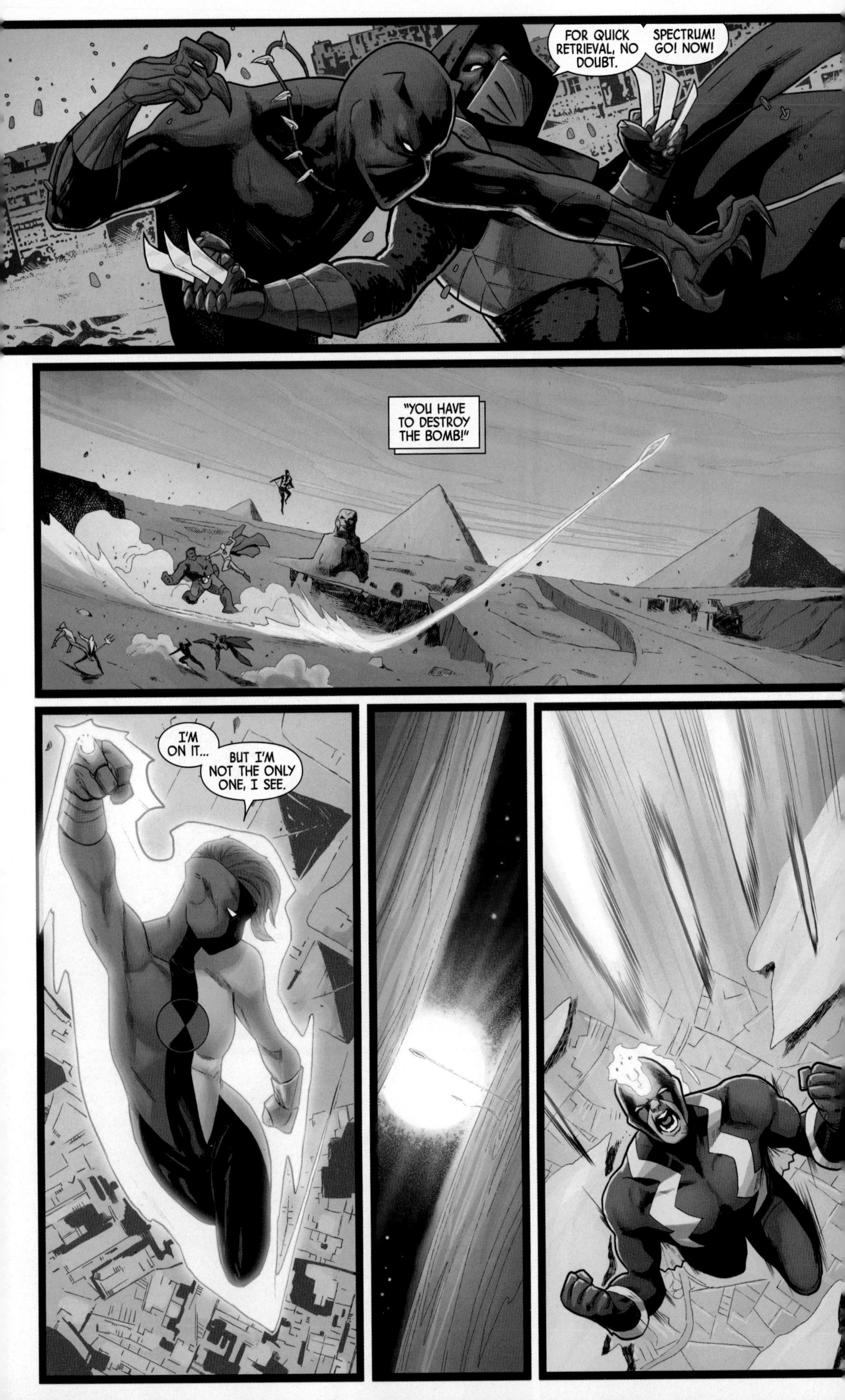
FOR QUICK RETRIEVAL, NO DOUBT.
SPECTRUM! GO! NOW!
"YOU HAVE TO DESTROY THE BOMB!"
I'M ON IT...
BUT I'M NOT THE ONLY ONE, I SEE.

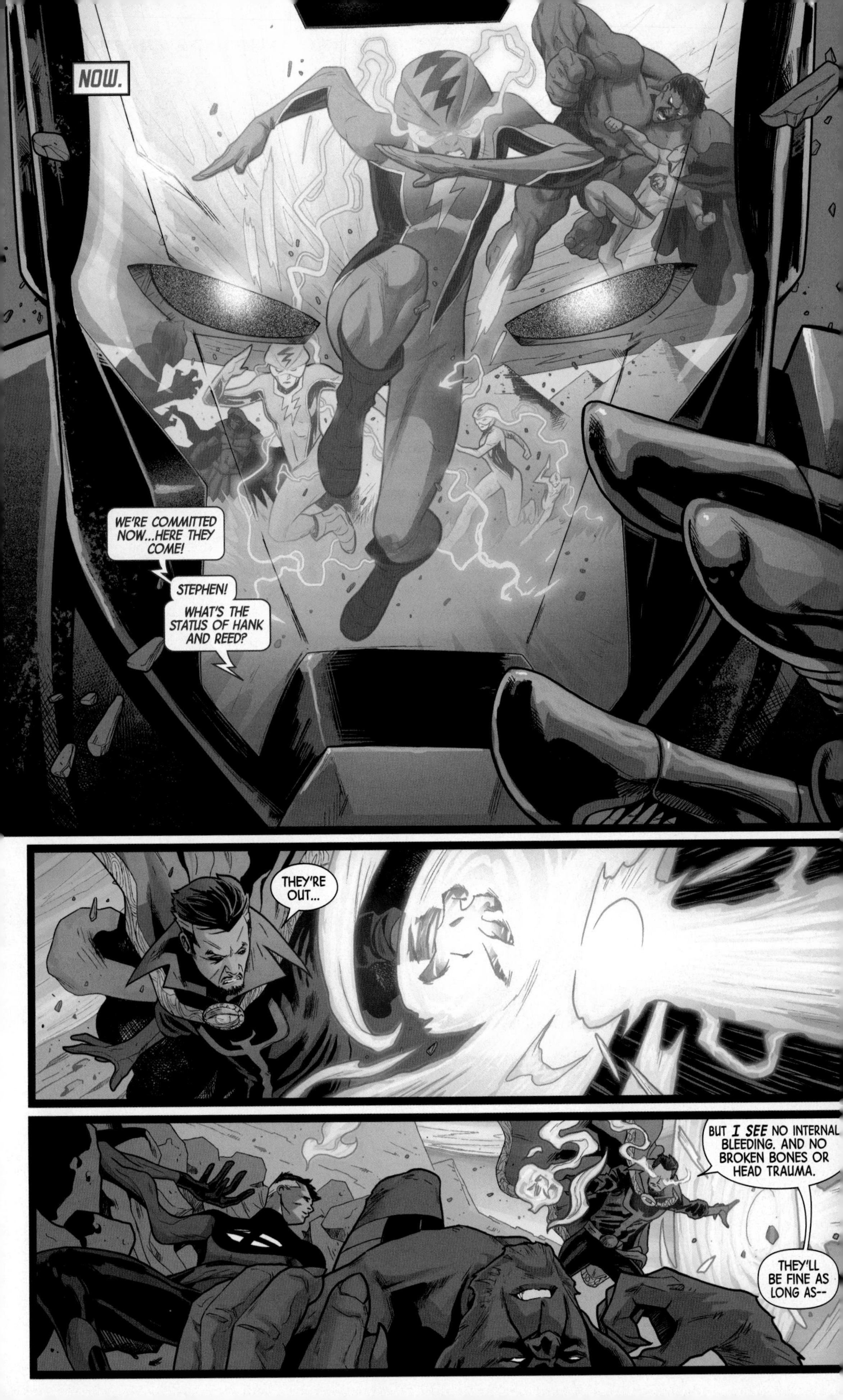
NOW.
WE'RE COMMITTED NOW...HERE THEY COME!
STEPHEN! WHAT'S THE STATUS OF HANK AND REED?
THEY'RE OUT...
BUT I SEE NO INTERNAL BLEEDING. AND NO BROKEN BONES OR HEAD TRAUMA.
THEY'LL BE FINE AS LONG AS--

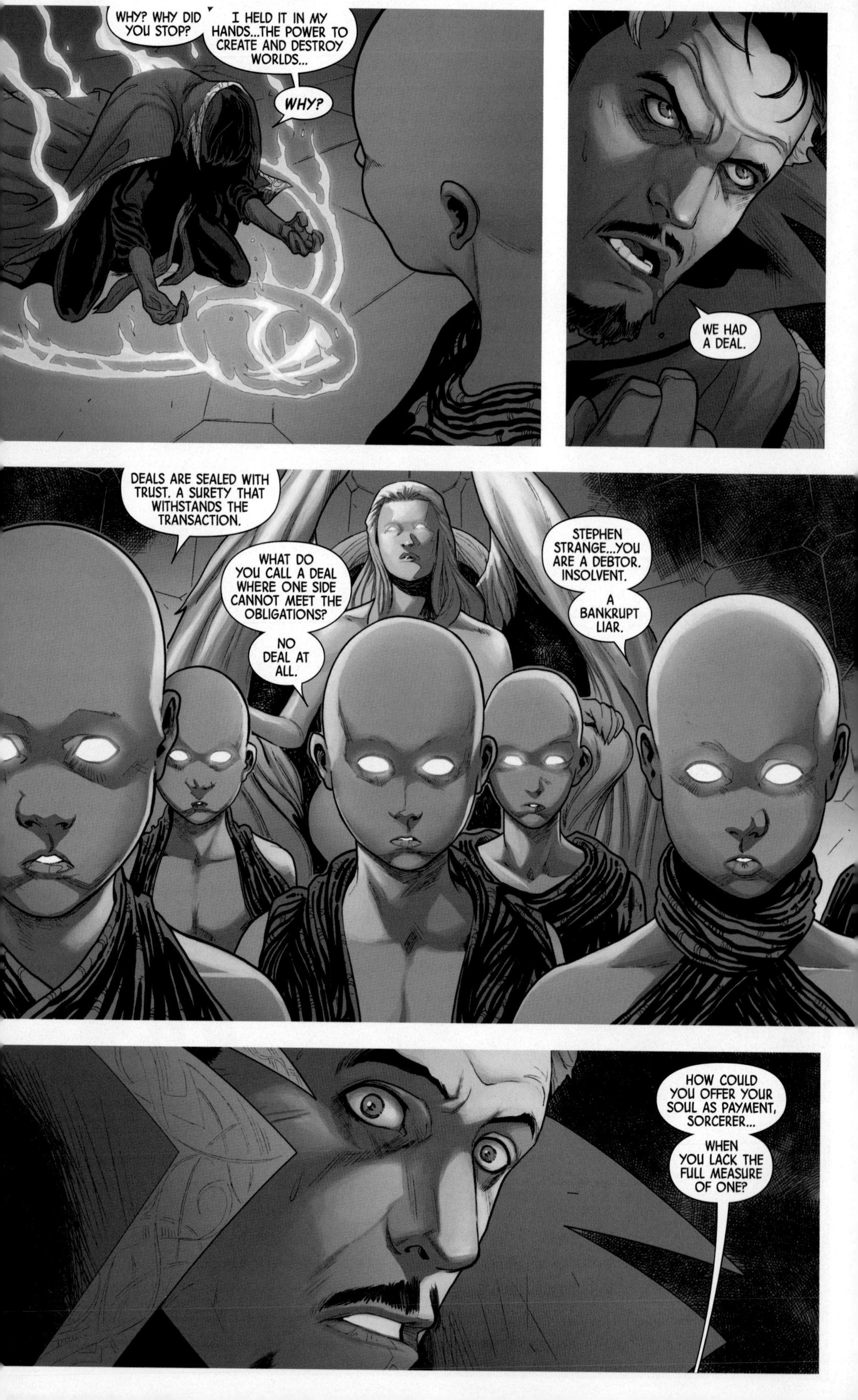
WHY? WHY DID YOU STOP?
I HELD IT IN MY HANDS...THE POWER TO CREATE AND DESTROY WORLDS...
WHY?
WE HAD A DEAL.
DEALS ARE SEALED WITH TRUST. A SURETY THAT WITHSTANDS THE TRANSACTION.
WHAT DO YOU CALL A DEAL WHERE ONE SIDE CANNOT MEET THE OBLIGATIONS?
NO DEAL AT ALL.
STEPHEN STRANGE...YOU ARE A DEBTOR. INSOLVENT.
A BANKRUPT LIAR.
HOW COULD YOU OFFER YOUR SOUL AS PAYMENT, SORCERER...
WHEN YOU LACK THE FULL MEASURE OF ONE?

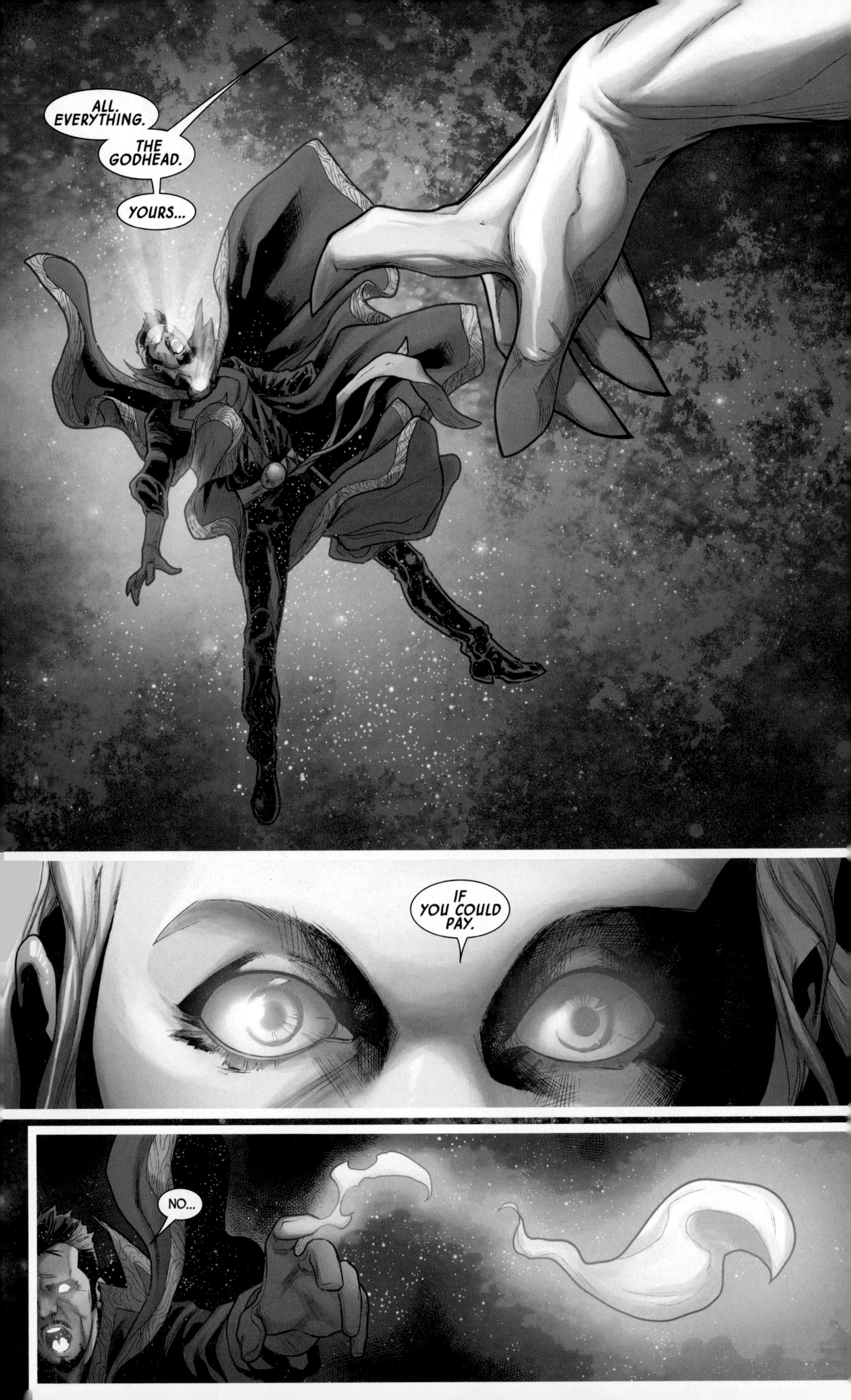
ALL. EVERYTHING.
THE GODHEAD.
YOURS...
IF YOU COULD PAY.
NO...

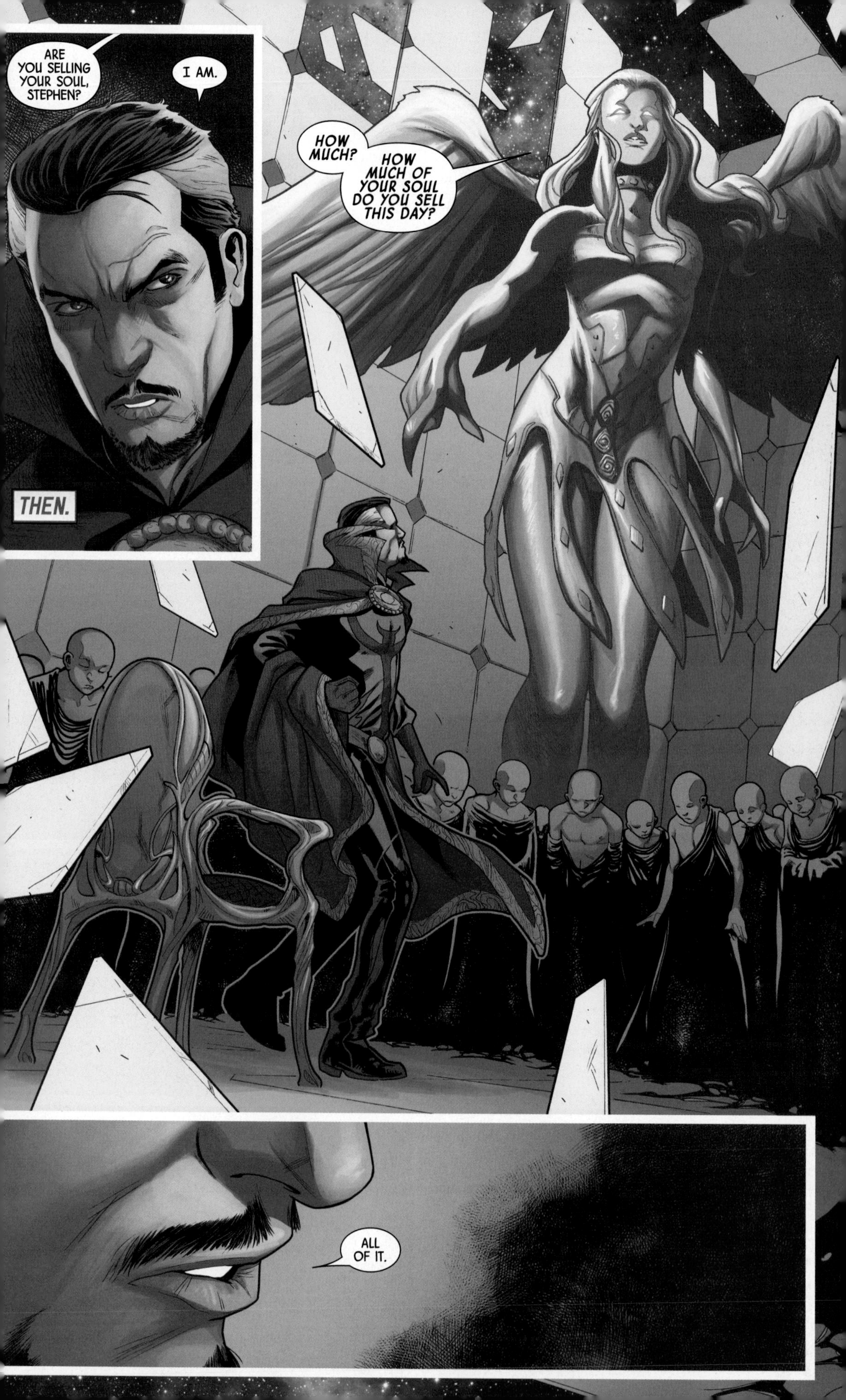

ARE YOU SELLING YOUR SOUL, STEPHEN?
I AM.
THEN.
HOW MUCH?
HOW MUCH OF YOUR SOUL DO YOU SELL THIS DAY?
ALL OF IT.

"BLU'DAKORR"

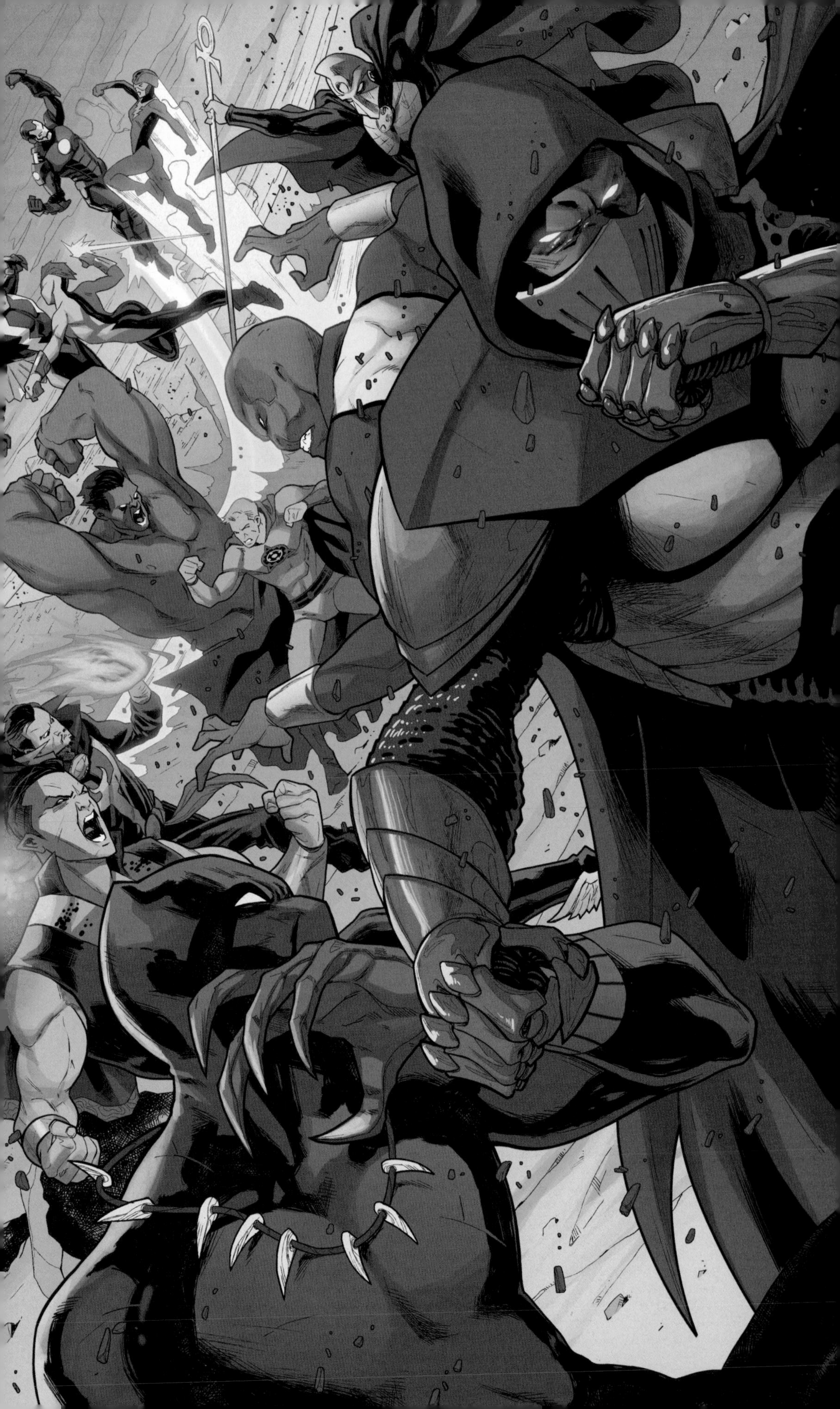

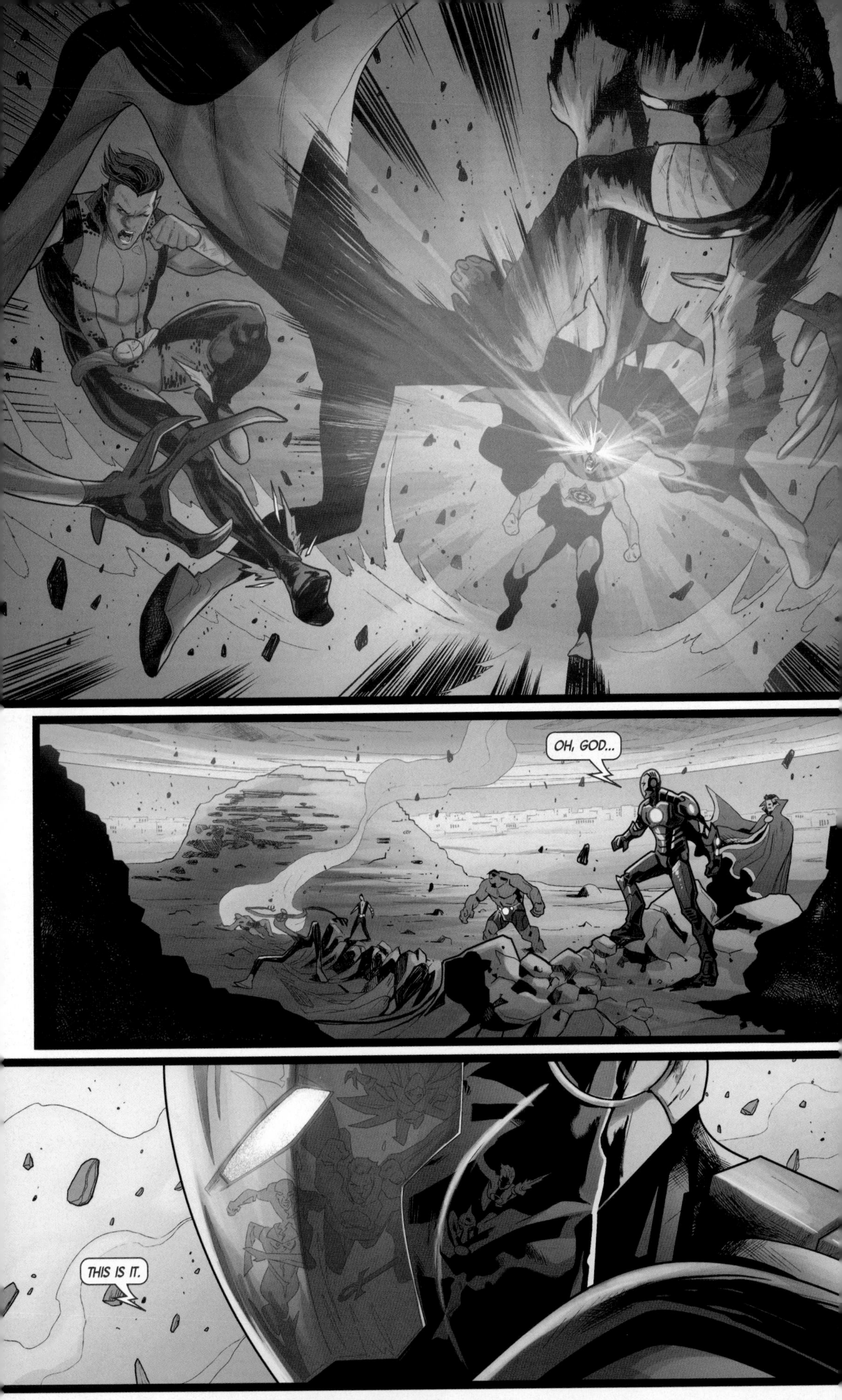
OH, GOD...
THIS IS IT.

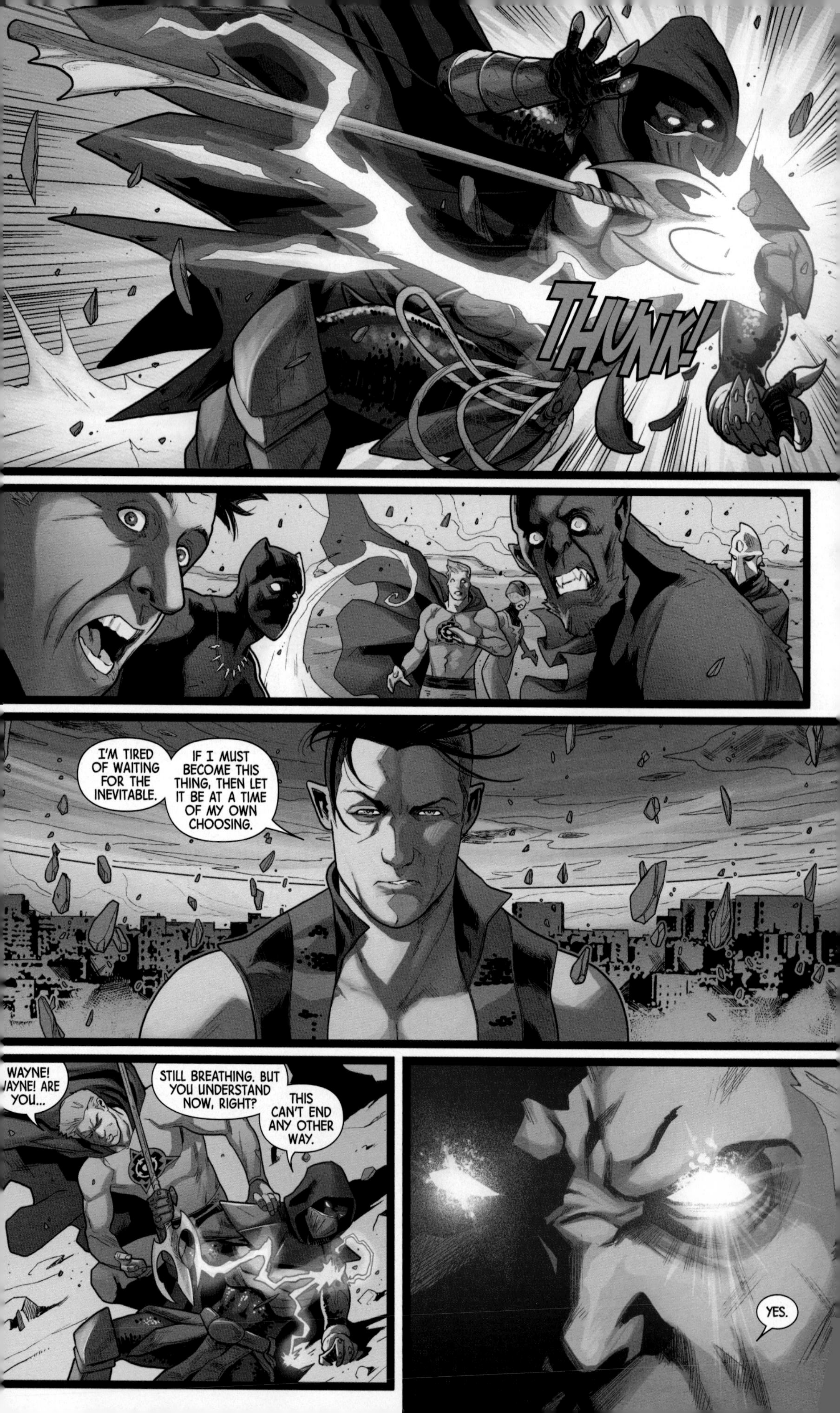
THUNK!
I'M TIRED OF WAITING FOR THE INEVITABLE.
IF I MUST BECOME THIS THING, THEN LET IT BE AT A TIME OF MY OWN CHOOSING.
WAYNE! WAYNE! ARE YOU...
STILL BREATHING. BUT YOU UNDERSTAND NOW, RIGHT?
THIS CAN'T END ANY OTHER WAY.
YES.

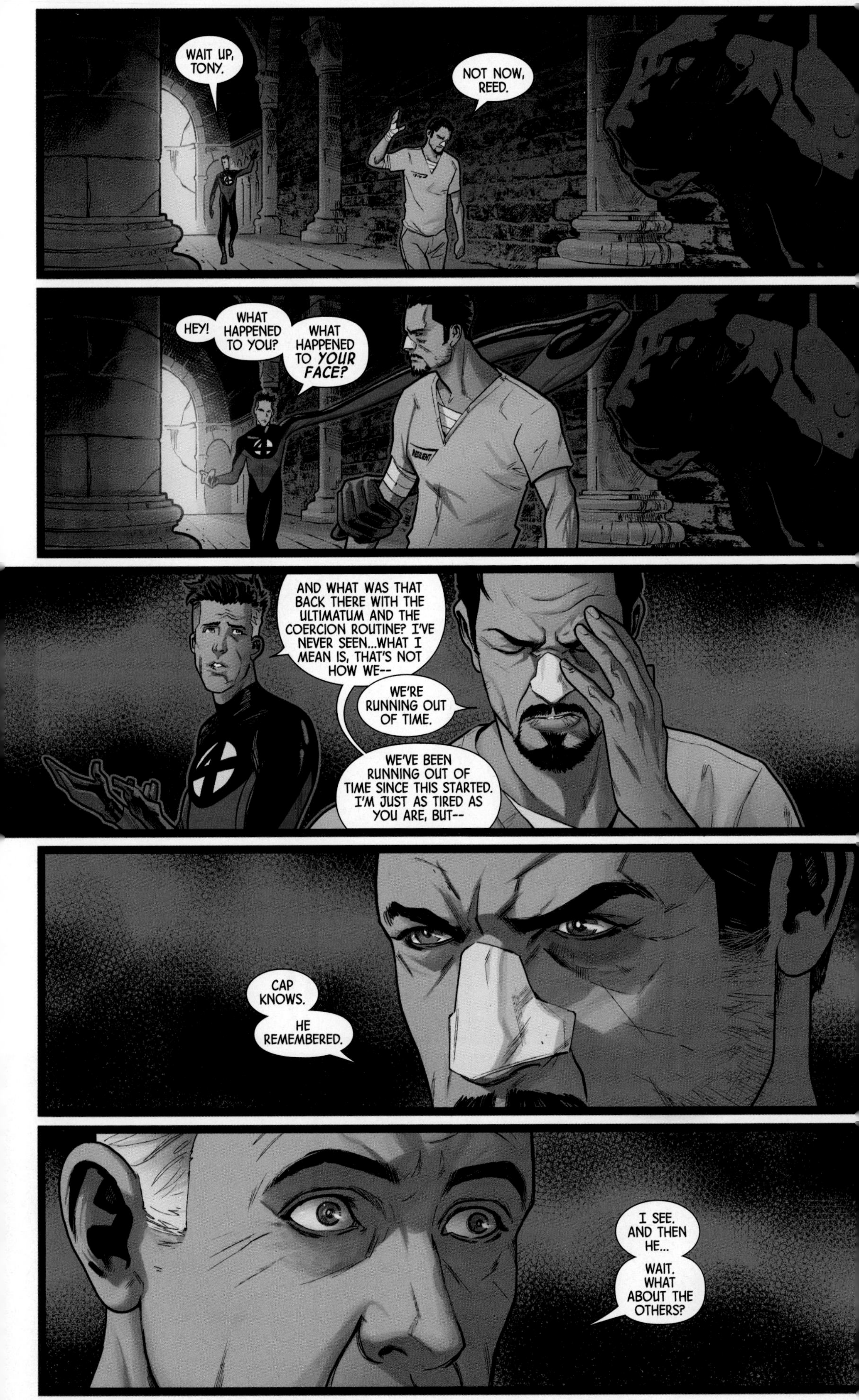

WAIT UP, TONY.
NOT NOW, REED.
HEY!
WHAT HAPPENED TO YOU?
WHAT HAPPENED TO *YOUR FACE?*
RESILIENT
AND WHAT WAS THAT BACK THERE WITH THE ULTIMATUM AND THE COERCION ROUTINE? I'VE NEVER SEEN...WHAT I MEAN IS, THAT'S NOT HOW WE--
WE'RE RUNNING OUT OF TIME.
WE'VE BEEN RUNNING OUT OF TIME SINCE THIS STARTED. I'M JUST AS TIRED AS YOU ARE, BUT--
CAP KNOWS.
HE REMEMBERED.
I SEE. AND THEN HE...
WAIT. WHAT ABOUT THE OTHERS?

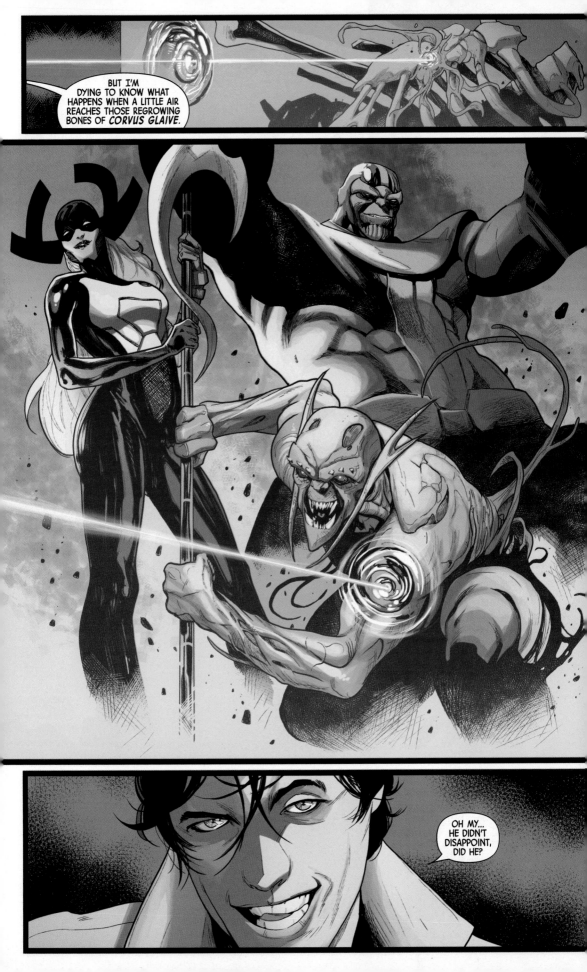

BUT I'M DYING TO KNOW WHAT HAPPENS WHEN A LITTLE AIR REACHES THOSE REGROWING BONES OF *CORVUS GLAIVE*.

OH MY... HE DIDN'T DISAPPOINT, DID HE?

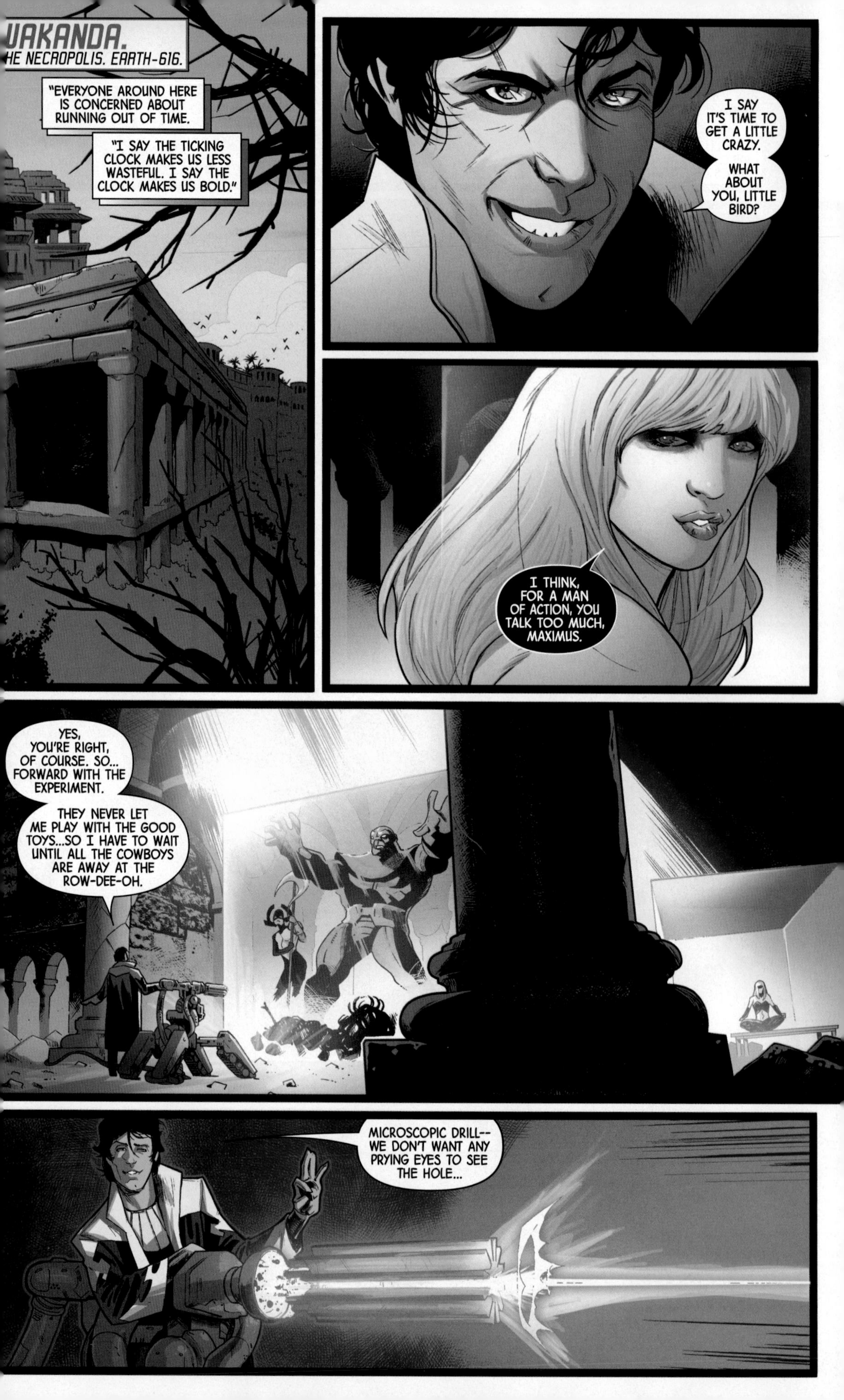

UAKANDA.
HE NECROPOLIS. EARTH-616.
"EVERYONE AROUND HERE IS CONCERNED ABOUT RUNNING OUT OF TIME.
"I SAY THE TICKING CLOCK MAKES US LESS WASTEFUL. I SAY THE CLOCK MAKES US BOLD."
I SAY IT'S TIME TO GET A LITTLE CRAZY.
WHAT ABOUT YOU, LITTLE BIRD?
I THINK, FOR A MAN OF ACTION, YOU TALK TOO MUCH, MAXIMUS.
YES, YOU'RE RIGHT, OF COURSE. SO... FORWARD WITH THE EXPERIMENT.
THEY NEVER LET ME PLAY WITH THE GOOD TOYS...SO I HAVE TO WAIT UNTIL ALL THE COWBOYS ARE AWAY AT THE ROW-DEE-OH.
MICROSCOPIC DRILL-- WE DON'T WANT ANY PRYING EYES TO SEE THE HOLE...

"WE ARE ALL MONSTERS NOW"

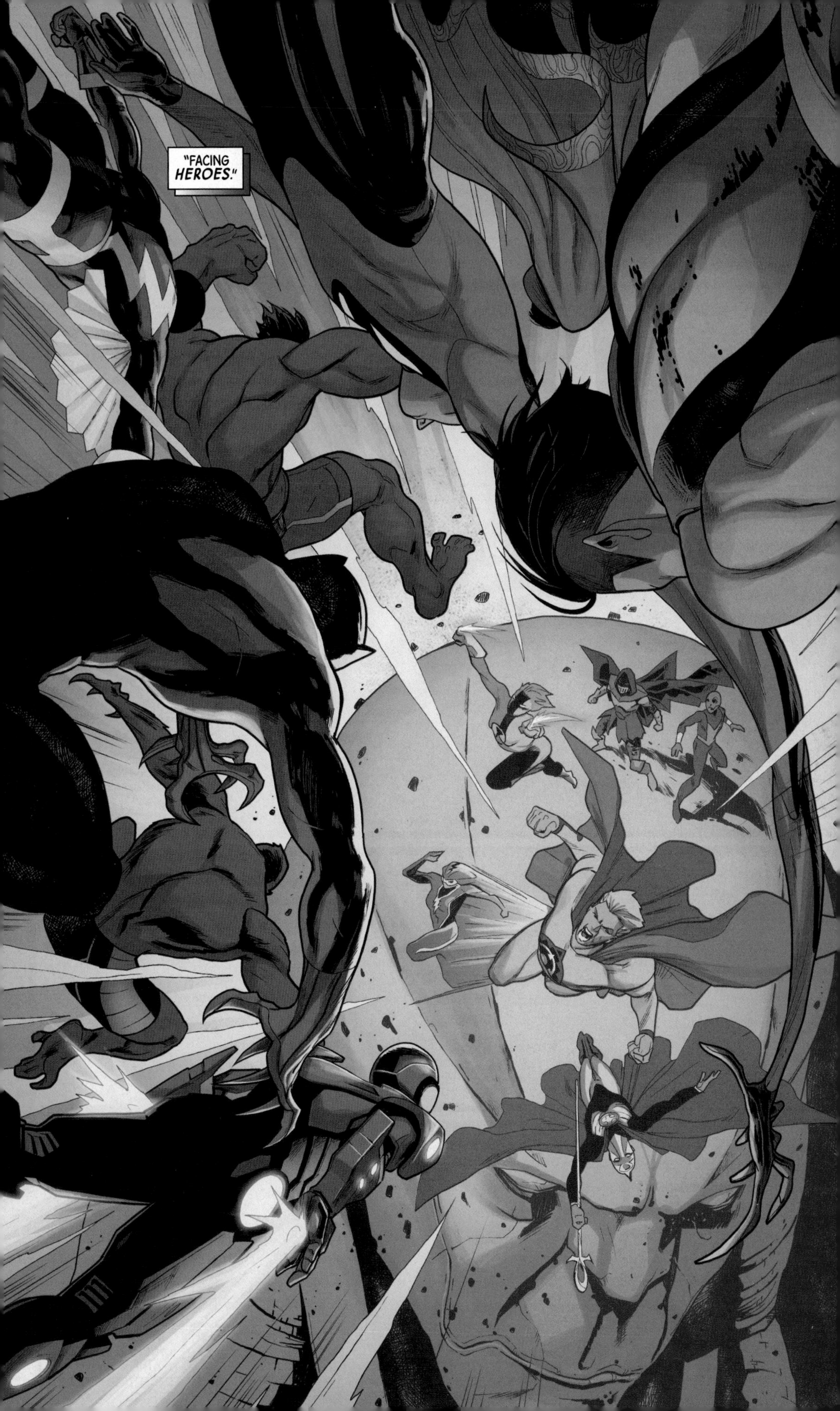
"FACING *HEROES.*"

... HERE'S WHAT'S GOING TO HAPPEN NEXT:

WE'RE GOING TO DEAL WITH THIS UPCOMING INCURSION.

THEN I'M GOING TO TALK TO THE OTHERS--DO WHATEVER IT TAKES TO CONVINCE THEM WE NEED TO BRING IN SOMEONE WHO CAN DIG AROUND IN YOUR MIND.

BYPASS ALL THE GAMES, ALL THE LIES, AND GET RIGHT TO THE TRUTH.

THE TRUTH? I'VE NEVER LIED TO ANY OF YOU.

EVER HEARD OF LIES OF OMISSION, SWAN?

YES. THAT'S WHAT ALL THE IGNORANT PEOPLE CALL DISPLAYS OF THEIR IGNORANCE.

TONY. IT'S TIME. INCURSION'S TWENTY MINUTES OUT.

WE HAVE TO GO.

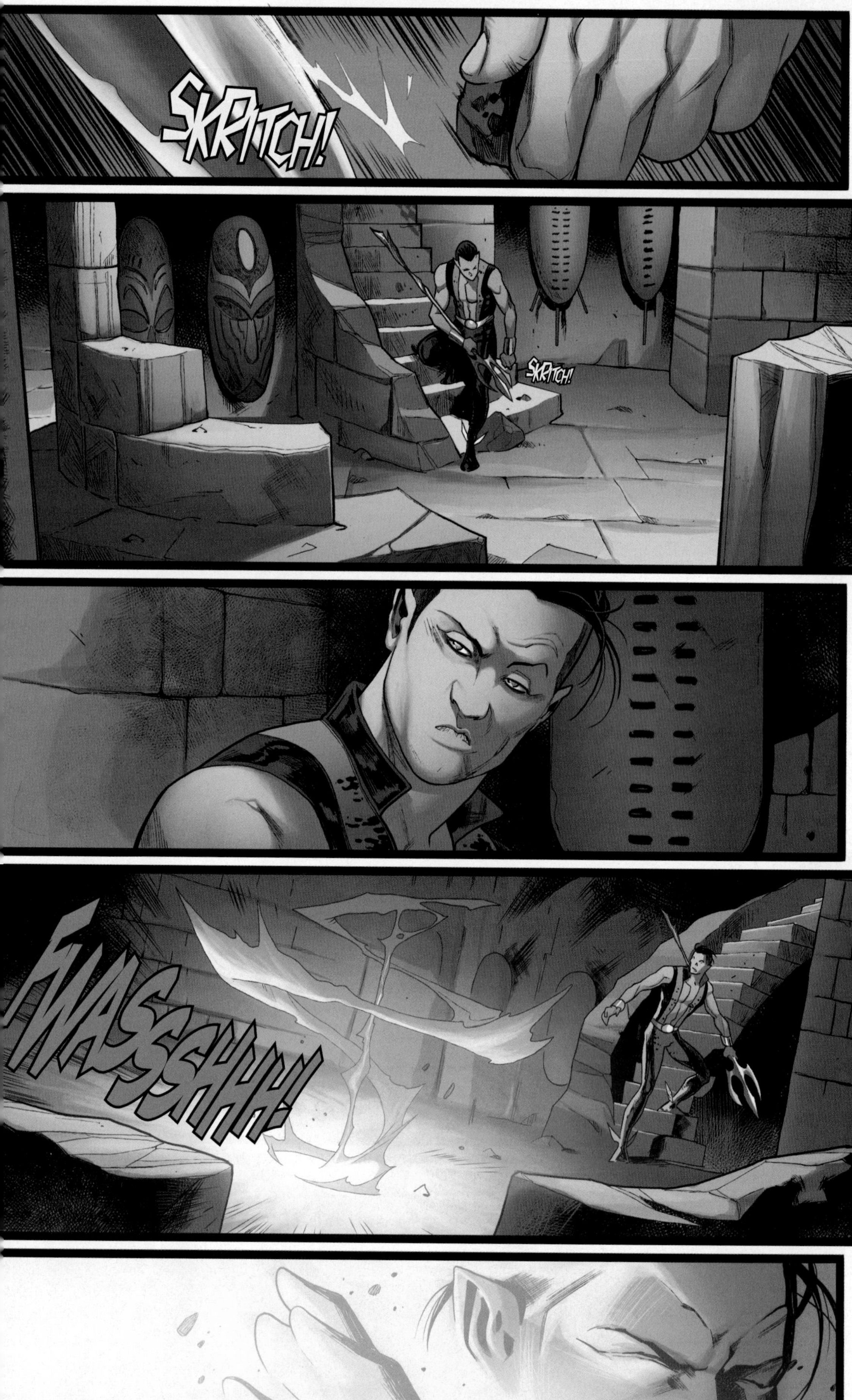
SKRITCH!
SKRITCH!
FWASSHHH!

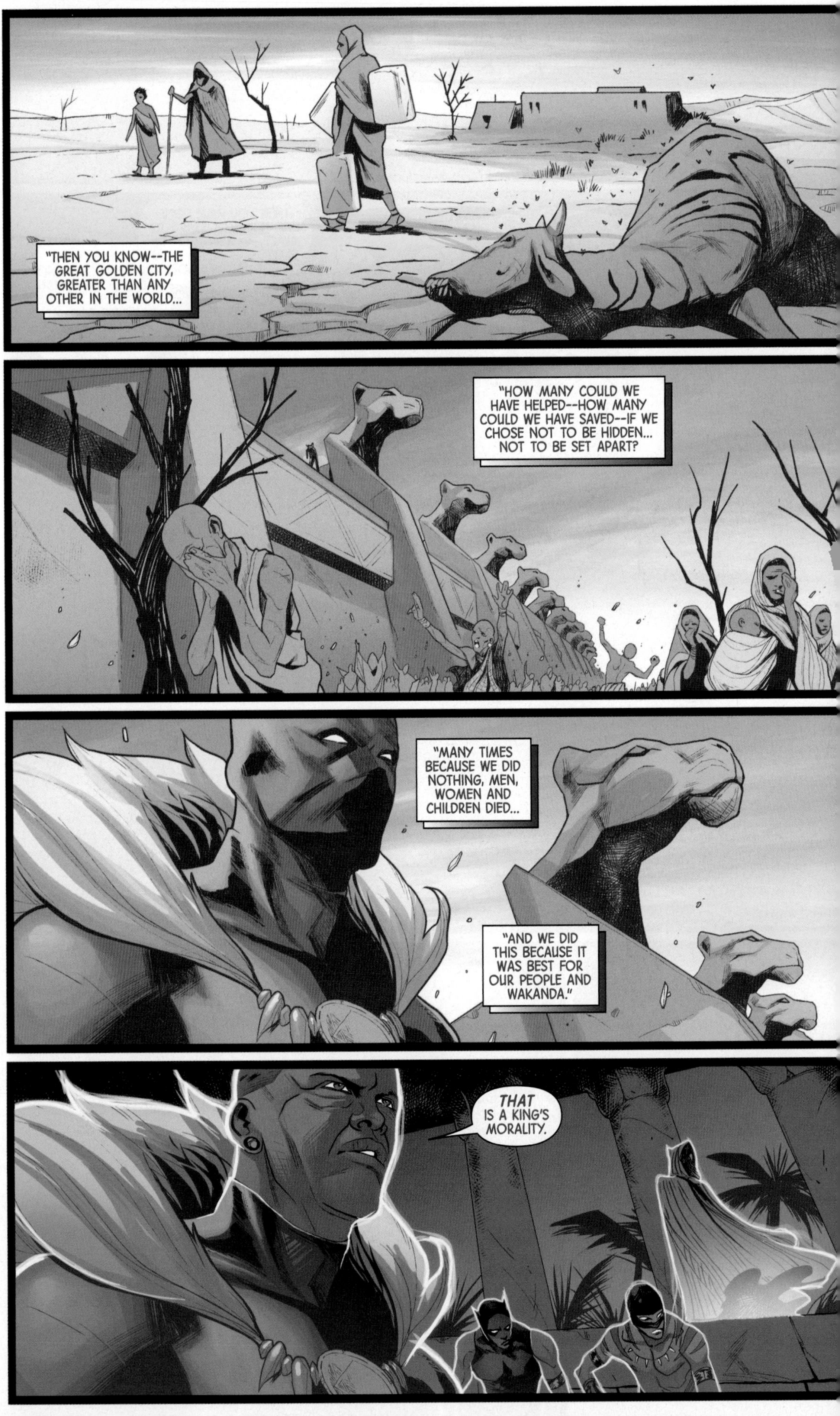
"THEN YOU KNOW--THE GREAT GOLDEN CITY, GREATER THAN ANY OTHER IN THE WORLD...
"HOW MANY COULD WE HAVE HELPED--HOW MANY COULD WE HAVE SAVED--IF WE CHOSE NOT TO BE HIDDEN... NOT TO BE SET APART?
"MANY TIMES BECAUSE WE DID NOTHING, MEN, WOMEN AND CHILDREN DIED...
"AND WE DID THIS BECAUSE IT WAS BEST FOR OUR PEOPLE AND WAKANDA."
THAT IS A KING'S MORALITY.

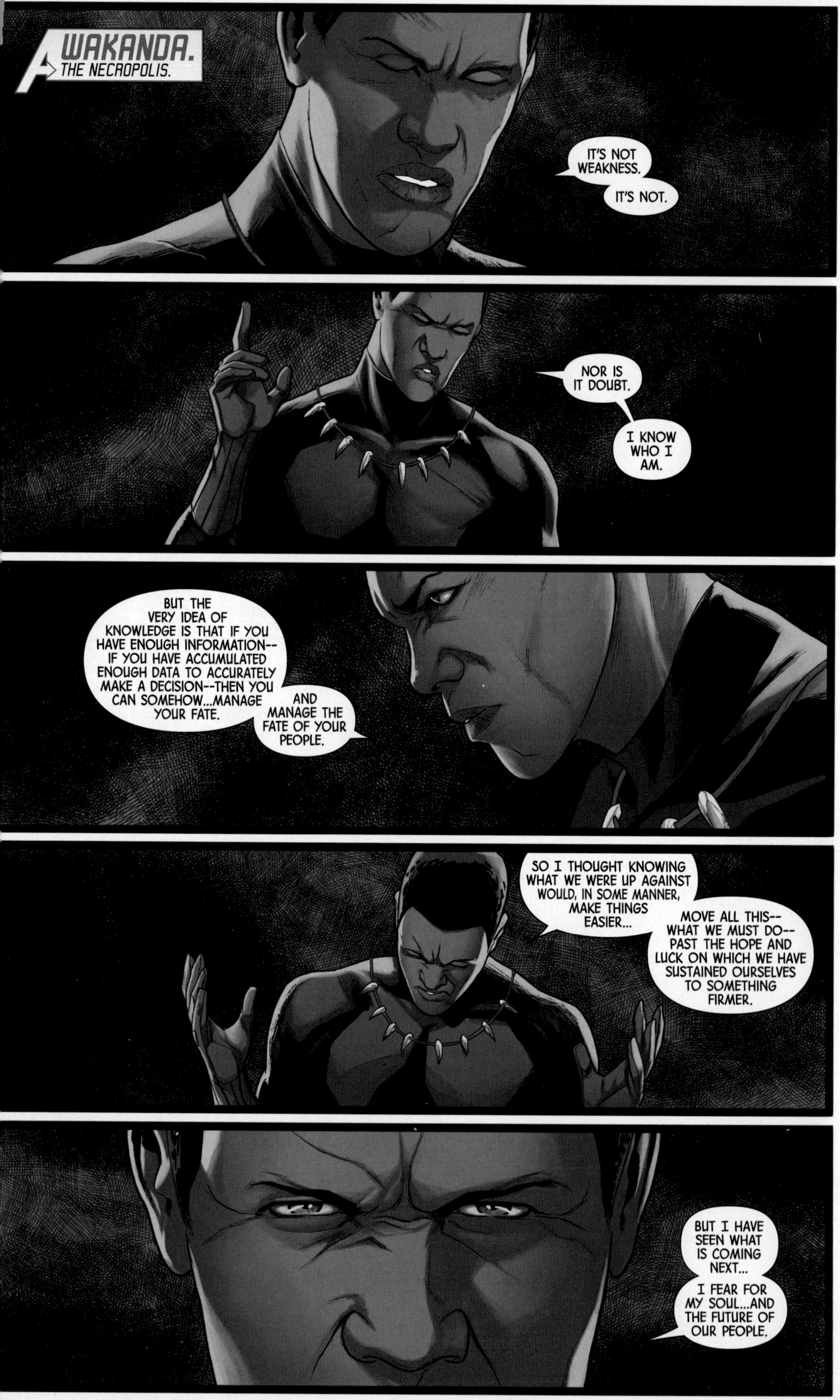
WAKANDA.
THE NECROPOLIS.
IT'S NOT WEAKNESS.
IT'S NOT.
NOR IS IT DOUBT.
I KNOW WHO I AM.
BUT THE VERY IDEA OF KNOWLEDGE IS THAT IF YOU HAVE ENOUGH INFORMATION-- IF YOU HAVE ACCUMULATED ENOUGH DATA TO ACCURATELY MAKE A DECISION--THEN YOU CAN SOMEHOW...MANAGE YOUR FATE.
AND MANAGE THE FATE OF YOUR PEOPLE.
SO I THOUGHT KNOWING WHAT WE WERE UP AGAINST WOULD, IN SOME MANNER, MAKE THINGS EASIER...
MOVE ALL THIS-- WHAT WE MUST DO-- PAST THE HOPE AND LUCK ON WHICH WE HAVE SUSTAINED OURSELVES TO SOMETHING FIRMER.
BUT I HAVE SEEN WHAT IS COMING NEXT...
I FEAR FOR MY SOUL...AND THE FUTURE OF OUR PEOPLE.

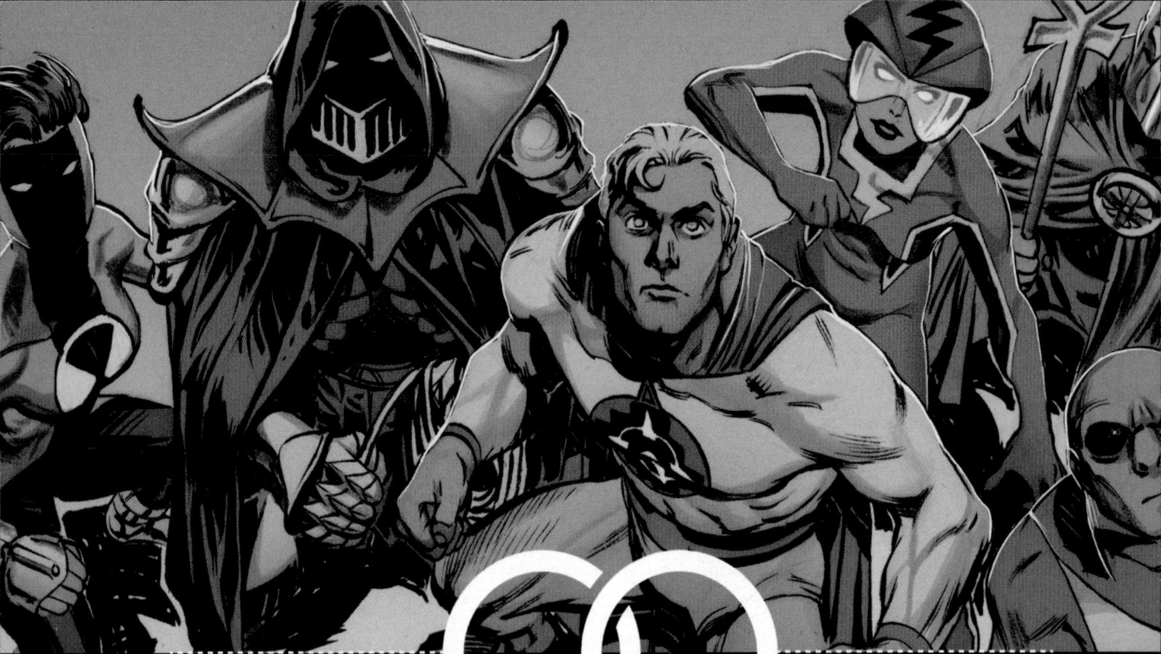

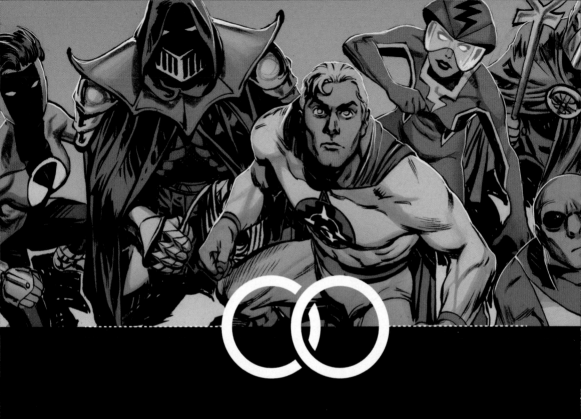

"INTO THE BREACH"

THE ILLUMINATI

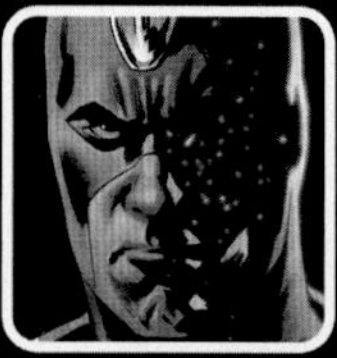
BLACK BOLT
Celestial Messiah

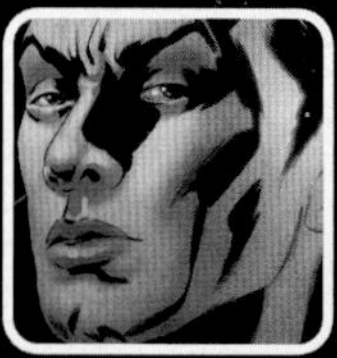
NAMOR
Imperius Rex

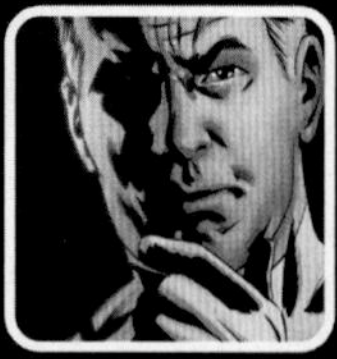
REED RICHARDS
Universal Builder

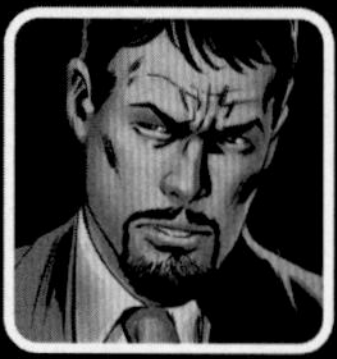
IRON MAN
Master of Machines

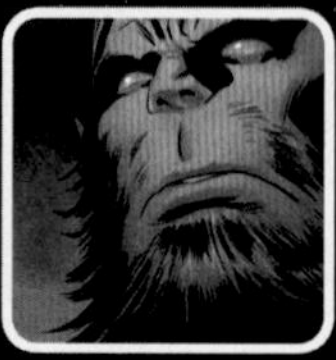
BEAST
Mutant Genius

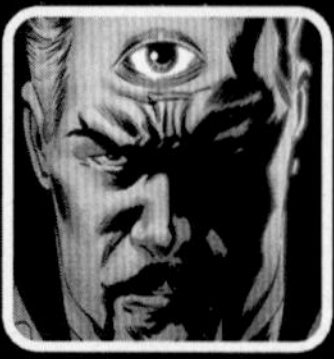
DOCTOR STRANGE
Sorcerer Supreme

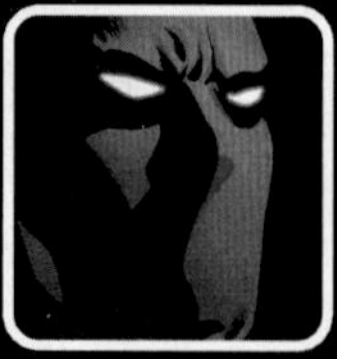
BLACK PANTHER
King of the Dead

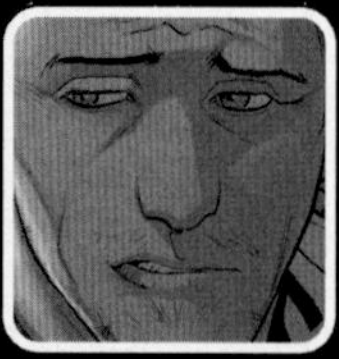
HULK/BRUCE BANNER
Strongest There Is

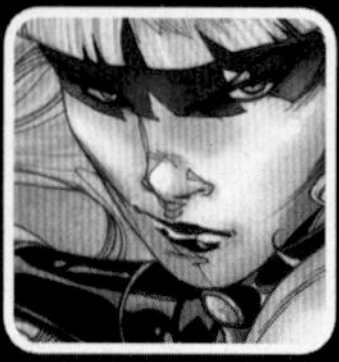
BLACK SWAN
Incursion Survivor

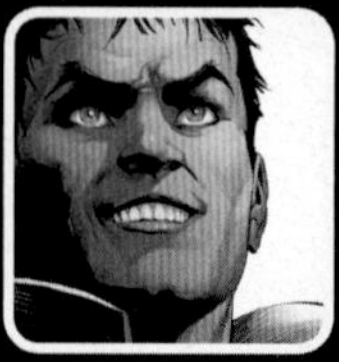
MAXIMUS
Inhuman Madman

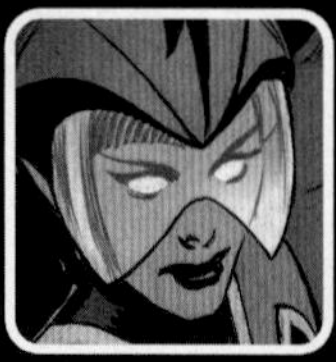
BOUNDLESS

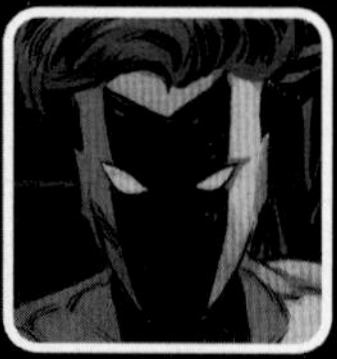
DR. SPECTRUM

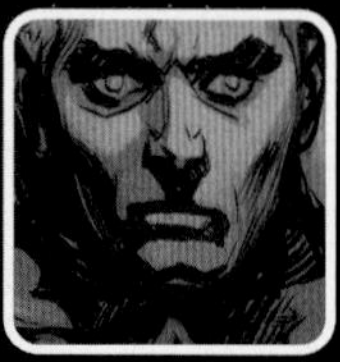
SUN GOD

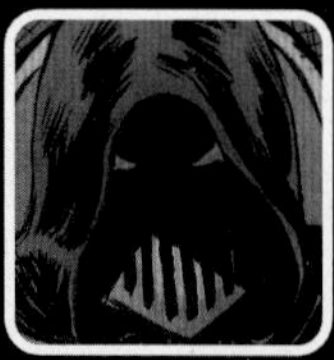
THE RIDER

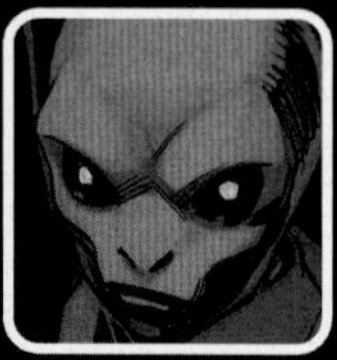
THE JOVIAN

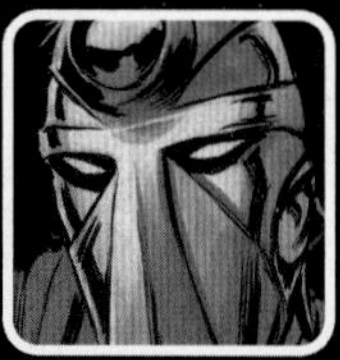
THE NORN

WRITER: **JONATHAN HICKMAN**

ISSUES #18-21

ARTIST: **VALERIO SCHITI** WITH SALVADOR LARROCA (#21)

COLOR ARTIST: **FRANK MARTIN** WITH PAUL MOUNTS (#20-21)

COVER ART: **DUSTIN WEAVER & JASON KEITH**

ISSUES #22-23

ARTIST: **KEV WALKER**

COLOR ARTIST: **FRANK MARTIN**

COVER ART: **DALE KEOWN & JASON KEITH** (#22) AND **CHRISTIAN WARD** (#23)

LETTERER: **VC'S JOE CARAMAGNA**

ASSISTANT EDITOR: **JAKE THOMAS**

EDITORS: **TOM BREVOORT** WITH **WIL MOSS**

COLLECTION EDITOR: **JENNIFER GRÜNWALD**
ASSISTANT EDITOR: **SARAH BRUNSTAD**
ASSOCIATE MANAGING EDITOR: **ALEX STARBUCK**
EDITOR, SPECIAL PROJECTS: **MARK D. BEAZLEY**
SENIOR EDITOR, SPECIAL PROJECTS: **JEFF YOUNGQUIST**
SVP PRINT, SALES & MARKETING: **DAVID GABRIEL**
BOOK DESIGN: **JEFF POWELL**

EDITOR IN CHIEF: **AXEL ALONSO**
CHIEF CREATIVE OFFICER: **JOE QUESADA**
PUBLISHER: **DAN BUCKLEY**
EXECUTIVE PRODUCER: **ALAN FINE**

NEW AVENGERS VOL. 4: A PERFECT WORLD. Contains material originally published in magazine form as NEW AVENGERS #18-23. First printing 2014. ISBN# 978-0-7851-5485-3. Published by MARVEL WORLDWIDE, INC., a subsidiary of MARVEL ENTERTAINMENT, LLC. OFFICE OF PUBLICATION: 135 West 50th Street, New York, NY 10020. Copyright © 2014 Marvel Characters, Inc. All rights reserved. All characters featured in this issue and the distinctive names and likenesses thereof, and all related indicia are trademarks of Marvel Characters, Inc. No similarity between any of the names, characters, persons, and/or institutions in this magazine with those of any living or dead person or institution is intended, and any such similarity which may exist is purely coincidental. **Printed in the U.S.A.** ALAN FINE, EVP - Office of the President, Marvel Worldwide, Inc. and EVP & CMO Marvel Characters B.V.; DAN BUCKLEY, Publisher & President - Print, Animation & Digital Divisions; JOE QUESADA, Chief Creative Officer; TOM BREVOORT, SVP of Publishing; DAVID BOGART, SVP of Operations & Procurement, Publishing; C.B. CEBULSKI, SVP of Creator & Content Development; DAVID GABRIEL, SVP Print, Sales & Marketing; JIM O'KEEFE, VP of Operations & Logistics; DAN CARR, Executive Director of Publishing Technology; SUSAN CRESPI, Editorial Operations Manager; ALEX MORALES, Publishing Operations Manager; STAN LEE, Chairman Emeritus. For information regarding advertising in Marvel Comics or on Marvel.com, please contact Niza Disla, Director of Marvel Partnerships, at ndisla@marvel.com. For Marvel subscription inquiries, please call 800-217-9158. **Manufactured between 9/5/2014 and 10/20/2014 by R.R. DONNELLEY, INC., SALEM, VA, USA.**